Rhetoric & Composition
PhD Program

PROGRAM
Pioneering program honoring the rhetorical tradition through scholarly innovation, excellent job placement record, well-endowed library, state-of-the-art New Media Writing Studio, and graduate certificates in new media and women's studies.

TEACHING
1-1 teaching loads, small classes, extensive pedagogy and technology training, and administrative fellowships in writing program administration and new media.

FACULTY
Nationally recognized teacher-scholars in history of rhetoric, modern rhetoric, women's rhetoric, digital rhetoric, composition studies, and writing program administration.

FUNDING
Generous four-year graduate instructorships, competitive stipends, travel support, and several prestigious fellowship opportunities.

EXPERIENCE
Mid-sized liberal arts university setting nestled in the vibrant, culturally-rich Dallas-Fort Worth metroplex.

English
DEPARTMENT

Contact Dr. Mona Narain
m.narain@tcu.edu
eng.tcu.edu

Reviewers from March 2015 through February 2016

A journal is only as good as its reviewers. We acknowledge and celebrate the dedication, good will, and expertise of our generous reviewers:

Karen Adams, Arizona State University
Kristin Arola, Washington State University
Nicholas Behm, Elmhurst College
Patrick Bizzaro, Indiana University of Pennsylvania (Retired)
Ella Browning, University of South Florida
Jennifer Clary-Lemon, University of Winnipeg
Frankie Condon, University of Waterloo
Christiane Donahue, Dartmouth College
Jessica Enoch, University of Maryland
Joe Harris, University of Delaware
Brian Huot, Kent State University
Elizabeth Kalbfleisch, Southern Connecticut State University
Miles Kimball, Texas Tech University
Daisy Levy, Southern Vermont College
Brad Lucas, Texas Christian University
Donna Qualley, Western Washington University
Dan Royer, Grand Valley State University
Wendy Ryden, Long Island University
Lucille Schultz, University of Cincinnati (Professor Emerita)
Gillian Steinberg, Yeshiva University
Kathleen Vandenberg, Boston University
Amy Vidali, University of Colorado, Denver
Gary Weissman, University of Cincinnati

composition STUDIES

Volume 44, Number 1
Spring 2016

Editor
Laura R. Micciche

Book Review Editor
Kelly Kinney

Editorial Assistants
Christina M. LaVecchia
Janine Morris

Former Editors
Gary Tate
Robert Mayberry
Christina Murphy
Peter Vandenberg
Ann George
Carrie Leverenz
Brad E. Lucas
Jennifer Clary-Lemon

Advisory Board

Linda Adler-Kassner
University of California, Santa Barbara

Tom Amorose
Seattle Pacific University

Chris Anson
North Carolina State University

Valerie Balester
Texas A&M University

Robert Brooke
University of Nebraska, Lincoln

Sidney Dobrin
University of Florida

Lisa Ede
Oregon State University

Paul Heilker
Virginia Polytechnic Institute and State University

Peggy O'Neill
Loyola College

Victor Villanueva
Washington State University

SUBSCRIPTIONS

Composition Studies is published twice each year (May and November). Annual subscription rates: Individuals $25 (Domestic), $30 (International), and $15 (Students). To subsccribe online, please visit http://www.uc.edu/journals/composition-studies/subscriptions.html

BACK ISSUES

Back issues, five years prior to the present, are freely accessible on our website at http://www.uc.edu/journals/composition-studies/issues/archives.html. If you don't see what you're looking for, contact us. Also, recent back issues are now available through Amazon.com. To find issues, use the advanced search feature and search on "Composition Studies" (title) and "Parlor Press" (publisher).

BOOK REVIEWS

Assignments are made from a file of potential book reviewers. If you are interested in writing a review, please contact our Book Review editor at kkinney@uwyo.edu.

JOURNAL SCOPE

The oldest independent periodical in the field, *Composition Studies* publishes original articles relevant to rhetoric and composition, including those that address teaching college writing; theorizing rhetoric and composing; administering writing programs; and, among other topics, preparing the field's future teacher-scholars. All perspectives and topics of general interest to the profession are welcome. We also publish Course Designs, which contextualize, theorize, and reflect on the content and pedagogy of a course. Contributions to Composing With are invited by the editor, though queries are welcome (send to compstudies@uc.edu). Cfps, announcements, and letters to the editor are most welcome. *Composition Studies* does not consider previously published manuscripts, unrevised conference papers, or unrevised dissertation chapters.

SUBMISSIONS

For submission information and guidelines, see http://www.uc.edu/journals/composition-studies/submissions/overview.html.

Direct all correspondence to:

>   Laura Micciche, Editor
>   Department of English
>   University of Cincinnati
>   PO Box 210069
>   Cincinnati, OH 45221–0069
>   compstudies@uc.edu

Composition Studies is grateful for the support of the University of Cincinnati.

©2016 by Laura Micciche, Editor
Production and printing is managed by Parlor Press, www.parlorpress.com.
ISSN 1534–9322.
Cover design by Jennika Smith and photo by joo0ey.

http://www.uc.edu/journals/composition-studies.html

composition STUDIES

Volume 44, Number 1
Spring 2016

Reviewers from March 2015 through February 2016	4
From the Guest Editors	**10**
Composition's "Global Turn": Writing Instruction in Multilingual/ Translingual and Transnational Contexts	10
Articles	**13**
Translation as (Global) Writing *Bruce Horner and Laura Tetreault*	13
Teaching for Agency: From Appreciating Linguistic Diversity to Empowering Student Writers *Shawna Shapiro, Michelle Cox, Gail Shuck, and Emily Simnitt*	31
Negotiating World Englishes in a Writing-Based MOOC *Ben McCorkle, Kay Halasek, Kaitlin Clinnin, and Cynthia L. Selfe*	53
"This is a Field that's Open, not Closed": Multilingual and International Writing Faculty Respond to Composition Theory *Lisa R. Arnold*	72
Negotiating Languages and Cultures: Enacting Translingualism through a Translation Assignment *Julia Kiernan, Joyce Meier, and Xiqiao Wang*	89
Course Design	**108**
World Rhetorics *Ghanashyam Sharma*	108
Where We Are: The "Global Turn" and Its Implications for Composition	**127**
Moving Beyond Methodological Nationalism *Rebecca Lorimer Leonard*	127

Across Time and Space: The Transnational Movement of
Asian American Rhetoric 131
Morris Young

The Global Turn and the Question of "Speaking From" 134
Bo Wang

Doing Transnational Writing Studies: A Case for the
Literacy History Interview 138
Kate Vieira

Localizing Transnational Composition Research and Program Design 141
Amy Zenger

Fast Movements, Slow Processes 144
Jay Jordan

The "Trans" in Transnational-Translingual: Rhetorical and
Linguistic Flexibility as New Norms 147
Christiane Donahue

Book Reviews 151

The Translanguaging Conversation: A Dialogic Review 151
Reviewed by Mark Brantner, Alanna Frost, and Suzanne Blum Malley
Review of *Reworking English in Rhetoric and Composition: Global Interrogations, Local Interventions*, edited by Bruce Horner and Karen Kopelson; *Literacy as Translingual Practice: Between Communities and Classrooms*, edited by Suresh Canagarajah

Race, Language Policy, and Silence in Composition Studies 160
Reviewed by David F. Green, Jr.
Review of *Vernacular Insurrections: Race, Black Protest, and the New Century in Composition Studies*, by Carmen Kynard; *Shaping Language Policy in the U.S.: The Role of Composition Studies*, by Scott Wible; *A Search Past Silence: The Literacy of Young Men*, by David E. Kirkland

Writing as Language in Use: On the Growing Engagement between
Sociolinguistics and Writing Studies 169
Reviewed by Joel Heng Hartse
Review of *The Sociolinguistics of Writing*, by Theresa Lillis; *Writing and Society*, by Florian Coulmas

Del Otro Lado: Literacy and Migration across the U.S.-Mexico Border,
by Susan V. Meyers   177
   Reviewed by Rubén Casas

WAC and Second Language Writers: Research towards Linguistically and Culturally Inclusive Programs and Practices, edited by
Terry Myers Zawacki and Michelle Cox   181
   Reviewed by Shirley K Rose

Transnational Writing Program Administration, edited by
David Martins   185
   Reviewed by Chris Thaiss

Transiciones: Pathways of Latinas and Latinos Writing in High School and College, by Todd Ruecker   189
   Reviewed by Kat Williams

Contributors   193

Call for Proposals – 2016 Graduate Research Network   200

From the Guest Editors

Composition's "Global Turn": Writing Instruction in Multilingual/Translingual and Transnational Contexts

In our initial call for papers for this special issue, we asserted that composition has witnessed a surge in attention to the multilingual/translingual and transnational dimensions of higher education, a shift aligned with what Wendy Hesford described in 2006 as a "global turn" in our disciplinary research and explanatory frameworks. This shift or "turn" seems inevitable for us to engage, as colleges and universities recruit increasing numbers of international students and establish satellite campuses worldwide, the U.S. resident population diversifies in ways consistent with broader emigration and immigration trends, and discourse about higher education becomes more fully immersed in and responsive to global flows of individuals and cultures. In short, as U.S. institutions are becoming more globally minded so, too, are the people who work and learn there.

In addition, our own experiences in higher education have spurred our interest in exploring these topics with colleagues in the field. As part of a three-year grant sponsored by the U.S. Embassy in Iraq, Connie partnered with English department faculty members at Salahaddin University in Erbil, Kurdistan, to negotiate curricular and pedagogical reform—meaningful work that invited critical reflection about the intended and unintended consequences of transnational collaborations in fostering institutional change. Meanwhile, Brian has taught college writing courses comprised of international and residential multilingual writers for several years and participated in a short study-abroad at the University of Malaga in Spain in order to better appreciate the situations of international students. Together, our experiences have shown us that there is no part of our professional or personal lives that can somehow "escape" the global, if that were ever even possible or desirable. Languages and cultures engage us daily, and we engage them with great appreciation for the diversity that enriches our own teaching and research.

As composition continues to address increasingly multilingual and international realities, the authors contributing to this special issue remind us that maintaining an appreciation of the relationship between the theory and practice, past and future, and global and local contexts of writing instruction remains a vital endeavor. In addition to the overlapping perspectives these authors share about the need for global attentiveness in writing and rhetoric, this special issue also highlights the presence of productive differences in the theoretical foundations, methodologies, and terminologies being used to address this need.

Included in this issue are five articles from teacher-researchers who share commitments to explore the multilingual/translingual and transnational aspects of writing and writing instruction and who develop ways of tapping into currents already present in our classrooms to further guide, refine, and reinforce them. It is our pleasure to introduce these articles here.

In their article "Translation as (Global) Writing," Bruce Horner and Laura Tetreault draw on translation studies to both contest neoliberal appropriations that render translation an invisible process and to articulate an alternate framework that posits all writing as acts of translation. Horner and Tetreault argue that treating writing as translation not only helps students and teachers recognize language difference as a feature of all writing, but also reveals the translingual dimensions and implications of conventional writing practices, such as paraphrase and interpretation.

A key construct critical for the empowerment of multilingual students is agency, which Shawna Shapiro, Michelle Cox, Gail Shuck, and Emily Simnitt foreground in their article, "Teaching for Agency: From Appreciating Linguistic Diversity to Empowering Student Writers." Acknowledging the resources multilingual writers bring to the classroom, as well as their needs and goals for English language development, these authors advocate pedagogical approaches that create opportunities for students to evaluate their writerly decisions not only in terms of language choice but also with regard to mode, medium, and genre. Extending the notion of agency outside of the writing classroom, this article also describes program policies that further support student choice and academic success.

"Negotiating World Englishes in a Writing-Based MOOC," by Ben McCorkle, Kay Halasek, Kaitlin Clinnin, and Cynthia L. Selfe, explores the impact of a peer-review process designed to foster robust dialogue about individual and common language learning experiences as a means of empowering participants in a globalized classroom. Leveraging the principles of emergent pedagogical theory, these authors underscore the centrality of second language writing instruction for compositionists and demonstrate how MOOCs can serve as open, democratic spaces where assumptions about cultural, linguistic, and geographical difference can be made visible and, in turn, productively negotiated.

Lisa R. Arnold's article, "'This is a Field that's Open, not Closed': Multilingual and International Writing Faculty Respond to Composition Theory," reports on a professional development seminar she organized at the American University of Beirut (AUB), where writing faculty studied "core" composition scholarship and gained insight on the cultural and linguistic assumptions shaping North American pedagogies and theoretical perspectives. Using rich descriptions of AUB's writing program, faculty, and students to situate participant responses and reflections as practitioners, Arnold's study illuminates the challenges faced by—and, importantly, the values attached to—writing instruction in this multilingual, international university setting.

In "Negotiating Languages and Cultures: Enacting Translingualism through a Translation Assignment," Julia Kiernan, Joyce Meier, and Xiqiao Wang present a multipart writing assignment in which English language learners translate texts—ranging from culture stories to scholarly articles—compare versions, and then critically reflect on their writing practices to build capacity for knowing and naming their individual language negotiation processes and, in turn, strengthen their translingual competences. Drawing from their own teaching experiences using this translation assignment, the authors demonstrate how writing about transnational and translingual experiences not only builds English language learners' agency and develops metalinguistic awareness but also responds to the field's call for asset-based, culturally sustaining pedagogical practices.

Our special issue also includes one course design: Ghanashyam Sharma's "World Rhetorics," which highlights a course designed to help internationalize Stony Brook University's graduate certificate program in the teaching of writing. Sharma's course is organized around a three-point axis of geopolitical/regional, historical/temporal, and thematic/ideational views. Through the lenses of history, sociocultural theory, and comparative rhetoric, this course's unique framework invites students to develop a critical understanding of the world's rhetorical traditions as not only situated within particular geopolitical and material contexts but also perpetually in flux and thus always open to revision and change.

Seven short essays comprise the Where We Are forum, a roundtable where scholars with diverse backgrounds and perspectives are invited to share their thoughts about the issue's theme. Individually and collectively, these contributions from Rebecca Lorimer Leonard, Morris Young, Bo Wang, Kate Vieira, Amy Zenger, Jay Jordan, and Christiane Donahue promise to deepen readers' appreciation of the questions and issues attending our understanding of writing instruction in multilingual, translingual, and transnational contexts.

Finally, we wish to thank Laura Micciche for enabling this opportunity and the *CS* team for supporting our efforts. This special issue would not have been possible without their thoughtful guidance and advice. We hope that readers will find these articles and essays as engaging and energizing as we do, and that this issue will lead to continued, vigorous conversation about the research and teaching of composition.

Brian Ray, University of Arkansas at Little Rock
Connie Kendall Theado, University of Cincinnati

Works Cited

Hesford, Wendy. "Global Turns and Cautions in Rhetoric and Composition Studies." *PMLA* 121.3 (2006): 787-801. Print.

Articles

Translation as (Global) Writing

Bruce Horner and Laura Tetreault

This article explores translation as a useful point of departure and framework for taking a translingual approach to writing engaging globalization. Globalization and the knowledge economy are putting renewed emphasis on translation as a key site of contest between a dominant language ideology of monolingualism aligned with fast capitalist neoliberalism and an emerging language ideology variously identified as *translingualism, plurilingualism, translanguaging,* and *transcultural literacy*. We first distinguish between theories of translation aligned with neoliberalism, on the one hand, and, on the other hand, a critical approach to translation focused on the difference that a translingual approach insists translation makes to languages, language relations, and language users. We then describe ways that a translingual approach to language difference in writing can be pursued in the classroom through student experimentation with translation of ordinary texts and with paraphrase and interpretation. Treating all writing as translation, we argue, can help students and their teachers better engage with language difference as a feature of all writing rather than imagining such engagement to fall outside the norm of communicative practice.

In this article, we treat translation as a useful point of departure and framework for taking a translingual approach to writing, an approach, we argue, that is aligned with globalization "from below" contesting neoliberal fast capitalism. Following an overview locating a renewed emphasis on translation and emerging postmonolingual approaches to language and language relations in current conditions of globalization, we consider strategies by which writing can be taught as translation, including experimentation with conventional translation from one language to another as well as with the translation in meaning effected through such conventional practices as paraphrase and interpretation. Treating writing as translation, we argue, can help students and their teachers better engage with the productive labor on and with language difference as a feature of all writing, rather than imagining such engagement to fall outside the norm of communicative practice.

Translating Translation, Globalization, and Postmonolingualism

Translation is conventionally defined as finding equivalents in meaning and form in two languages: for example, the French *éducation* for the English *education*, *diversité* for *diversity*, *le monde* for *the world*. Without disputing the impossibility of an exact equivalence between languages of the sort obtaining in, say, mathematics (A = B, 3 = 1 + 2), such an approach to translation heralds—at least as an ideal—the erasure of any sign of a lack of equivalence, so that the fact, necessity, and labor of translation are rendered invisible (see Müller 207-08). In this approach, translation, again at least ideally, does not change the substance of what is translated, nor the languages to and from which that substance is translated or their relations to one another, nor the users of those languages or their relation to them. What is demanded in this approach is someone with mature (i.e., fully developed and settled) "native speaker" fluency in both languages, fluency that facilitates but is not affected by movement between them. Differences in language are seen as surface level, underneath which, it is assumed, resides a solid foundation of sameness—that which may be encoded differently but remains the same in any code.

This conception of translation is aligned with neoliberal fast capitalism's pursuit of globalization "from above," in which Visa can claim that "It's Fluent in Every Language," and Mastercard can counter, "Any time. Anywhere. Any Language" (Ganahl). As translation scholar Michael Cronin notes, translation plays a key role in the new globalized information economy of neoliberalism. For this economy, he writes, translation is "not simply a by-product of globalization but is a constituent, integral part of how the phenomenon both operates and makes sense of itself" (34). For "[i]f information is often hailed as the basic raw material of the new economy and significant economic gains are to be made from the production of goods with a high cognitive content, then it follows that language itself is not only a key factor in the expression of that information but it is also a crucial means in accessing the information" (16). Translators are thus "indispensible intermediaries in the new informational economy" and as such are pressured to meet its demands for translation that can spread information and products quickly and efficiently to global markets any time, anywhere, and in any language (16).

However, globalization in a broader sense encompassing globalization from below as well as from above—the growing global movement and exchange of people, ideas, and goods on terms contested by subordinated and dominant groups—has put renewed emphasis on translation not merely as a distinct form of writing but also as a feature and outcome of all writing—a feature that entails difficulty and friction—labor—and that produces rather than bridges or erases difference—under what Yasemin Yildiz has described as our current "postmonolingual" condition.¹ From this perspective, translation is not a mechanical erasure of surface linguistic differences but, instead, an inevitable feature of all language practice insofar as the norm of such practice is not sameness but difference. Thus Yildiz uses "postmonolingual" to reference not any ostensible increase in conventional multilingualism but, instead, a break from monolingualist ideology's tenets of languages as discrete, stable, internally uniform entities each tied indelibly to specific, similarly discrete, stable, and internally uniform ethnic and civic identities, for and between which translations serve as neutral bridge. Under postmonolingual conditions, models of language are emerging that instead posit languages as internally diverse, interpenetrating, and fluid both in character and in relation to other languages and to social identities, which are likewise understood as multiple and fluid—the always emerging products of practices. Unlike conventional models of multilingualism favored by neoliberalism that favor an "additive" model of language difference (see Dor), a postmonolingual perspective treats even those utterances that appear to be glossally monolingual as potentially non-monolingual-ist in their production, as when English is appropriated and put to new work by those not identified as Anglo-American "native speakers" of English (see Lu, "Living"; Widdowson). Under such conditions, even reiterations of conventional English usages come to be seen as "different" rather than simply "more of the same" insofar as, relocated in time as well as space, such utterances now more clearly represent a choice by social historically located actors to both contribute to the sedimentation of the conventional and thereby also to recontextualize the conventional (Lu and Horner, "Translingual"). Difference, in short, is seen not as deviation from a norm of underlying sameness but, rather, as itself the norm and outcome of all language practice (Pennycook, *Language*).

Compositionists have grown familiar with a variety of competing terms that have emerged in response to this postmonolingual condition, including *plurilingualism, translingualism, translanguaging,* and *transcultural literacy.*² Not surprisingly, these are sometimes conflated with one another and with conventional understandings of translation practices (and with L2 writing), not only because of the "trans-" prefix many of them share but also because of the dominance of monolingualist definitions of language and language difference (e.g., French vs. Chinese). Just as translation is subject to competing inflections—some in alignment with neoliberalist aims of fast and efficient bridging of difference, some focusing on difference and difficulty as the norm of all translation and, indeed, all communicative practice—so terms like *translingualism* have likewise been subject to contradictory inflections. For example, while some writers have used "translingual" to designate writing with specific features (e.g., with what is recognized as code-meshing), others have argued against such a designation as an unwitting reversion to monolingualist tenets in its reinforcement of discrete and stable codes (see Canagarajah, "Introduction," "Translanguaging"; Lu, "Metaphors"; Vance), and use "translingual" to refer not to a specific set of glossal features in utterances recognizable within monolingualism as different but instead to a specific orientation or set of dispositions toward all language and language use (see, for example, Lu and Horner, "Translingual").[3] Both translation and translinguality can be understood as referencing either technical means by which to overcome language difference as monolingualism defines language difference, or a shift in orientation toward recognizing difference and its production as the norm of all communicative practice.

In the former, translation is understood as a special case, a currently necessary if regrettable cost (to be minimized) of the communication of people, goods, and services between discrete, stable, linguistically homogeneous communities—what Mary Louise Pratt long ago critiqued as linguistic utopias ("Linguistic"). However, globalization in its broad sense has called that utopian vision into question and placed translation as in fact the norm of language practice—not simply in the sense that translation, as conventionally understood, is increasingly commonplace and in demand as a consequence of increases in communication between hitherto isolated groups resulting from changes to migration patterns and the development of global communication technologies and economic exchange, but also in the sense that translation now seems a feature of communicative practice even within what is recognized as the same language. What were seen as discrete, internally uniform, and stable sets of meanings and glossal forms shared by and defining members of discrete, homogeneous communities—Pratt's "linguistic utopias"—are now understood to be anything but discrete, internally uniform, stable, shared, or defining. English itself, as Alastair Pennycook has argued, is a language always in translation, no matter by or with whom it is practiced ("English" 33).

This latter notion of all writing as translation can help to counter the seeming alignment between an emphasis on language difference in scholarship on translation, translinguality, and plurilinguality, on the one hand, and, on the other, the celebration of language difference and flexibility as means to neoliberalist ends of expanding markets and exploiting workers (anytime, anywhere, and in any language), a potential alignment that has been the subject of critique by various writers (see for example Cameron; Dor; Flores; Heller, "Globalization," "Repenser"; Kubota). For, as Cronin argues, translation—especially nonliterary translation, which is often viewed in mechanistic terms as ideologically neutral—"is ideally placed to understand *both* the transnational movement that is globalization *and* the transnational movement that is anti-globalization" (1, emphasis added). For example, as L. G. Crane, M. B.

Lombard, and E. M. Tenz observe, researchers in human geography increasingly feel both the means and the pressure to "go global," which puts renewed attention on translation. As they explain, there are "increasing possibilities for comparative cross-national and cross-cultural research projects to take place, giving rise to opportunities for intellectual endeavour at a scale that was previously more difficult to access. . . . [N]o doubt, related to drives through funding initiatives requiring academics to engage in multinational research ventures" (39). Such research, they note, "has pushed issues around translation into the foreground of academic debates" (39). But researchers' actual engagement in translation, they discover, "produces moments of friction and hesitation [. . . at which] meanings and conceptualisations are challenged by new ideas and thoughts," the antithesis of the neoliberalist ideal for translation as a means of efficient one-way communication of knowledge (40).

Because nonliterary translation is often viewed as mechanical and free of ideological baggage, Cronin argues that it is most indicative of the language tensions embedded in globalization—if, that is, we take a critical approach to translation and the processes of mediation the work of translation entails. Such a critical approach focuses on what a neoliberal ideal of translation elides and aims to render invisible—the differences and difficulties Crane et al. report, not only bridged but produced through the process of mediation that translation entails: what Anna Lowenhaupt Tsing identifies as the "friction" inevitable and necessary to global exchange (Cronin 124-25; Tsing 6). The speed, efficiency, accuracy, and ideological neutrality of the neoliberal ideal for translation are from this alternative, critical standpoint chimeras masking difficulty and differences in the translation process that constitute the actual norm of translations and their inevitably contingent and ideologically inflected character.

Translation and/in Composition

While it may not seem initially obvious how questions about translation enter into a space like the composition classroom, we argue that translation offers a particularly rich framework for work in composition insofar as it brings to the fore the negotiation of language difference as well as ideologies of language difference that a translingual approach calls for. Writing instruction has always been institutionally structured as a key site for the negotiation of language ideology, whether through reproduction of the tacit policy of English-only monolingualism that has long dominated composition (Horner and Trimbur) or through cultivation of orientations critical of that ideology. And as Nelson Flores has argued of TESOL, composition teachers, too, have the option of working "to expose the constructed nature and ideological assumptions of all language practices [to] . . . resist neoliberalism's corporatist agenda" by helping students learn "how language can be consciously used to experiment with new subjectivities and produce new subject positions" (517). In response to Flores's and other similar calls (Canagarajah, "Place"; Horner et al.), we argue that by focusing on translation, writing pedagogy can encourage translingual orientations to languages as always emergent and constructed "local practices" (Pennycook, *Language*) and thus the need for all writers to attend to and take responsibility in their writing—whether seemingly conventional or seemingly deviant—for the difference their choices inevitably make to such practices as local, contingent, emergent rather than sets of unquestionable standards or codes.[4]

Pennycook writes that translation is always implicated within the "traffic in meaning, a passing to and fro of ideas, concepts, symbols, discourses"—a traffic that is inevitably also a site for struggle ("English" 34). Pennycook locates this ideologically inflected view of an "activist translation" in relation to Lawrence Venuti's aim to "disrupt the assimilationary and domesticating tendencies that eradicate difference through translation" (qtd. in Pennycook, "English" 43). An activist translation approaches translation "neither in terms of the reductive and pejorative role it has been given within language teaching . . . nor only as the activity conducted by those who work to translate a text into one language or another . . . [but] as part of a much broader traffic in meaning" (Venuti qtd. in Pennycook, "English" 43). For Pennycook, translation characterizes all language use, with communication between languages merely "a special case: all communication involves translation," and conventional translation itself is "the key to understanding [all] communication" once difference is seen not as an alternative to normal practice but an inevitable outcome of writing ("English" 40). Treating all writing as translation allows us to see writers as always engaged in a process of negotiating and reworking common language practices, and to direct our attention and that of our students to exploring the responsibilities entailed by specific translational/writing practices for reproducing and revising languages and language relations.

While Pennycook is also arguing (in "English as a Language Always in Translation") for English Language Teaching (ELT) as translation—his twist on the conventional meaning ascribed to ELT—similar calls for a pedagogy of translation have emerged from literary studies. Emily O. Wittman and Katrina Windon, for example, argue that a translation studies course should be required of all undergraduate English literature majors to shift the monolingual nature of such departments (449). For Wittman and Windon, studying translation means paying attention to the ways in which meaning and origin are layered and multiple, and this attention is also necessarily implicated in power and the struggle over valuation. Translations reveal networks of power that circulate certain forms of language use and not others, bringing to light the usually hidden dynamics of what happens when writers work with what they perceive as specific discourses or genres. This process illustrates how writers do not simply choose to assimilate into or resist particular norms, but are instead always reworking what are usually recognized as norms. A method of teaching translation in the sense of working with, on, and between conventionally demarcated languages is one step toward teaching all writing as translation in the specific way we are arguing for. Building on such calls for a pedagogy of translation in literature and Cronin's call for focusing on forms of translation and writing usually assumed to be mechanical and thus ideologically neutral, we argue for a focus on translation in the production of nonliterary writing—that is, in what is ordinarily identified as composition.

A composition pedagogy of translation would focus attention on production by emphasizing how translation, like all writing, is a site of struggle—labor—that contends with competing ideologies, resources, representations, and assumed expectations of readers, in addition to the writer's sense of identity and desire to claim particular identities. Translation between conventionally demarcated languages thus represents not a deviation from the norm but a more intensive version of what is true of all writing. Because translation between languages as conventionally defined works actively within this site of struggle, it can continually draw attention to its own production. But it is also possible to see all discursive performance as a process of production within this struggle of translation.

Viewing translation as labor in this sense dismantles the myth behind neoliberal claims about language and the potential alignment of some conceptions of multilingualism or plurilingualism with neoliberalist ideology. Neoliberalist ideology occludes such labor by treating language as commodity: hence its conception of translation as ideally the friction-free, mechanical transfer of meaning from one language to another. The occlusion of this labor constructs the myth that there is a linguistic commodity that is translated cleanly without change to the meaning, the languages to and from which the meaning is translated, and their relations to one another and to language users. But the reality is that language, language relations, and their users are always reworked as that ostensible commodity gets translated.

Approaching translation as the labor of reworking language and meaning challenges the mechanisms of deproduction by which a translated text is understood to be (i.e., misrecognized as) transparent—as a direct recoding between languages (as in A = B).[5] A translation framework for writing views terms as always up for questioning, considers what slippages of meaning and perception occur in the spaces where one usage is substituted for another, and explores how these slips and transfers—intentionally or not—operate in relation to larger narratives and ideologies. As we discuss below, those adopting a translation framework might ask students to translate their own or others' texts as starting points for discussing the differences in meaning and power relations that are negotiated in producing such translations; read different translations of the same text while noting points of tension between them; discuss what narratives are activated by certain terms and not others; and consider the ways writing ostensibly within the same language engages the same dynamics of difference, using paraphrase as a particular instance of everyday translation in composition.

Teaching Writing as Translation, Teaching Translation as Writing

We have argued that translation, rather than signifying a distinct form of writing, represents a more intensive version of the negotiation of difference in language that a translingual approach claims all writing entails. But without discounting the value of and need for courses focused specifically on teaching translation, we posit here that because the negotiation of language difference is more immediately apparent in translation writing, translation provides a useful framework by which to explore such negotiation in all writing. We are aware that composition has often invoked translation as a metaphor for writing that crosses over from one text, identity, or context to another while leaving unaddressed translation as a form of writing itself (e.g., Cook-Sather; Eubanks; Schor; Soliday, "Translating"). Granted, such a conceptualization of translation risks problematically reinforcing the stability of the texts, identities, or contexts to and from which meaning is carried over, as well as the stability of the entity transferred—like the problematics scholars have faced in conceptualizing knowledge transfer (see Beach). As Pratt has observed of invocations of "cultural translation," the concept "bears the unresolvable contradiction that in naming itself it preserves the distances/distinctions it works to overcome" ("Response" 95). But the resolution to such an unresolvable contradiction, we suggest, is to deploy the translation metaphor not so much to name the process by which to resolve predetermined conditions of difference but rather as an analytical tool by which to bring such contradictions to visibility (cf. Wagner 98.): as point of departure rather than endpoint. For, as Birgit Wagner observes regarding "cultural translation," "everything depends on the use you make of it" (99).

Thus, to teach writing as translation, we might best begin by teaching conventional translation as writing. So, for example, students can be asked to read different translations of a text and to examine what narratives are activated by different choices, and how they see those narratives connecting to larger ideologies. Students can also experiment with translating their texts or others' texts as a heuristic for generating multiple translations, working with whatever language resources they choose to bring to the task. These strategies can then be extended into translation across discourses or across media by having students investigate how each act of translation changes a text, what narratives are activated by different choices each entails, and what ideologies and histories are illuminated by each.

The fact that students may see translation as unfamiliar or unusual in a writing class can itself serve to destabilize monolingualist ideologies by asking students to question why it is often taken for granted in the context of U.S. college composition that a writing class will only involve writing in something called Standard English. Using translation as an analytic framework, we can then have students explore the actual instability of the languages, discourses, genres, and meanings that translation ostensibly works with and between. Composition teachers and their students are familiar with the treatment of languages and discourses as discrete, stable, and associated with identity formation, invoked in the trope of students negotiating between home or cultural identities and a desired, or enforced, academic identity as they learn to write academic discourse and leave behind, or attempt to keep, what are categorized as their home languages. That trope figures students as having to decide whether to give up or somehow carry over elements of a home language or dialect—treated as stable, internally uniform, and discrete—into this new academic discourse. Academic discourse is represented as a stable, internally uniform category called college writing for students to be introduced to, on the way toward adopting an also supposedly uniform and stable academic identity. Debates such as those tied to "Students' Right to Their Own Language" then ask to what extent students should bring so-called home or nonacademic forms of discourse into academic writing, when these categories are seen as radically different from one another. These debates become especially fraught when language choices are tied so closely to invocations of identity.[6]

Alternatively, using translation as an analytic framework, we can reconsider the relations of difference that such conventional models posit. Such a reconsideration can work in two directions: to challenge the discrete character of languages, discourses, and identities posited as different, and, conversely, to challenge the uniformity—the sameness—to utterances ordinarily located within any of these. Having students produce multiple translations to and from English, drawing collaboratively on whatever language resources they have, can make apparent both the interpenetration of ostensibly discrete languages with one another, on the one hand (*éducation*/education, *chī* /chow, *haus*/house, etc.) and, on the other, the lack of uniformity within what are conventionally demarcated as individual languages (e.g., in French, *éducation, formation, apprentissage, enseignement*). Experimentation in producing multiple, multidirectional translations can thus challenge commonplace, dominant models of languages as singular codes and of translation as a matter of recoding, shifting the question from considering what the single correct translation might be, as the code metaphor encourages, to considering the variety of possible translations one might propose, and with what consequences: for example, the consequences for meaning and argument of translating "education" as *éducation, formation, enseignement,* etc. As Weiguo Qu observes of a course for Chinese students translating to and from English, "A foreign language such as English may be . . . used to de-automatize habituated way of thinking, challenging and subverting the power relations embedded in the Chinese traditional rhetoric," power relations that occlude the diversity within that rhetoric and within English to render both of them seemingly internally uniform as simply Chinese vs. English (72). Qu reports that his students, forced to make a decision and a choice rather than imagining their task as translators to be algorithmic, "are changed to cognize the world in line with their own decisions and with what they themselves believe in. They want their own definitions, English or Chinese" (73).

The consequences and motivations for such choices can be further explored through the narrative theory framework provided by translation scholar Mona Baker. Baker explains that the framing of events through narrative sets up "structures of anticipation" that guide interpretations (156). In terms of translation, this idea allows for an understanding of translational choices "not merely as local linguistic challenges but as contributing directly to the narratives that shape our social world" (156). For Baker, translators and interpreters play a key role in shaping social and political reality. In her examples, how translators reframe aspects of political conflicts when translating between Arabic and English invokes narratives of the War on Terror, American nationalism, and Islamic fundamentalism. But this narrative framework for translation can be applied not only to political conflicts but also to any site of ideological struggle—including that struggle as it plays out when we consider all writing as an act of translation.

We can consider translations, then, in terms of the narratives they activate: the identities, trajectories, values they (re)present. For example, a student in one of our classes, when asked to consider the various French terms she might use to translate the English "education," wrote:

> I, myself, would choose the French word *formation*. I find this term to relate to more situations that I am currently experiencing at Louisville. I am being trained to become a [_____] by first being trained in the general education requirements, and even before that I was being trained in high school to be educated to go to college.
>
> The relationship between word choice, thinking, and living to me suggests that the word you choose can cause you to not only understand more, but learn more. In doing so you can begin to change

> words for others and make sense of what you are experiencing in your day to day life.[7]

The narrative this student offers is that of her education as a sequence of training preparing her for and leading directly to a fixed career—one for which she is ultimately being trained. However, she activates this narrative after having considered a range of other possible ways of translating "education," such as education as a kind of socialization into manners. As she writes earlier in the same paper, she started

> noticing that all education is involved with manners or how you behave. Through formal education we go to school, and interact with peers, and teachers who expect the students to behave in a certain way in that environment. Society teaches us what is "in" or popular, and also how we can further our knowledge on the popular people or items. Professionally we are expected to behave a certain way along with having the knowledge of the field you are in, if you did not it would be inappropriate.

While the student arrives at a sense of these competing narratives through considering different ways of translating "education" (into French), it should be apparent that this investigation leads to consideration within a single language—here, English—how "education" might be translated—e.g., as socialization, employment preparation or training, acquisition of general knowledge, etc. For translation is present not only in composing that involves shifts between languages, discourses, or media, but also in writing strategies that have become so commonplace as to not appear to merit attention at all as translation (i.e., as a negotiation and production of difference). Thus, to Cronin's observation that it is especially important to pay attention to forms of translation and writing that seem initially mundane, mechanical, and thus ideologically neutral, we can add that it is likewise important to recognize the dynamics of translation in writing that does not, after all, appear to require or engage these dynamics at all, such as translation within English. Doing so counters the conventional, dominant identification of difference with discrete languages (e.g., French versus English) by recognizing difference obtaining within these—even in iterations of what might appear to be the same.

In other words, we can apply frameworks such as Baker's to the study of writing not only across languages, but within the same language, showing how translation not only operates between what are recognized as separate languages, but within a seemingly—yet not actually—uniform language like English itself. As Baker writes, "by contrast to static, power-insensitive concepts like 'norms,' narrative theory recognizes that dominance and resistance not only shape our behavior and discursive choices, but that they are also always in a relationship of tension" (167). Translation is a site where the linguistic activation of certain narratives of dominance and resistance plays out. This conception allows students of writing to pay deeper attention to this ever-present tension within any text—those read and those written.

Paraphrase as Translation

We take paraphrase as exemplary of the kind of writing task predominantly understood as mechanical and ideologically neutral but that, like the non-literary translations Cronin discusses, constitutes a site for negotiation of powerful differences. Paraphrase appears in many writing handbooks and online resources and is a feature of most writing classes that ask students to work with others' texts, often in lessons addressing ways to avoid plagiarism. Typically, paraphrase is treated as a means of representing the same ideas and information in words other than those used in the source text. For example, Purdue University's Online Writing Lab (OWL) describes paraphrase as "[y]our own rendition of essential information and ideas expressed by someone else, presented in a new form" and "[o]ne legitimate way (when accompanied by accurate documentation) to borrow from a source" ("Paraphrase"). Paraphrases are distinguished from summaries by being "a more detailed restatement" than summaries, and from plagiarism in using significantly different wording and in identifying the source text. (Of course, like many statements on plagiarism, the statement on paraphrase fails to acknowledge its source.)

Many popular writing handbooks and online resources illustrate this tension between making an idea new or putting it in your own words and accurately borrowing from a source or restating its ideas—assuming that changing the wording does not change the meaning. *The Everyday Writer* advises students that "a paraphrase accurately states all the relevant information from a passage *in your own words and sentence structures,* without any additional comments or elaborations. A paraphrase is useful when the main points of a passage, their order, and at least some details are important but—unlike passages worth quoting—the particular wording is not" (Lunsford 207, emphasis in original). The University of Wisconsin-Madison's online writer's handbook recommends that "you should *summarize or paraphrase* when what you want from the source is the *idea* expressed, and *not the specific language* used to express it [or] you can express in fewer words what the key point of a source is" ("Paraphrasing Vs. Quoting," emphasis in original).

While this advice is useful to student writers trying to understand the difference between quoting and paraphrasing, these examples also show a tendency to detach *idea* from *language,* revealing an underlying assumption that an idea can remain perfectly intact even if the language used to express it is altered. Such treatments of paraphrase imply that there is a single meaning unchanged by the rewording effected through paraphrase, a meaning that successful paraphrase, like successful summary, preserves. (The Purdue OWL statement on paraphrase recommends paraphrase in part as a way to help writers "grasp the full meaning of the original" being paraphrased ["Paraphrase"]). But composition classes can instead analyze paraphrase not as a mechanical act of transferring meaning from one set of words to another—to put in other words what is in other, yet somehow equivalent, words—but instead as an act of reshaping meaning (cf. Roman Jakobson's description of intra-lingual translation or "rewording," or Frédéric François's concept of "reprise-modification") through an act of translation engaging, and producing, difference.[8]

For instance, asking students to produce, individually as well as collectively, different paraphrases of the same source text can reveal how paraphrase does not simply move or reproduce an idea found in one set of words to another or distill an idea but (re)shapes the idea itself and repositions the writer and the texts between which the writer is ostensibly moving that idea. Students can come to see how paraphrases activate different narratives through word choice, syntax, organization, and so forth, revealing many layers of ideological complexity. (The same can be done with summary, a term which belies the difference produced in summary by alluding to mathematical equations [e.g., of 5 as the sum of 3 + 2]).

This treatment of paraphrase answers calls for a translingual approach that "recognizes difference *as* the norm, to be found not only in utterances that dominant ideology has marked as different but also in utterances that dominant definitions of language, language relations, and language users would identify as 'standard'" (Lu and Horner, "Translingual" 585, emphasis in original). More specifically, studying intra-linguistic acts of translation such as paraphrase can reveal the difference produced through utterances of what is claimed to be the same. Engaging students in considering such forms of intra-lingual translation reveals all writing as simultaneously producing difference, even in the attempt to iterate "the same," whether through rewording accomplished in paraphrase or summary or through recontextualization of the conventional (see Lu and Horner, "Translingual").

Conclusion

The authors of "Language Difference in Writing: Toward a Translingual Approach" encourage "renewed focus by students of writing on the problematics of translation to better understand and participate in negotiations of difference in and through language" (308) and identify translation studies among the disciplines on which the work of pursuing a translingual approach draws (Horner et al. 309-10). In this essay, we have argued that translation provides a particularly useful analytical framework by which composition teachers and students can address the negotiation of difference in and through language. This negotiation operates by challenging dominant, monolingualist ideological models of language, language relations, and language users as stable, discrete, internally uniform sets—models that provide the foundation for neoliberalist notions of and demands for translation as the ideologically neutral and friction-free bridging of difference to communicate the "same." Ultimately, this framework helps to identify the production of difference in writing that aims at merely re-presenting, in other words, nothing more than "the same," such as paraphrase. Using translation as an analytical framework, engagement in multiple and multidirectional translation between languages reveals the fluidity between and internal change and diversity within what monolingualist ideology posits as ostensibly discrete, stable, and internally uniform, and the contingent character of knowledge and its interdependent relation to its written representation in intra-lingual translation—what monolingualism posits as requiring and engaging no translation at all. Multiple and multi-directional inter- and intra-lingual translations can reveal the ideological work accomplished in what monolingualist and neoliberalist ideology posits as in fact ideologically neutral.

In short, translation can serve as a means of re-imagining the difference always already made by composition students, like all writers, through their labor with and on language. As our discussion above suggests, such work, like the work Crane et al. experienced in taking up translation, "produces moments of friction and hesitation . . . [at which] meanings and conceptualisations are challenged by new ideas and thoughts" (40). But while such experience is at odds with neoliberalist ideals of clear and efficient communication, it remains the actual norm of communicative practice, as the concrete labor of translation, conventional and otherwise, testifies, notwithstanding what commodifications of the products of that labor might have us believe. In its concern with and production of difference, translation can make a difference in how composition teachers and students understand their work, and in the kind of difference they might work toward.

Notes

1. The literature on globalization is enormous and growing. For a sampling of recent work addressing globalization in composition studies, see Darin Payne and Daphne Desser, Wendy Hesford et al., Bruce Horner and Karen Kopelson, and David S. Martins.

2. For accounts of these and other terms, see Suresh Canagarajah, "Afterword," "Translanguaging"; Council of Europe; Ofelia Garcia; Keith Gilyard; Juan Guerra; Horner et al.; Bruce Horner, Christiane Donahue, and Samantha NeCamp; Lu,

"Metaphors"; MLA; Danièle Moore and Laurent Gajo; Geneviève Zarate, Danielle Lévy, and Claire Kramsch.

3. The matter is further complicated by the fact that individual writers have sometimes shifted from one term to another, bespeaking both the inadequacy of existing terms (e.g., *multilingualism*) to capture postmonolingual conditions and practices and the disputed meanings of any one of them. Compare, for example, different terms and meanings argued for in Horner and Lu, "Resisting"; Lu and Horner, "Translingual Literacy"; Horner, Donahue, and NeCamp; Canagarajah, "Afterword," "Codemeshing," "Translanguaging," *Translingual;* Suresh Canagarajah and Andrew Wurr. Yet further complications arise from the challenges of translation (see, for example, Claire Kramsch; Moore and Gajo, esp. 142-43, 145-46).

4. Cf. Horner et al.'s warning that the translingual approach "calls for *more,* not less, conscious and critical attention to how writers deploy diction, syntax, and style, as well as form, register, and media" (305).

5. We can see the deproduction of translation, for instance, in the elision within English teaching of attention to translated texts *as* translations (Venuti 328).

6. For an account of the dilemmas this model poses, see Lu, "From." For a counter model, see Soliday, "Politics."

7. The student's work is here cited with her written permission on the condition of it remaining anonymous. In accordance with the assignment to which her text responds, the student is also referencing here a discussion of the relation of vocabulary to "thinking" and "living" in Lu and Horner, *Writing Conventions.*

8. There is a rich tradition of francophone scholarship on paraphrase useful for theorizing writing as translation (Donahue). See, for example, Marie-Madeleine de Gaulmyn; Catherine Fuchs; Bertrand Daunay; Zarate, Lévy, and Kramsch; as well as François.

Works Cited

Baker, Mona. "Reframing Conflict in Translation." *Social Semiotics* 17.2 (2007): 158-69. Print.

Beach, King. "Consequential Transitions: A Sociocultural Expedition beyond Transfer in Education." *Review of Research in Education* 24 (1999): 101-39. Print.

Cameron, Deborah. "Globalization and the Teaching of 'Communication Skills.'" *Globalization and Language Teaching.* Ed. David Block and Deborah Cameron. London: Routledge, 2002. 67-82. Print.

Canagarajah, A. Suresh. "Afterword: World Englishes as Code-meshing." *Code-meshing as World English: Pedagogy, Policy, Performance.* Ed. Vershawn Ashanti Young and Aja Y. Martinez. Urbana: NCTE, 2011. 273-81. Print.

---. "Codemeshing in Academic Writing: Identifying Teachable Strategies of Translanguaging." *Modern Language Journal* 95.3 (2011): 401-17. Print.

---. "Introduction." *Literacy as Translingual Practice: Between Communities and Classrooms.* Ed. Suresh Canagarajah. New York: Routledge, 2013. 1-10. Print.

---. "The Place of World Englishes in Composition: Pluralization Continued." *CCC* 57.4 (2006): 586–619. Print.

---. "Translanguaging in the Classroom: Emerging Issues for Research and Pedagogy." *Applied Linguistics Review* 2 (2011): 1-28. Print.

---. *Translingual Practice: Global Englishes and Cosmopolitan Relations.* New York: Routledge, 2013. Print.

---, and Andrew Wurr. "Multilingual Communication and Language Acquisition: New Research Directions." *The Reading Matrix* 11.1 (2011): 1-15. Print.

Cook-Sather, Alison. "Education as Translation: Students Transforming Notions of Narrative and Self." *CCC* 55.1 (2003): 91-114. Print.

Council of Europe. *Common European Framework of Reference for Languages: Learning, Teaching, Assessment.* 2001. Web. 2 December 2015. <http://www.coe.int/t/dg4/linguistic/Source/Framework_EN.pdf>.

Crane, L. G., M. B. Lombard, and E. M. Tenz. "More than Just Translation: Challenges and Opportunities in Translingual Research." *Social Geography* 4 (2009): 39-46. Print.

Cronin, Michael. *Translation and Globalization.* New York: Routledge, 2003. Print.

Daunay, Bertrand. *Éloge de la paraphrase.* Paris: Presses Universitaires de Vincennes, 2002. Print.

de Gaulmyn, Marie-Madeleine. "Reformulation et Planification Métadiscursives." *Décrire la Conversation.* Dir. J. Cosnier and C. Kerbrat-Orecchioni. Lyon: Presses Universitaires de Lyon, 1987. 167-98. Print.

Desser, Daphne, and Darin Payne, eds. *Teaching Writing in Globalization: Remapping Disciplinary Work.* Boulder: Lexington Books, 2012. Print.

Donahue, Christiane. "'Words for Other Words' and the Nature of Composing." CCCC. Tampa, FL. 21 March 2015. Conference Presentation.

Dor, Daniel. "From Englishization to Imposed Multilingualism: Globalization, the Internet, and the Political Economy of the Linguistic Code." *Public Culture* 16.1 (2004): 97-118. Print.

Eubanks, Philip. "Understanding Metaphors for Writing: In Defense of the Conduit Metaphor." *CCC* 53.1 (2001): 92-118. Print.

Flores, Nelson. "The Unexamined Relationship Between Neoliberalism and Plurilingualism: A Cautionary Tale." *TESOL Quarterly* 47.3 (2013): 500-20. Print.

François, Frédéric. *Morale et mise en mots.* Paris: L'Harmattan, 1994. Print.

Fuchs, Catherine. *La paraphrase.* Paris: Presses Universitaires de France, 1982. Print.

Ganahl, Rainer. "Free Markets: Language, Commodification, and Art." *Public Culture* 13.1 (2001): 24-38. Print.

Garcia, Ofelia. *Bilingual Education in the 21st Century: A Global Perspective.* Oxford: Wiley-Blackwell, 2009. Print.

Gilyard, Keith. "Cross-Talk: Toward Transcultural Writing Classrooms." Severino et al. 325-32.

Guerra, Juan C. "Cultivating Transcultural Citizenship: A Writing across Communities Model." *Language Arts* 85.4 (2008): 296-304. Print.

Heller, Monica. "Globalization, the New Economy, and the Commodification of Language and Identity." *Journal of Sociolinguistics* 7.4 (2003): 473-92. Print.

---. "Repenser le plurilinguisme: Langue, postnationalisme et la nouvelle économie mondialisée." *Diversité urbaine* (Automne 2008): 163-76. Print.

Hesford, Wendy, Eddie Singleton, and Ivonne M. García. "Laboring to Globalize a First-Year Writing Program." *The Writing Program Interrupted: Making Space for Critical Discourse*. Ed. Donna Strickland and Jeanne Gunner. Portsmouth: Boynton/Cook, 2009. 113-25. Print.

Horner, Bruce, Christiane Donahue, and Samantha NeCamp. "Toward a Multilingual Composition Scholarship: From English Only to a Translingual Norm." *CCC* 63.2 (2011): 269-300. Print.

Horner, Bruce, and John Trimbur. "English Only and U.S. College Composition." *CCC* 53.4 (2002): 594-630. Print.

Horner, Bruce, and Karen Kopelson, eds. *Reworking English in Rhetoric and Composition: Global Interrogations, Local Interventions*. Carbondale: SIUP, 2014. Print.

Horner, Bruce, and Min-Zhan Lu. "Resisting Monolingualism." *Rethinking English in Schools: A New and Constructive Stage*. Ed. Viv Ellis, Carol Fox, and Brian Street. London: Continuum, 2007. 141-57. Print.

Horner, Bruce, Min-Zhan Lu, Jacqueline Jones Royster, and John Trimbur. "Opinion: Language Difference in Writing: Toward a Translingual Approach." *College English* 73.3 (2011): 303-21. Print.

Kramsch, Claire. "Contrepont." Zarate et al. 319-23.

Kubota, Ryuko. "The Multi/Plural Turn, Postcolonial Theory, and Neoliberal Multiculturalism: Complicities and Implications for Applied Linguistics." *Applied Linguistics* (2014): 1-22. Print.

Jakobson. Roman. "On Linguistic Aspects of Translation." *The Translation Studies Reader*. Ed. Lawrence Venuti. 2nd ed. New York: Routledge, 2008. Print.

Lu, Min-Zhan. "From Silence to Words: Writing as Struggle." *College English* 49 (1987): 437-48. Print.

---. "Living English Work." *College English* 68 (2006): 605-18. Print.

---. "Metaphors Matter: Transcultural Literacy." *JAC* 29.1-2 (2009): 285-93. Print.

---, and Bruce Horner. "Translingual Literacy, Language Difference, and Matters of Agency." *College English* 75.6 (2013): 582-608. Print.

---. *Writing Conventions*. New York: Penguin Academics, 2008. Print.

Lunsford, Andrea A. *The Everyday Writer*. 5th edition. Boston: Bedford St. Martin's, 2015. Print.

Martins, David S., ed. *Transnational Writing Program Administration*. Logan: Utah State UP, 2015. Print.

MLA Ad Hoc Committee on Foreign Languages. "Foreign Languages and Higher Education: New Structures for a Changed World." *MLA Commons*. Modern Language Association. 2007. Web. 2 December 2015. <https://www.mla.org/Resources/Research/Surveys-Reports-and-Other-Documents/Teaching-Enrollments-and-Programs/Foreign-Languages-and-Higher-Education-New-Structures-for-a-Changed-World>.

Moore, Danièle, and Laurent Gajo. "Introduction: French Voices on Plurilingualism: Theory, Significance and Perspectives." *International Journal of Multilingualism* 6.2 (2009): 137-53. Print.

Müller, Martin. "What's in a Word? Problematizing Translation between Languages." *Area* 39.2 (2007): 206-13. Print.

"Paraphrase: Write It in Your Own Words." *Purdue Online Writing Lab.* Purdue University. n.d. Web. 4 June 2015. <https://owl.english.purdue.edu/owl-print/619/>.

"Paraphrasing Vs. Quoting—Explanation." *The Writer's Handbook.* The Writing Center at the University of Wisconsin-Madison. 29 August 2014. Web. 4 June 2015. <https://writing.wisc.edu/Handbook/QPA_PorQ.html>.

Pennycook, Alastair. "English as a Language Always in Translation." *European Journal of English Studies* 12.1 (2008): 33-47. Print.

---. *Language as a Local Practice.* London: Routledge, 2010. Print.

Pratt, Mary Louise. "Linguistic Utopias." *The Linguistics of Writing: Arguments Between Language and Literature.* Ed. Nigel Fabb, Derek Attridge, Alan Durant and Colin MacCabe. New York: Methuen, 1987. 48-66. Print.

---. "Response." *Translation Studies* 3.1 (2010): 94-97. Print.

Qu, Weiguo. "Critical Literacy and Writing in English: Teaching English in a Cross-cultural Context." Horner and Kopelson 64-74.

Schor, Sandra. "Composition Strategy as Translation." *College English* 48.2 (1986): 187-94. Print.

Severino, Carol, Juan C. Guerra, and Johnnella E. Butler, eds. *Writing in Multicultural Settings.* New York: MLA, 1997. Print.

Soliday, Mary. "The Politics of Difference: Toward a Pedagogy of Reciprocity." Severino et al. 261-72.

---. "Translating Self and Difference Through Literacy Narratives." *College English* 56.5 (1994): 511-26. Print.

Tsing, Anna Lowenhaupt. *Friction: An Ethnography of Global Connection.* Princeton: Princeton UP, 2005. Print.

Vance, John. "Code-Meshing Meshed Codes: Some Complications and Possibilities." *JAC* 29.1-2 (2009): 281–84. Print.

Venuti, Lawrence. "Translation and the Pedagogy of Literature." *College English* 58.3 (1996): 327-44. Print.

Wagner, Birgit. "Response." *Translation Studies* 3.1 (2010): 97-99. Print.

Widdowson, Henry G. "The Ownership of English." *TESOL Quarterly* 28 (1994): 377-89. Print.

Wittman, Emily O., and Katrina Windon. "Twisted Tongues, Tied Hands : Translation Studies and the English Major." *College English* 72.5 (2010): 449-69. Print.

Yildiz, Yasemin. *Beyond the Mother Tongue: The Postmonolingual Condition.* New York: Fordham UP, 2012. Print.

Zarate, Geneviève, Danielle Lévy, and Claire Kramsch, dirs. *Précis du plurilinguisme et du pluriculturalisme.* Paris: Éditions des archives contemporaines, 2008. Print.

Teaching for Agency: From Appreciating Linguistic Diversity to Empowering Student Writers

Shawna Shapiro, Michelle Cox, Gail Shuck, and Emily Simnitt

In this article, we build on conversations about linguistic diversity in writing studies, proposing a framework by which instructors and administrators can promote the empowerment of multilingual writers. Our framework, which we call "teaching for agency," recognizes the resources that linguistically diverse students bring to our writing classrooms, but also takes into account these students' needs and goals regarding English language development. We articulate a process in which students gain greater awareness and control of the opportunities for action available to them, and learn to evaluate the effects of their decisions as writers and scholars. Practitioners can help to facilitate this process, we argue, by creating optimal conditions within which students can make informed decisions. After presenting the teaching for agency framework, we describe how we have employed it at our own institutions, through assignments that provide an authentic and relevant rhetorical context for student writing, as well as programmatic policies that offer multiple pathways for student success. By foregrounding agency as a central construct in the teaching of writing, we hope to demonstrate our respect for what students already know and can do with language, and our commitment to expanding every student's linguistic and rhetorical repertoire.

In recent years, discussions within writing studies about language difference have burgeoned. As Paul Kei Matsuda argues, this growth is due partly to the recent attention given to translingualism as an approach to linguistic diversity and partly to the increase of multilingual writers at many institutions of higher education. Many of these conversations have focused on the importance of promoting a positive, inclusive view of language—a stance we also endorse. There is widespread agreement that multilingualism[1] should be seen as an asset or resource, rather than a deficit or obstacle, and that our classroom instruction should reflect the valuing of multiple linguistic codes.

Linguistic diversity is a useful place to begin conversations about multilingual writers, as it may compel instructors and administrators to enact more equitable classroom practices and institutional policies. But often overlooked in these discussions is multilingual students' own goal to continue developing as English language users. In other words, a focus on appreciation alone may leave behind classroom practices that are explicitly aimed at promoting English language development. And yet pedagogies focused primarily on language development run the risk of perpetuating a deficit orientation toward multilingual writers, causing those students to be seen only in terms of the gaps in their English knowledge. The questions that we continue to wrestle with, then, are as follows: How can we treat students as developing writers/language users without promoting a deficit view of second language (L2) writers and writing, and without reproducing stigmatizing pedagogies and policies? How do we honor the knowledge and linguistic resources all students bring to our courses and programs, while also promoting their growth as writers and language users?

We suggest that foregrounding the concept of student agency can enhance conversations about language difference, recognizing the resources multilingual students bring to writing, while also promoting linguistic growth. While the term "agency" has been employed within writing studies and other disciplines in various ways (see Canagarajah, "Agency"; Duranti; Lu and Horner; Miller), it has not been widely used within composition to inform how we address multilingual writers across a full spectrum of language backgrounds. Our aim in this article is to flesh out what we mean by agency, including the conditions, pedagogies, and institutional practices that make agency possible for multilingual writers.

In the remainder of our article, we articulate the central elements of teaching for agency and describe how we each have enacted this approach in our own writing pedagogies and programs. We conclude by discussing how this theoretical framework may be applied in other contexts in which multilingual students write. Our aim is to complement the recent—and welcome—moves in writing studies toward adopting linguistically inclusive practices, by presenting a pedagogical framework that is informed not only by an appreciation for linguistic diversity, but also by a commitment to empowering multilingual writers.

Understanding Agency

The practices we propose here are rooted in the idea that each linguistic, rhetorical, political, and institutional act is a choice that in turn shapes the language, writing, thoughts, beliefs, and actions of other people. Within a broad understanding of social action, its impacts, and the available choices human actors have, we will discuss the relationship of agency to writing pedagogy and institutional practice, particularly in relation to undergraduate multilingual writers in U.S. institutions of higher education.

The framework we develop here articulates relationships between action, awareness, and optimal conditions—critical components of agency—as they apply to the work of writers, writing instructors, and writing programs:

1. Students as agents have a degree of control over their own acts related to writing and writing development.
2. In order to have greater control over these acts, students need to notice that an action needs to be taken, understand the range of possible actions, be aware of the context of the action, and be able to evaluate the possible effects of a given action.
3. In order to help student writers develop greater awareness, writing instructors and program administrators need to create optimal conditions—from classroom activities and assignments that help students to notice and utilize particular rhetorical and linguistic practices, to program structures that help writers make informed choices about their academic lives.

We will take each component of agency in turn. At the core of our conceptualization of agency is action. Agency has been defined broadly to include all actions, intentional and not, and encompasses the idea that all actions have impacts on others (Cooper; Duranti). As teachers and program administrators, we are interested in raising writers' awareness of those impacts and increasing students' sense of control over their acts as writers. Acts can be as specific as choosing a particular word or as broad as choosing a particular writing course. In order for an act to be agentive, from our perspective, there must be options for action. Those options are opened and constrained by particular micro- or macro-contextual factors. Multilingual writers have access to multiple linguistic codes, language and literacy practices, and rhetorics, thereby acting as linguistically agile agents of their own communicative messages (Cook; Jordan). However, students still developing their knowledge of the dominant language or language variety may experience constraints because they have fewer linguistic resources to choose from in that language. These students also face the same constraints experienced by all students, such as an instructor's evaluation criteria, the bounds of an assignment, their own educational histories, or time pressures.

Central to the ability to take action is the idea of "noticing" that an action needs to be taken and awareness of the available actions one might take. Indeed, as explained by psychologist John Godolphin Bennett, "Unless we notice, we cannot be in a position to choose or act for ourselves" (i). Linguists have taken up this concept of "noticing" to explain how language development occurs, including students' development as writers (Schmidt; Swain). Noticing includes identifying problems in a text which might compel a writer to revise their work, or rejecting certain rhetorical conventions (Qi and Lapkin; Swain). Here, we broaden noticing to encompass any moment when a student feels called upon to take action as a writer, including selecting a particular path through a writing program.

Once a writer is aware that action needs to be taken, she then must be aware of the range of available actions and the existing constraints on those actions. She must also have the necessary knowledge for informed decision-making. Key areas of knowledge for multilingual writers include linguistic, generic, rhetorical, and cultural knowledge, as well as an understanding of U.S. educational culture. Awareness not only guides writing acts, such as specific linguistic choices while drafting and revising, but also aids writers in evaluating their own writing. Greater awareness of the effects of actions includes a better understanding of how readers might perceive their writing (including recognizing what would be "marked" for a native English speaker), a sense of the perspectives the writer has to offer on a topic, and information about the possible consequences of a course placement decision. As illustrated in fig. 1, greater awareness leads to greater control. Thus, the framework for writer agency may be summarized as such (see fig. 1).

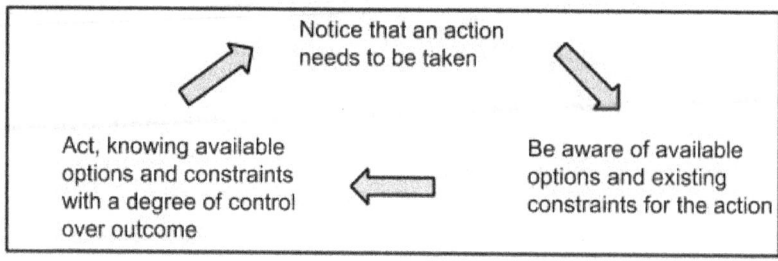

Fig. 1. Writer Agency.

To facilitate this awareness, writing instructors and program administrators need to create opportunities for students to exercise agency. Tanita Saenkhum, in her study of multilingual writing placement, lists as acts of agency "negotiating, choosing to accept or deny [their placements], self-assessing, planning, questioning, and making decisions" (126) and argues that "these acts of agency will be possible when conditions for agency are optimal" (126). Our goal as instructors and administrators, then, is to create optimal conditions for success, no matter a student's English proficiency level on being admitted. Instructors and administrators must recognize the constraints that students must inevitably work under, while also expanding opportunities for students to shape the contexts in which they write and act. Teaching for agency, then, might look like this:

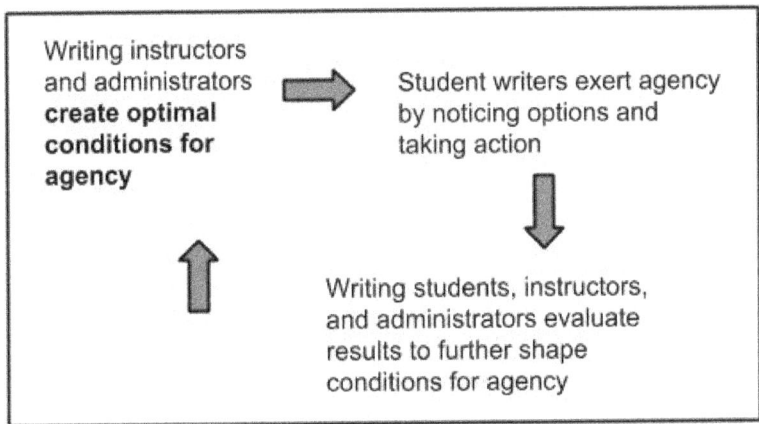

Fig. 2. Creating Optimal Conditions for Agency.

In the remainder of this article, we introduce assignments, pedagogical strategies, and curricular options that we have developed at our respective institutions. We also explore the necessary conditions for students to become aware of the choices available to them and the possibilities for negotiation, so they can not only act, but also understand how those actions affect their own and others' lives.

Pedagogical and Programmatic Practices for Agency

Writing Beyond the Classroom (Shawna Shapiro)

This assignment is part of a writing course entitled "The English Language in a Global Context," which students select through guided self-placement at Middlebury College, a small liberal arts college in Vermont. The course supplements the instruction students receive in writing-intensive seminars taught by faculty across the curriculum. I designed this course in response to a request from colleagues for an offering that would appeal to both L1 and L2 writers with a range of abilities and would provide language support in a non-remedial environment. "Writing beyond the Classroom" is the final course assignment and requires that students write about a lingering issue from the course for an outside audience.

Students exercise agency at various points throughout this project. They first write a proposal, articulating an audience and purpose for their work. After receiving feedback, they revise the proposal and develop an annotated bibliography of sources that have informed their thinking on the topic. As they develop their projects, students are asked to pay close attention to genre and register—to "break out" from the academic norms that shaped their other papers. To heighten students' rhetorical awareness, we examine sample texts, noting choices the writers made to fit audience expectations. When submitting the final draft, students submit a Writer's Memo, reflecting on their rhetorical choices. I have received a wide range of projects, including persuasive letters, editorials, narrative essays, informational brochures, and a variety of creative works (see "snapshots" below). In my feedback and evaluation, I focus on rhetorical awareness, informed decision-making, and self-evaluation, guided by the following questions:

1. Is the project relevant to the course? Does it reflect the learning and thinking we have done throughout the semester?
2. Is the writer able to articulate linguistic and/or rhetorical choices they made, and to explain the rationale behind those choices? Are they aware of how their work meets and/or diverges from genre conventions?
3. Can the student explain how this project reflects their growth as a writer?

To illustrate the range of student work, as well as the negotiation and reflection that occurs throughout the writing process, I offer brief snapshots of three students' projects.

Fernando, an international student from Mexico, wrote a letter addressed to our college's Center for Social Entrepreneurship—an entity with which he had become heavily involved. Fernando had noticed that the center had very few resources on social entrepreneurship in non-English languages. He found this problematic, as many of the initiatives undertaken by the center were in countries where English is not a dominant language. His letter opens as follows:

> Dear everyone at CSE,
>
> In our meeting last Friday I told you that you would help me with one of my final assignments. . . . I was fortunate enough to have the freedom to create my own final project for my [writing] class, and . . . I chose to write a letter—to you. In it I will tell you the story of the journey that led me to Social Entrepreneurship, and I will also talk about a problem that hinders its reach and development.

Fernando goes on to argue for shared "transcreation" of materials, which he says involves making key concepts relevant to "the context of [readers'] own culture and daily experience." Fernando wanted his letter to have a confident, professional tone while also referencing his personal experiences. Reflecting on his final draft, he said,

> The tone is right for the intended audience—it is personal to keep the connection I have with them... but it is also slightly academic to convey the importance that the issue has for me. I am very satisfied with the way I connected my own story with the issue that I present, and I believe this makes the writing stronger.

In a personal email to me near the end of the semester, Fernando wrote, "[W]hat a great feeling it is when one can integrate classes and what one loves most."

Emily, a second generation Chinese American, wrote an essay for other Middlebury students, entitled "Loss of a Mother Tongue." In her Writer's Memo, Emily said, "My goal for this project is to capture that feeling of uncertainty, of not knowing where one stands in the scheme of things, of feeling alone and angry at being different, yet feeling proud to be so." In the first half of the essay, Emily shares stories from her childhood that highlight the complexity of her linguistic and cultural identity. Later, these stories culminate in a social critique: "In the eyes of the American education system, language is the least important of standards. . . . But not if it's English. . . . Any other language, and the educations system force it out of children."

Emily's tone in the essay was fairly colloquial—an intentional choice she justified as follows: "I wanted this piece . . . to capture the feeling of in-betweenness, and above all [to be] relatable." To help illustrate her "in-betweenness," Emily recounted typical conversations she had with older relatives, which included dialogue in Cantonese. To make these conversations more accessible, she represented the Cantonese in Pinyin, which uses the Roman alphabet, rather than in Chinese characters. Emily also used her narration to convey the gist of the conversation, rather than offering a direct translation:

> My mother . . . asked me: "Nei num-ji nei hai zhong-goc yen ah-hai mei-goc yen?" Are you Chinese or American? There was no preface to this question. It came out of nowhere—that's the thing with my mother, she just comes out and hits you with things like that.

Emily exercised agency as well when presenting her work to the class, by performing her reading dramatically, using a variety of voices and gestures. She received a warm round of applause from her classmates afterward.

Eirene, an international student from Malaysia, wrote an editorial article, "The Non-National National Language," which targeted a Malaysian audience. Eirene's goal was to highlight and challenge negative attitudes toward "Manglish"—a colloquial mix of Malay and Malaysian English. Keeping her audience in mind, Eirene made frequent references to cultural and political dynamics in Malaysia. She also employed frequent code-switching among

English, Malay, and Manglish, which she felt was an important way to underscore her claim that Manglish should be a source of pride, rather than embarrassment. When reading Eirene's early drafts, I realized I lacked the cultural and linguistic knowledge to grasp the nuances in her argument. To make the writing more accessible, Eirene chose to include footnotes explaining cultural or historical references and translating the sections written in Manglish and Malay. One example of this is in this passage: "But in all honesty, though I grew up learning the language, I feel no affinity to *Bahasa Melayu* (BM) as my national language. I say *Bahasa Melayu* and not, *Bahasa Malaysia* because well . . . who am I kidding?" In a footnote here, Eirene explained that "Bahasa Melayu" meant "Malay Language," while "Bahasa Malaysia" meant "Malaysian Language." She continued, "The government changed the name of the language from the Malay language to the Malaysian language in order to reinforce the idea that this was our national language and not an ethnic-centric language." Without this information, I would not have grasped the relevance of this subtle difference to her broader argument. While the inclusion of footnotes may be incongruent with the genre of a newspaper article, those footnotes were crucial not just for me, but for the first-year writing awards committee: I submitted Eirene's piece, and she was named one of five finalists.[2]

These snapshots illustrate the process by which students exert agency as writers: They create a project about which they are knowledgeable and passionate; they make informed rhetorical choices throughout the writing and presentation process; and they reflect deeply on those choices, as well as on their growth as writers.[3]

Writing in the Twittersphere (Emily Simnitt)

In a section of first-year writing designed to support multilingual writers at Boise State University, I use a Writing about Writing (WAW) approach, which requires students to engage in primary research into their own and others' literacy practices (Downs and Wardle). The content of the course provides students the academic language and methods through which to honor, discuss, and explore their experiences with language acquisition, multilingual negotiation, and English-language literacy. The formal writing assignments provide scaffolding and support for students to gain experience in genres of academic writing. This curriculum sets the stage for additional ways in which students can choose to share their developing knowledge about writing in an academic environment.

To encourage further exploration of multiple literacies, I invite students to join an optional, ongoing Twitter chat about writing, language, and identity. The choice to participate via Twitter offers a low-stakes opportunity for agency, as students explore the content of the course (academic writing) in a flexible, often more familiar, format. Students may feel little rhetorical control over academic writing in English, but many of these same students are comfortable micro-composing on mobile devices, whether on Twitter, other social media, or simply texting.

This Twitter chat originated during a campus-wide conference at Boise State University presented by multilingual students taking English 123, a course designed to support multilingual writers, as Gail will further describe below (see also Shuck). At the spring 2012 conference, my students, who had been researching technology and writing, invited attendees to live-tweet about what they saw, learned, and experienced during the conference and to label each tweet with the hashtag #123chat or #197chat. The hashtag acts as a searchable marker, allowing those interested to follow and join in the conversation from semester to semester.

Before each conference, I bring archived tweets into class as an object of analysis, showing how the tweets become meaningful as a compilation. Together, we notice patterns of language use and content, categorizing types of tweets and considering what tweets indicate about the expressed identity of the Twitter user (teacher? student? presenter? multilingual?). This analysis in turn facilitates student awareness of the available choices for constructing tweets.

In reading through the chat from spring 2015, students might notice how Twitter can strengthen community (see also Lomicka and Lord). For example, tweets express encouragement and congratulations to presenters from friends and strangers alike: "You are the best group dude" (Almutari), "It was a great opportunity to learn about all these cultures" (Abochnb), or, "So confident" (aldihani). They might also notice how tweets highlight resonating ideas from presentations, offering ideas for students' own projects. A presentation on homesickness elicited this batch of tweets: "This conference remained me of my first semester at boise state" (Abochnb); "I can relate to missing where you from! I miss California" (Herrera); "Who doesn't miss his home?" (AbulGreen); and "Missing home is normal feelings to many students" (Alrashidi). Students might also notice meta-commentary on what is happening during the conference and how the audience for student work goes beyond the classroom and the conference itself. For example, this tweet calls attention to a chat participant outside of the state: "This guy from Tennessee [emoji of a hand pointing down to the username at the end of the tweet] And he is watching the conference from hashtag #197chat @hsulmutairi_" (Almutari).

While they are reading the #197chat feed, I draw students' attention to presenters' rhetorical choices and how they are received by the tweeting audience. One presentation that elicited many responses argued that use of social media in one's personal life influences how one writes in academic genres. The presenters argued that the most important factor influencing writing is the tool used, most often a computing device where writers send emails, check social media, and write academic papers. To visually represent how use of the same device results in the blending of genres, this group drew on one member's skill with Video Scribe, a program that animates whiteboard drawing, to make a video. In the video, a picture of a cell phone appeared and then disappeared. Next came a picture of a blender. Written to one side of the blender was "Formal Writing," with "essay, resume, research paper" listed below. On the other side, under the label "Informal Writing," students listed "e-mail, social media, journals." As the video continued, each of the terms flew into the blender, and the blender whirred.

As students presented, the audience of their peers, instructors, and faculty from across the university tweeted. Two pictures of the blender appeared in the Twitter feed, with one respondent asking, "How did you do this animation?" (Nogle). The presenters responded using subsequent tweets. Several more conference participants tweeted praise of the video, including, "Wow, great video. I'm going to have to try video scribe" (Donahue). Another attendee tweeted, "Do you think that writing style will be changed with the social media?" (abullah_q45), and other tweets appeared to restate the argument that technology use leads to genre blending. These tweets extended the WAW-based class discussion about technology and writing and showed the students how their choice and use of technology communicated their main point.

This exchange and traces of the presentation remain on Twitter for future students to find and analyze, creating a space to reimagine students' academic work for other audiences. The conference and the Twitter chat do not replace the study and practice of academic writing in English. Rather, they give students opportunities to share ideas, gain confidence, and support each other. Using the Twitter chat as an object of analysis prior to their participation shows students ways to exercise control and agency beyond more standard academic genres. When students analyze the language of tweets from previous conferences, they reach the conclusion that tweets do not need to be in Standard Written English to be rhetorically successful. Drawing students' attention to the informality and register of the tweets highlights the difference between the rhetorical situation on Twitter and that of academic genres in the university. While students develop academic language in formal essay assignments, Twitter increases opportunities for written language interaction in a different genre with an immediate, familiar audience.

I do not grade or evaluate the chat. Instead, my evaluation of whether Twitter provides useful rhetorical opportunities for students involves my own noticing of how the chat makes its way into class discussions, final portfolios, and student reflective writing. I point this out to my students. In this way, I help students see how the linguistic and rhetorical choices in the chat affect conversations in other contexts. I encourage them to seek opportunities to actively participate in a larger scholarly conversation.

Agency through a Film Project (Michelle Cox)

This film assignment served as a capstone for an international section of First Year Writing (FYW) at Dartmouth College that is enrolled through directed self-placement and stretches across two quarters. In designing the section, I considered the many challenges facing international multilingual students at Dartmouth, a small Ivy League college set in a rural area in the third "whitest" state in the country (U.S. Census Bureau). Dartmouth's student culture is dominated by fraternities, and the college prides itself on its long-held traditions and competitive atmosphere. The quarter system compresses courses to 9.5 weeks, ramping up the pace, and with it, the reading and writing load. Students without previous experience in English-medium academic environments need to quickly turn their textbook knowledge of English into their primary means for communicating and learning. And students without previous experience in U.S. education systems need to quickly acquire the knowledge of genres, writing processes, and research strategies assumed by faculty across the curriculum. Further, the first year of college is a time when international and U.S.-born students alike negotiate their identities. Therefore, I wanted my course to lead to greater awareness of issues related to multilingualism and second language writing development, allowing students to have greater control when making decisions about self-representation in their writing.

My goals during the first quarter, then, were for students to better understand their own English language and literacy development, position themselves as English users within the global arena (rather than only as Dartmouth students), and explore cultural differences in writing. During this term, students read about second language writing development, World Englishes, and textual ownership, while writing a language and literacy narrative, a research report on a variety of English, and a researched argumentative essay on plagiarism (see the Appendix for a list of course readings). My goal for the second quarter was for students to apply this knowledge while producing original research, writing a proposal for an undergraduate research grant, and engaging in a term-long film project.

For the film project, groups produced short films that targeted a Dartmouth audience (such as faculty or peers) and chose topics related to material covered during the first term. Scaffolding allowed students first to analyze samples (student films, as well as *Writing across Borders*, a film for faculty on multilingual writing) and then to complete separate stages of the project: a pitch (which identified the primary audience and message), a treatment plan (a more developed plan), a storyboard and script (which laid out the visual and sound elements), the rough cut (a draft of the film), and then the final cut. Each stage was presented for review by peers, a consultant from the college's media center, the course writing fellow, and me.

While creating the films, students were challenged to think carefully about audience and identity. One group, who wanted their film to target international peers and promote pride in international identity, struggled with how to handle the voiceover (Kudakwashe, Orzisk, and Sung). Concerned that their audience would have difficulty understanding their accents, the group considered asking a native-English speaking student to serve as narrator. During a class workshop, however, their peers asked if this decision would conflict with their message. They ultimately decided to do their own narration. The final cut of their film, "Speak Up! (a movie by internationals for internationals)," opens with the narrator telling us, "About ten percent of Dartmouth students are international. These students—*we*—create an environment that contributes to a valuable and unique Dartmouth experience." The narrator appears on camera a minute into the film, when he shares results from a survey conducted by the group and states that they also interviewed international students on their challenges. He then says, "Please, hear *our* voices," and walks off camera. These uses of first person show how the decision to serve as narrator led to stronger performance of identification with international students in the film. The remainder of the film shares clips of international students discussing challenges in adapting to U.S. culture, strategies they used to overcome these challenges, and final words for international peers: "Be proud of your heritages," "Be proud of your culture," and "Be proud of your accent."

A second group, who wanted to persuade domestic peers to value international students more, struggled to find an effective rhetorical approach (Bekele, Golanda, and Janjua). During a workshop, peers pointed out that the tone of their film could be considered negative and perhaps accusatory toward domestic students, as they seemed to be blaming domestic students for not knowing more about international students. To soften the tone, the group chose to frame the film with a series of questions. Their film, "Unity in Diversity: Internationalism at Dartmouth," opens with the question, "Did you know that in the Class of 1925, there was only one international student at Dartmouth?" followed by a clip of a hand flipping through a 1925 class yearbook and stopping at a photo of a Chinese international student. The words, "And now?" come on the screen, after which we see a series of short clips, showing international students answering the questions, "Where are you from?" and "What is your first language?" The film then moves to short clips of domestic students guessing answers to questions about Dartmouth international student demographics, followed by the correct answers and data on how many Dartmouth students answered the question correctly on a survey distributed by the group. The final question of the film, "So what? Why is internationalism important to Dartmouth anyway?" is followed by interview excerpts featuring the Director of International Student Programs and writing program faculty, who the group felt would add credibility to the film. The positive feeling that runs throughout the film is created by the humor with which the domestic students' responses are presented, the statements made by Dartmouth staff highlighting the benefits of working with international students, the upbeat music that runs in the background ("Best Days of My Life" by American Authors), and the message in the final frame, "Let's appreciate internationalism."

A third group, who wanted to empower international peers as writers, struggled to find approaches that would convince students to make use of available writing support (Bing and Pejanovic). Their classmates told them that raising awareness of available resources would not be enough, as information about the resources already existed. Their film, "Second Language Adaptation: Writing at Dartmouth for International Students," opens with information meant to persuade international students that they need writing support, sharing data from a survey they conducted (e.g., "41% of international students did not feel ready for college-level writing before coming to Dartmouth") interspersed with clips of international students discussing their writing struggles. Then, a frame announces, "Don't panic! We will introduce you to people who will make writing at Dartmouth easier." Headshots of the film's producers are shown traveling along a campus map, followed by clips of representatives from the programs they visit, including the library, writing program, and writing center. The most powerful moment in the film comes at the end, when one of the international students who had described her struggles with writing in English earlier is revealed to be a writing center tutor. Smiling broadly, she tells us, "Here I am. I am an international student, but I am teaching American students how to write."

With this curriculum, I was pushing back against the tendency in academic communities for others to craft the representations of multilingual students' identities (Costino and Hyon; Ruecker; Saenkhum). I sought to create optimal conditions for agency by inviting students into the academic conversation on second language writing, equipping students with the same literature and tools that academics have access to, and providing a venue for self-positioning as international students at Dartmouth. Overall, I would say the project successfully met these goals. Students also successfully advocated for multilingual students through their films, promoting inclusion, pride in diversity, and community, and produced films they felt proud of, as indicated by three groups' choice to publish their films on YouTube.

Curricular Structures and Informed Student Choice (Gail Shuck)

In addition to creating optimal conditions for agency in assignments and classroom practices, those of us with administrative roles can create optimal conditions for students to decide among multiple curricular options. In this section, I describe a pilot FYW course at Boise State University that addresses students' language development needs without relying on deficit-oriented practices and provides options that honor students' ability to make informed choices.

This pilot option is a six-credit, one-semester course called Accelerated English 101 for Multilingual Students (hereafter, "Accelerated English"), which fulfills the first-semester FYW requirement. More similar to the Accelerated Learning Program (ALP), with its support studio linked to a mainstream course (Adams, Gearhart, Miller, and Roberts) than to a stretch program (Glau), Accelerated English bypasses the second of two pass/fail ESL[4] courses and moves students to the required FYW courses (English 101 and 102) more quickly. Placement into the Level I or Level II ESL course or into FYW is determined by an in-house timed essay test. International students take this test during their orientation, and U.S.-resident multilingual students are guided toward this test by certain responses on our online self-placement website or through advising.[5] Accelerated English offers three hours of extra class time per week and a class size of fifteen. In letting students bypass one ESL course, Accelerated English helps to alleviate the pressures that some multilingual students are under, from scholarship restrictions to financial concerns to the stigma of "remedial" courses.

The course is a direct response to recent increases in two populations at Boise State: Saudi and Kuwaiti students on government scholarships, on one hand, and students who came to the U.S. as refugees, on the other. This latter group is often not identified for English proficiency evaluation. They may have very low SAT or ACT scores, or they may be exempt from needing a standardized test at all for admission because the admissions policy exempts applicants over twenty-one years old. These increases have posed some population-specific challenges. Government-sponsored students, warned that they must "compete with native speakers," are likely to try to avoid ESL courses, sometimes waiting a semester or more to take the placement test again, hoping their English will have improved enough to bypass ESL courses, or seeking FYW courses at other institutions with fewer barriers to enrollment. While avoidance of ESL courses is certainly a form of agency, the lack of curricular alternatives, coupled with insufficient information about the implications of avoiding, makes for less than optimal conditions.

For refugee or immigrant students, a central problem is a lack of awareness about multilingual-specific classes or support programs, which stems from the lack of a solid infrastructure of support and information for U.S.-resident English learners. Once informed of their options, however, these students often take the pass/fail ESL courses to ease into the university, receive credit toward graduation, and protect their GPAs. Without a system that adequately identifies students most in need of such information, U.S.-resident multilingual writers often find themselves in English 101 or its four-credit ALP version, English 101-Plus ("English 101P"), often without the English proficiency to be successful in those courses.

These contextual constraints highlight an additional challenge: international as well as resident students' being admitted without the English proficiency or reading and writing experience—even in their native languages—required to be academically successful. Providing a faster path through the FYW program was appealing, but only if we increased the support for English language and writing development, which would benefit multilingual students from a wide variety of backgrounds.

Without the new course, the entire sequence would look like this for a student who placed into ESL Level I (English 122):

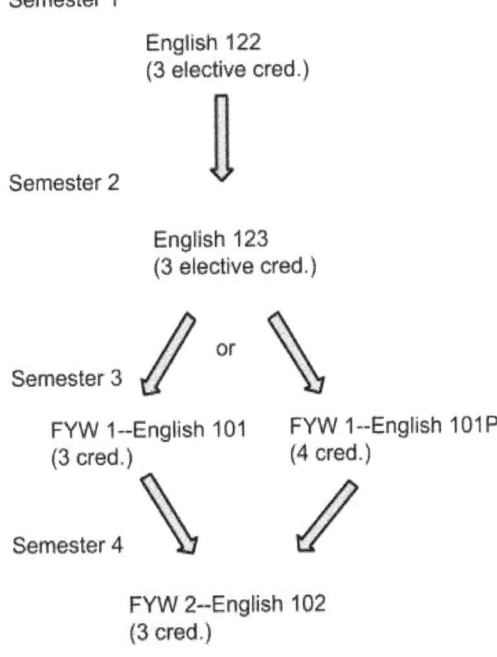

Fig. 3. Limited Choice and a Longer Path without Accelerated English.

The one institutionally sanctioned course choice a student can make comes after passing English 123, at which point the student may choose English 101 (3 credits) or a 4-credit, class-plus-studio option called English 101P. Some English 101P instructors have reported that one weekly studio hour is not sufficient for these two newer populations to be successful. Although these stories are anecdotal, these instructors, despite their preparation to teach L2 writers, have seen students with lower English proficiency levels struggle in FYW.

Since we began offering Accelerated English two semesters ago, many students have preferred it to the two-course ESL sequence and to the avoidance strategies many previous students chose. Demand has been very high. The following illustration can help to explain why.

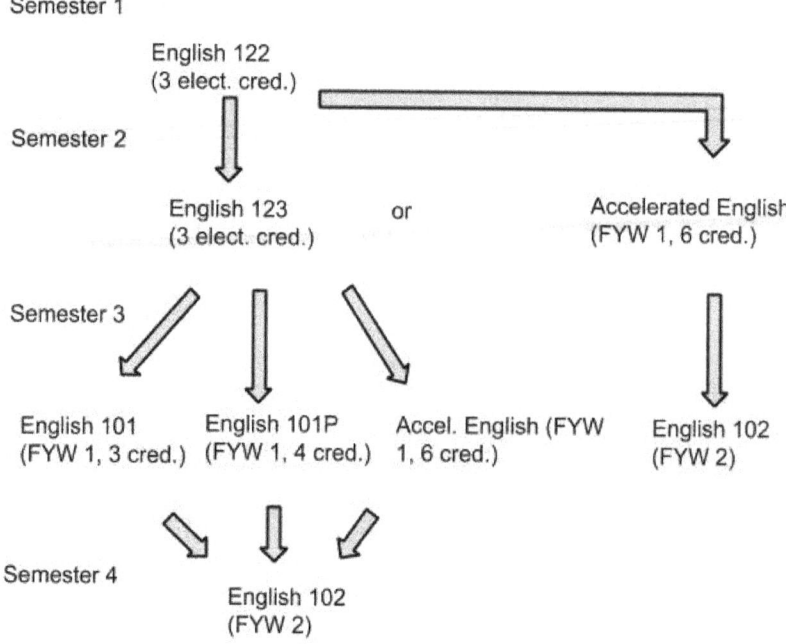

Fig. 4. More Choice and a Shorter FYW Path with Accelerated English.

As illustrated in Figure 4, students who pass English 122 may choose to move more slowly through the course sequence and take English 123 next before attempting English 101, or they may jump to Accelerated English, after which they would take English 102. A student who takes the English 123 path can then choose among three options for fulfilling the first-semester FYW requirement. With both a shorter path and a greater number of options, students have more opportunities to make agentive decisions. We will be collecting data on students' performance in English 102 over the next few semesters, which we hope will demonstrate comparable success in English 102 regardless of the students' choice at each juncture.

Despite the delays entailed by a two-course preparatory sequence, I have continued to offer English 122 and 123. Even when there are alternatives, some students have chosen these courses. They want the time, the support, and the opportunity to take low-risk but credit-bearing courses, as well as the comfort of being in a class with other second-language writers (Costino and Hyon). Having options as well as information empowers multilingual students to decide how they want to complete their FYW requirement.

Students who choose Accelerated English over the slower ESL sequence have experienced one unexpected advantage of Accelerated English: the greater impact that the six graded credits have on GPAs. The higher stakes seem to be leading these students to be more engaged than they typically are in the pass/fail ESL courses. It is too early in the pilot to document these claims, but in informal conversations, all four of the Accelerated English instructors have reiterated this point. If true, this outcome would suggest that students are investing in their own success—agents at work.

A survey of all of the students enrolled in the spring 2015 and fall 2015 Accelerated English and English 123 classes was revealing. Asked the most important reason for their choosing the course they were in, the students in Accelerated English were split between "finishing faster" and "wanting time and support." The most commonly chosen answers were as follows:

Table 1. Top Reasons for Choosing the 6-credit Option

Reason for Choosing Accelerated English	Percentage of Students (Number)
I wanted to finish composition requirements faster.	25% (21)
I wanted the extra time and support of the 6-credit option.	24% (20)
A friend or advisor told me to take it.	11% (9)
English 101 seats were full.	8% (7)

The finding that seven students enrolled in Accelerated English even though they were eligible for English 101 is striking, as they chose a 6-credit course over a 3-credit course a semester later. This could be explained by a desire for a more supportive experience or a desire to finish faster. In either case, they made their own agentive decisions.

The students in English 123 were asked the same question. Their primary reason for choosing English 123 was that they did not know or understand that Accelerated English was a way of bypassing English 123. Two of the 14 English 123 respondents had hoped to enroll in Accelerated English, but it was full. Ten (71%) answered simply that English 123 was the next course in the sequence or that the test placed them into English 123, revealing a lack of awareness among some students that Accelerated English was an option.

As my coauthors have illustrated, offering options is one way to create conditions for agency. Having an institutionally recognized choice, where there were only back-door choices in the past, is crucial. So is accurate information. Some students, for example, have expressed a concern that a six-credit course would be too difficult. The reality is that Accelerated English offers more support—not more work—than English 101. I have addressed these concerns where possible in impromptu information sessions, announcements by instructors of English 122, and more formal presentations to students, advisors, and international services staff, but more awareness-raising needs to be done. Once they recognize that the additional credits are for in-class support, students can better evaluate the effects of enrolling in Accelerated English. I am also deepening my partnerships with the FYW Program and other units to increase students' awareness of options and of the implications of their choices. That awareness is a critical component of empowering multilingual writers to make informed decisions and be academically successful.

Concluding Thoughts

As the above examples show, agency is a useful framework for both microlevel and macro-level analysis, from a single assignment to an institutional structure. The examples illustrate how we, as writing instructors and program administrators, seek to create optimal conditions for multilingual student agency, by building options for students and by working to increase awareness so those students can make informed decisions about those options. This awareness includes increased knowledge of second language writing itself, of the politics of English, and of the effects of different linguistic and rhetorical choices. That knowledge, in turn, increases students' control over how they navigate an assignment or writing program, how they position themselves in a text and in the wider community, and how they continue developing as English users.

Although our examples reference undergraduate writing courses and programs, this agency framework would also be useful for increasing multilingual student agency in other contexts, such as writing-in-the-disciplines courses, graduate writing programs, writing centers, and K-12 settings. Within these contexts, what options for linguistic, rhetorical, generic, and programmatic action exist? What, in the assignment, curriculum, or wider rhetorical, cultural, and political contexts, constrains writers' options? What constitutes "sufficient information"—what do students need to notice—for students to make informed decisions about these options? How can we, as instructors and program administrators, use this information to create optimal conditions for multilingual student agency? And how do we respect student choices, even when their choices (such as avoiding an ESL section) do not seem advantageous, from our perspective as instructors or administrators? Promoting student agency does require a degree of trust in the student, providing spaces for students to both thrive and stumble. We are convinced, however, that stumbling leads to learning and resilience, and that the rewards of teaching for agency far exceed the risks.

Notes

1. We have chosen not to use the term "translingual" to refer to our overall project or to students. As Suresh Canagarajah (*Translingual Practice*) has argued, "translingualism" has become an umbrella term that includes the use of multiple languages, discourses, and registers (in other words, the term refers to a set of language practices employed by all language users). In this article, we limit our discussion to students who use English as an additional language. Thus, we alternate between "multilingual" and "second language (L2)," terms widely used to describe this population. We acknowledge that neither term is wholly accurate to describe learners of English in the U.S. However, "multilingual" values the many linguistic resources students bring, and "L2" connects our work to the field of second-language writing studies, which has made important contributions to theory and pedagogy for working with learners of English as an additional language.

2. The article was eventually published in an online Malaysian newspaper—without the footnotes.

3. Another published piece from this project is at http://translingual.org/2013/05/06/reflexiones-en-bilingue/.

4. We use the term *ESL* here, in part to highlight these courses' "pre-101," non-requirement-fulfilling status. "ESL" does not appear in the catalog title of those courses.

5. The online self-placement process has some junctures at which students can identify themselves as multilingual and answer questions about their experiences with reading and writing in English and other languages. However, the online placement questionnaires have very text-heavy questions that some multilingual students do not understand. Some admitted that they clicked answers at random and ended up with a 101 placement, despite their lack of comprehension of the language of the questionnaire. The FYW Placement Coordinator and I (Gail) are working toward a more nuanced way to identify students who would be best served in a course designed to facilitate their English language development without overwhelming them.

Works Cited

Adams, Peter, Sarah Gearhart, Robert Miller, and Anne Roberts. "The Accelerated Learning Program: Throwing Open the Gates." *Journal of Basic Writing* 28.2 (2009): 50-69. Print.

(abdullah_q45). "Do you think that writing style will be changed with the social media?" 15 April 2015. 9:47 a.m. Tweet.

(Abochnb). "It was a great opportunity to learn about all these cultures." 15 April 2015. 10:03 a.m. Tweet.

(AbulGreen). "Who doesn't miss his home?" 15 April 2015. 10:01 a.m. Tweet.

---. "This conference remained me of my first semester at boise state." 15 April 2015. 9:59 a.m. Tweet.

Aldihani, Abdulatif (abdullateefq8). "So confident." 15 April 2015, 10:05 a.m. Tweet.

Almutari, Omar. (OmarAlmutari). "You are the best group dude." 15 April 2015. 9:59 a.m. Tweet.

Alrashidi, Anwur. (anwur123). "Missing home is normal feelings to many students." 15 April 2015. 10:03 a.m. Tweet.

Bekele, Ekshesh, Donie Golanda, and Maieda Janjua. "Unity in Diversity: Internationalism at Dartmouth." Online video. *YouTube*. YouTube, 8 Mar. 2014. Web. June 2015. <https://www.youtube.com/watch?v=-bYB5snc1ec>.

Bennett, John Godolphin. *Noticing*. Sherborne: Coombe Springs P, 1976. Print. The Sherborne Theme Talks Ser. 2.

Bing, Jun, and Luka Pejanovic. "Second Language Adaptation: Writing at Dartmouth for International Students." Online video. *YouTube*. YouTube, 6 Mar. 2014. Web. June 2015. <https://www.youtube.com/watch?v=eUNP23Dac6Q&feature=youtu.be>.

Canagarajah, A. Suresh. "Agency and Power in Intercultural Communication: Negotiating English in Translocal Spaces." *Language and Intercultural Communication* 13.2 (2013): 202-24. Print.

---. *Translingual Practice: Global Englishes and Cosmopolitan Relations*. New York: Routledge, 2013. Print.

Cook, Vivian. "Evidence for Multi-Competence." *Language Learning* 42 (1992): 557-91. Print.

Cooper, Marilyn. "Rhetorical Agency as Emergent and Enacted." *CCC* 62.3 (2011): 420-49. Print.

Costino, Kimberly A., and Sunny Hyon. "'A Class for Students Like Me': Reconsidering Relationships among Identity Labels, Residency Status, and Students' Preferences for Mainstream or Multilingual Composition." *Journal of Second Language Writing* 16.2 (2007): 63-81. Print.

Donahoe, Jillian. (littlestDonahoe). "Wow, great video. I'm going to have to try video scribe." 15 April 2015. 9:50 a.m. Tweet.

Downs, Douglas, and Elizabeth Wardle. "Teaching about Writing, Righting Misconceptions: (Re)Envisioning 'First-Year Composition' as 'Introduction to Writing Studies.'" *CCC* 58.4 (2007): 552-84. Print.

Duranti, Alessandro. "Agency in Language." *A Companion to Linguistic Anthropology*. Ed. Alessandro Duranti. Malden: Blackwell, 2004. 451-73. Print.

Glau, Gregory J. "The 'Stretch Program': Arizona State University's New Model of University-level Basic Writing Instruction." *WPA: Writing Program Administration* 20.1/2 (1996): 79-91. Print.

Herrera, Robert. (RobertH88771204). "I can relate to missing where you from! I miss California." 15 April 2015. 10:00 a.m. Tweet.

Jordan, Jay. *Redesigning Composition for Multilingual Realities.* Urbana: NCTE, 2012. Print.

Kudakwashe, Clement, Odon Orzisk, and Taeho Sung. "Speak Up! (a movie by internationals for internationals)." Online video. *YouTube.* YouTube, 6 Mar. 2014. Web. June 2015. <http://www.youtube.com/watch?v=j3_keBWOTvM>.

Lomicka, Lara, and Gillian Lord. "A Tale of Tweets: Analyzing Microblogging Among Language Learners." *System* 40.1 (2012): 48-63. Science Direct. Web. 10 July 2014.

Lu, Min-Zhan, and Bruce Horner. "Translingual Literacy, Language Difference, and Matters of Agency." *College English* 75.6 (2013): 582-607. Print.

Matsuda, Paul Kei. "The Lure of Translingual Writing." *PMLA* 129.3 (2014): 478-83. Print.

Miller, Carolyn R. "What Can Automation Tell Us about Agency?" *Rhetoric Society Quarterly* 37 (2007): 137-57. Print.

Nogle, Christi. (ChristiNogle). "How did you do this animation?" 15 April 2015. 9:47 a.m.

Qi, Donald S., and Sharon Lapkin. "Exploring the Role of Noticing in a Three-Stage Second Language Writing Task." *Journal of Second Language Writing* 10 (2001): 277-303. Print.

Ruecker, Todd. "Improving the Placement of L2 Writers: The Students' Perspective." *WPA: Writing Program Administration* 35.1 (2011): 92-118. Print.

Saenkhum, Tanita. "Investigating Agency in Multilingual Writers' Placement Decisions: A Case Study of The Writing Programs at Arizona State University." Diss. Arizona State University 2012. Web. 1 Aug. 2015.

Schmidt, Richard. "Attention, Awareness, and Individual Differences in Language Learning." *Proceedings of CLaSIC 2010.* Ed. Wai Meng Chan, Seo Won Chi, Kwee Nyet Chin, Johanna W. Istanto, Masanori Nagami, Jyh Wee Sew, Titima Suthiwan, and Izumi Walker. Singapore: National U of Singapore, Centre for Language Studies, 2010. 721-37. Web. May 2015. <http://nflrc.hawaii.edu/PDFs/SCHMIDT%20Attention,%20awareness,%20and%20individual%20differences.pdf>.

Shuck, Gail. "Ownership of Texts, Ownership of Language: Two Students' Participation in a Student-Run Conference." *The Reading Matrix* 4.3 (2004): 24-39. Print.

Swain, Merrill. "Languaging, Agency and Collaboration in Advanced Language Proficiency." *Advanced Language Learning: The Contribution of Halliday and Vygotsky.* Ed. Heidi Byrnes. London: Continuum, 2006. 95-108. Print.

U.S. Census Bureau. *State Rankings: The 2012 Statistical Abstract.* Washington: GPO, 2012. Web. Oct. 2015. <www2.census.gov/library/publications/2011/compendia/statab/131ed/2012-statab.pdf>.

Writing across Borders. Dir. Wayne Robertson. Oregon State U, 2005. Film.

Appendix: Reading List from Dartmouth FYW Course

Bloch, Joel. "Plagiarism: Is There a Difference across Cultures?" *Indonesian Journal of English Language Teaching* 3.2 (2007): 139-51. Print.

Carson, Joan. "Becoming Biliterate." *Journal of Second Language Writing* 1.1 (1992): 37-60. Print.

Harushumana, Immaculee. "Blinding Audacity: The Narrative of a French-Speaking African Teaching English in the United States." *Reinventing Identities in Second Language Writing*. Ed. Michelle Cox, Jay Jordan, Christina Ortmeier-Hooper, and Gwen Gray Schwartz. Urbana: NCTE, 2010. 232-9. Print.

---. "Colonial Language Writing Identities in Postcolonial Africa." *Reinventing Identities in Second Language Writing*. Ed. Michelle Cox, Jay Jordan, Christina Ortmeier-Hooper, and Gwen Gray Schwartz. Urbana: NCTE, 2010. 207-31. Print.

Howard, Rebecca Moore. "A Plagiarism Pentimento." *Journal of Teaching Writing* 11.2 (1993): 233-46. Print.

---. "Understanding 'Internet Plagiarism.'" *Computers and Composition* 24.1 (2007): 3-15. Print.

Krachu, Braj. "World Englishes: Agony and Ecstasy." *Journal of Aesthetic Education* 30.2 (1996): 135-55. Print.

Kubota, Ryuko. "My Experience of Learning to Read and Write in Japanese and English as L2." *Reflections on Multiliterate Lives*. Ed. Ulla Connor and Diane Belcher. Clevedon: Multilingual Matters, 2001. 96-109. Print.

Leki, Ilona. "History of Writing Instruction in English as a Second Language." *Understanding ESL Writers: A Guide for Teachers*. Portsmouth: Heinemann, 1992. 3-9. Print.

---. "Models of Second Language Acquisition." *Understanding ESL Writers: A Guide for Teachers*. Portsmouth: Heinemann, 1992. 10-24. Print.

Sasaki, Miyuki. "An Introspective Account of L2 Writing Acquisition." *Reflections on Multiliterate Lives*. Ed. Ulla Connor and Diane Belcher. Clevedon: Multilingual Matters, 2001. 110-9. Print.

Tsai, Ming-Daw. "Learning is a Life-Long Process." *Reflections on Multiliterate Lives*. Ed. Ulla Connor and Diane Belcher. Clevedon: Multilingual Matters, 2001. 135-40. Print.

You, Xiaoye. "The Choice Made from No Choice: English Writing Instruction in a Chinese University." *Journal of Second Language Writing* 13.2 (2004): 97–110. Print.

Negotiating World Englishes in a Writing-Based MOOC

Ben McCorkle, Kay Halasek, Kaitlin Clinnin, and Cynthia L. Selfe

This article recounts the experiences of a team of faculty, graduate students, and instructional technologists facilitating Rhetorical Composing, a writing-focused Massive Open Online Course (MOOC). When first offering the MOOC, we recognized quickly that we needed to emphasize the global makeup of our learning cohort to foster a stronger sense of community, diminish concerns about peer review, and inform participants about various ways that people all over the world learn English. In response, we developed a curricular unit focusing on "World Englishes" that included video lectures, guest speakers, discussion forums, and an invitation for individuals to submit their own learning experiences. We also designed an in-house peer-review software platform, which provided focused training for all participants, regardless of language background. Here, we analyze demographic data for the course, participant writing, and other content generated within the MOOC.

"As the linguistic diversity of the student population has become undeniably clear, and as the institutional urge for globalization continues to grow, second language writing is beginning to gain recognition as a concern for everyone involved in the field of composition studies."

—Paul Kei Matsuda (2012)

In contemporary composition classrooms, teachers and scholars such as A. Suresh Canagarajah ("Ecology"), Bruce Horner and John Trimbur ("English Only"), and Paul Kei Matsuda ("Myth") encourage faculty to make what Wendy Hesford calls the "global turn" (787), to explore not only issues of multilingual education but also pursue with increased energy, focus, and understanding the expanded possibilities of an "imagined global geography" (788). Such efforts have proven both complex and difficult, however, as rhetoric and composition faculty—often without adequate preparation in teaching students with different language backgrounds—struggle to deal in productive ways with the different cultures, languages, and educational values introduced by an increasingly international student body in the U.S. and elsewhere (Horner, NeCamp, and Donahue; Jordan; Matsuda, "Myth"). One educational environment dramatically illustrating the importance of Hesford's call and Matsuda's point in the epigraph above—that second language writing instruction is increasingly becoming a central focus for the entirety of composition studies—is the Massive Open Online Course (MOOC), where participants from all over the world representing a diverse spectrum of ethnic, class, professional, and linguistic identities come together to participate in a collective learning experience.

Since their rise in popularity only a few years ago, MOOCs have offered a new, if no less contested, context for composition instruction that is globalized and multilingual (Matsuda, "Teaching"), yet disagreements about the value of these instructional environments persist. Some educators maintain, however, that MOOCs—if designed around the values of the open educational resources movement (de Langen and van den Bosch; Springs; Yuan and Powell)—can serve as locations for increasingly disruptive, transnational, and open access to higher education.

In this article, we describe the instructional context of the Rhetorical Composing MOOC taught by a team of Ohio State University faculty and graduate students in 2013 and 2014. In discussing this course, we identify an instructional approach addressing both Non-Native English Speakers (NNES) and Native English Speakers (NES) that focuses on World Englishes[1] as an intellectual space wherein both teachers and participants can productively investigate rhetoric, writing instruction, peer review, and participants' identities as writers and readers. This focus on World Englishes and the scale of the Rhetorical Composing MOOC, we maintain, afforded MOOC participants an opportunity to acknowledge an increasingly globalized world, navigate an academic context in which NNES concerns were centrally important, and confront assumptions about cultural, linguistic, and geographical difference. Although the MOOC was not entirely successful in every respect, we saw enough positive signs to convince us that a World Englishes approach informed by principles of emergent pedagogy is worth refining for writing instruction in MOOCs and other instructional contexts.

Situating the Rhetorical Composing MOOC

In the spring of 2013—amidst an increasingly volatile national conversation regarding MOOCs that variously described them as either transformational (Waldrop) or destructive (Vardi), questioning whether they're "scourge or savior" (McGettigan)—our instructional team designed and implemented a MOOC titled "Writing II: Rhetorical Composing."[2] During the course design phase, we modeled Rhetorical Composing on Ohio State's second-year writing class, a required general education course that focuses on developing critical analysis and research skills in written, oral, and visual modes of expression. The ten-week MOOC positioned rhetorical theory as the centerpiece of the curriculum, highlighting concepts of audience, purpose, genre, and other contextual concerns. During the course, participants discussed and completed several writing and multimodal composing assignments including a literacy narrative, comparative analysis, visually-oriented public-service announcement, and public discourse text that incorporated outside research. By completing these assignments and peer reviews of others' work, participants earned a Statement of Completion (or Completion with Distinction) through Coursera, our MOOC hosting partner. The MOOC was not offered for academic credit.

In addition to the formal assignments and peer review—which was conducted in The Writers Exchange (WEx), an in-house peer review platform—the MOOC included course content dealing with rhetorical theory and analysis delivered through a variety of methods: video lectures and presentations, supplemental readings from open content websites such as *Writing Commons*, and topic-based videos provided to us by Bedford/St. Martin's. Participants were encouraged to engage with course content, share preliminary ideas and early drafts of their work, and participate in community building in various discussion forum threads created during the course. Similar activities took place outside of the course platform itself in social media groups, typically created by MOOC participants.

Early in the development process, we did not explicitly connect course content and assignments to or concentrate on NNES needs, but we quickly realized that we had to address this oversight. Early demographic data for the MOOC emphasized just how wide-ranging and varied the Rhetorical Composing community was. During the 2013 iteration of Rhetorical Composing, the nearly 33,000 enrollees represented 181 countries, 36% from what the World Bank Country and Lending Group classifies as "emerging economies." Only 34% were from North America, and only 37% indicated English as a first language. The 2014 iteration of Rhetorical Composing had a smaller total enrollment (nearly 22,000), but demographic percentages were largely aligned with the 2013 offering.

Although we anticipated a great many NNES participants in the course, the enrollment statistics raised a question that we hadn't considered: Had we created a course that would meet the needs of a globalized classroom? Our answer was, "No"—or perhaps "Not as much as we'd like." We realized the need to adapt our approaches to pedagogy, content, and participant interaction. We recognized that the scale and range of MOOCs could inspire learning communities with a diversity of language backgrounds and that this very diversity could foster a dialogue that negotiated between individual and common experiences with language learning. This immense scale in turn could open spaces for promoting real learning—if we leveraged these features meaningfully toward these goals. Given the globalized, diverse character of participants and the multiple interventions made possible by the MOOC platform, we responded by revising curriculum, assignment design, and pedagogical philosophy. By adhering to the principles of emergent pedagogy, we learned valuable lessons about the importance of implementing real-time adjustments to teaching in a MOOC environment, involving learners in course design, encouraging participants to share their own backgrounds and language learning experiences with one another, and involving students in teaching and learning from one another.

Engaging World Englishes and Emergent Pedagogy

With the globalized character of our participants in mind, we reconceptualized the design and implementation of the Rhetorical Composing MOOC with a philosophy informed by emergent pedagogical theory. Employed by philosophy, media studies, various branches of the sciences and elsewhere to explain the development of complex systems for which underlying, guiding logics are not apparent, emergent theory is particularly well-suited as a lens through which to examine online learning environments, particularly large-scale MOOCs, for these contexts involve multiple spaces for interaction between and among groups of participants of varying sizes over time. In these environments, the capacity for learning is exceedingly difficult to predict with precision, and harder still to manage.

As French Dalke et al. maintain, effective emergent pedagogy approaches learning by emphasizing "autonomous, explorative interactions" in an effort to connect with students who have vastly different experiences and organizational schema (116). For Dalke et al., principles of emergent pedagogy create occasions for active learning through content that promotes exploration and is driven by developmental processes rather than static outcomes. Emergent pedagogy also seeks to support all learners through shared teaching and learning roles for both instructors and students (116). Writing about MOOCs specifically, Bill Hart-Davidson echoes a philosophy informed by the principles of emergent pedagogy: "Within peer networks, there is a dynamic that arises from the rich set of resources each individual learner has to draw upon that boosts the learning potential—and the performance level—of each individual" (213). For Davidson, the one-to-many learning environment typifying many MOOC designs, where content experts provide lecture content and participants are subsequently tested on their retention of it, does not cultivate the peer scaffolding model that ultimately results in better writing instruction and, it follows, better writers. Thus, creating the conditions for meaningful participant-to-participant interaction is an essential condition to effective learning. This involves managing a *many-to-many* learning environment, providing multiple outlets for learners to develop their skills and hone their craft in both formal and informal digital spaces. The approach has the added benefit of offsetting deficits in expertise typically situated at the level of instructor(s) by encouraging students to recognize and share their own expertise (Clinnin).

We therefore developed curricular content, spaces, and approaches to accommodate the multilingual participants by utilizing the principles of emergent pedagogy and related approaches such as Universal Design for Learning (UDL) and participatory design.[3] For example, acknowledging a globalized set of participants in the MOOC, we created a "World Englishes" content module that included a philosophy of and advice for creating a welcoming, generous community of learners from various language backgrounds, video interviews with multilingual learners, a video discussion with Paul Kei Matsuda, discussion forums specifically addressing NNES topics, and a "Level Up" challenge to submit narratives to the Digital Archive of Literacy Narratives.[4] Collectively, we envisioned these elements comprising an infrastructure upon which participants could build by developing and transferring rhetorical knowledge. From an emergent pedagogy perspective, initiating a World Englishes conversation and making these changes was an attempt to bring about increased awareness and understanding among MOOC participants about the complexities of multilingual learning and communication. Also, we hoped that broaching the topic might help create a greater sense of community through knowledge building and exchange. As Deborah Osberg and Gerta Biesta contend, "[k]nowledge is understood, rather, to 'emerge' as we, as human beings, participate in the world. Knowledge, in other words, does not exist except in our participatory actions" (313). Cultivating spaces for sustained, dynamic participatory actions poses a challenge in any educational setting, including MOOCs, as such a process often involves negotiating an uncertain terrain of knowing when, and to what extent, to intervene.

Engaging World Englishes through Peer Review

We envisioned "World Englishes" as an instructional context within which participants could productively engage one another across Englishes as they conversed about writing and language learning on discussion forums and completed course assignments. The World Englishes philosophy also implicitly informed peer review in the MOOC. To address some of the most critical challenges facing peer review in a multicultural, multilingual, and translingual context, we designed the WEx peer-review platform to support "constructive" activities (Chi 74). Through the assignments, peer reviews, and reflections submitted to WEx, participants extended their learning and engagement with course materials and other participants (Chi 76-77, 78).

We also created assets to support peer review, among them, a manual, *The WEx Training Guide to Peer Review,* a detailed introduction to the processes and pedagogies of peer review collaboratively authored by the entire MOOC team;

video introductions and tutorials; a practice peer-review module; and discussion forums on the topic of peer review. Through these materials, we sought to provide targeted, meaningful instruction on conducting peer review—a facet of overt writing instruction that Sheri Rysdam and Lisa Johnson-Shull argue is critical to successful peer review but often overlooked. Without such training, they argue, students are likely to mimic responses and employ strategies they've witnessed (84) that sometimes contribute to a "culture of negativity" (77), which compromises successful peer review, teaching, and learning. As in any class, we were, as instructors, unable to ensure that each participant read and fully embraced course materials or the philosophy of *The Guide* and its concept of peer review; however, we did encourage and acknowledge on discussion forums participants' engagement with the materials and processes. More valuable in the adoption of the peer review process were the participants themselves, whose commentary on forums emphasized the value of peer review.

Taking into account numerous studies addressing the challenges of peer review for NNES students (Hu and Lam; Ihm; Min, "Training Students"), we paid particular attention to providing explicit instruction in and practice of peer review, employing a response structure similar to Hui-Tzu Min's four-step procedure in which participants articulate an author's intention, identify and explain problems they encountered as readers, and make suggestions to the author (298). *The WEx Training Guide* asked participants to "describe the part of the writing that you are responding to," "assess what you are reading by pointing out both strengths and weaknesses," and "suggest how the writer might make changes if he or she were to revise or how the writer might think differently about writing in future assignments" (DeWitt et al. 6).

WEx and *The WEx Training Guide* were attempts to create a system that provided all peer reviewers time to construct and edit their responses before submitting them and writers time to consider that written feedback before responding to it—features that supported the kind of multicultural and translingual peer review that Min notes NNES students value ("Training" 296). Although we were influenced by research that suggests peer review provides meaningful opportunities for NNES students to improve their writing skills (Bradley; Hu and Lam; Min, "Effects"), we were also acutely aware of research that identified limitations in the practice of peer review, particularly in contexts in which NES and NNES students read and respond to one another's work. Studies suggest that NES and NNES students often do not trust one another with respect to peer feedback. George Braine found NNES students felt NES students were "impatient" with them and "complain[ed] about" the "numerous grammatical errors" in their papers (98), indicating that "native speakerist ideologies" complicated the students' engagement with peer review (Braine qtd. in Ruecker 94-95). Specifically, NNES students expressed anxiety about peer review, and although they reported "becoming more comfortable with peer review" over time, "giving feedback was consistently the[ir] least favorite part of peer review" (Ruecker 96). NNES students like Lily in Todd Ruecker's study reported that giving feedback entailed a significant commitment of time and that they were uncertain about their ability to provide meaningful feedback, leading them to focus on "'general ideas and comment on it [sic]'" (97). These students also expressed a reluctance to find fault or "'say anything bad'" because, as NNES students, they felt they could not provide accurate or helpful commentary (97). At the same time, although many NNES students in Ruecker's study looked forward to peer review of their own work by NES students—again, in part because of nativist assumptions—others found NES students' feedback harsh and rude—characteristics far different from the conventions of their own cultures (98).

The WEx Training Guide itself—which emphasized peer review as an "exchange," as a means of engaging writers through brainstorming, problem solving, advice and support—was one pedagogical means of addressing the power imbalances and the nativist assumptions scholars identify (Braine; Ruecker). Emphasizing the enriching value to writers of the cultural, ideological, and linguistic differences among an audience of readers, *The Guide* situated peer review as an integral part of conversations about writing and identified WEx as the primary vehicle for providing feedback. *The Guide* also encouraged participants to use the discussion forums as additional sites for commenting on and exchanging ideas about writing. One section of *The Guide* confronts head-on the complicated nature of undertaking online peer review and possibility that participants might be hesitant about providing feedback to one another:

> Admittedly, sometimes providing this kind of feedback creates an awkward situation. You might not know the person very well, and you're uncomfortable offering critique. Perhaps you feel that you're not sure of the most effective way to offer feedback, or you're not sure how to word your feedback. Perhaps you feel the piece is so strong that you have nothing to add. And often, you're just not sure what's at stake. Is this person really listening to your feedback? Will the feedback matter? Will the writer take your suggestions seriously? (DeWitt et al. 2)

The Guide encouraged participants to approach the task of peer review with a positive outlook, concluding, "If we assume that we're all doing the best work we can, and we keep this as the foundation of WEx, then there's no room for being overly critical or harsh. *It's an exchange*" (emphasis in original, 2). *The Guide*, in other words, offered NES and NNES participants alternative metaphors for the processes of peer review: Peer review is an exchange, a conversation among writers—not an expert reviewer imparting wisdom or a reviewer serving as proxy for the teacher.

Although WEx provided a productive venue for engaging in peer review, participants also sought out and created among themselves forum-based peer response, treating forums as community spaces where they posted drafts of their assignments and solicited peer feedback. This context for peer feedback served a different set of needs for some writers, including those who had particular issues to which they wanted peers to respond in particular units.

The discussion forums became productive spaces of engagement for participants, sites for distributing ideas and sharing writing outside of the official WEx peer review system. As such, the discussion forums served many of the functions that blogging serves for L2 and Gen 1.5 students (Bloch).[5] Although still a "gated community" (Lowe and Williams qtd. in Bloch 128), the MOOC—as an open access and massive learning space—provided participants with a linguistically and culturally diverse audience, giving them a "greater sense of the variety of possible audiences they can reach, both for understanding these audiences and learning strategies to respond to them" at the same time it facilitated the development of social communities (Bloch 128, 132). Participants used the forums as a venue for crowdsourcing responses and creating conversations among their peers about their writing, a function not available in WEx. In effect, the discussion forums offered participants de facto writing groups, a point we take up below.

In the end, our efforts to address the power imbalance between NNES and NES were only partially successful. For instance, the discussion forums served as a sounding board for expressing frustrations about peer review, with some participants noting variously that some reviews continued to be too harsh and rude or too accommodating—opinions that echoed students' responses in Ruecker's study. In addition, some participants' posts about peer review continued to invest in the expert/teacher proxy model and to maintain nativist assumptions. Such results testify to the multitude of cultural formations shaping NNES/NES relationships.

In a thread titled "Disappointing Reviews on Assignment 2," in the "Discuss Unit 2: Responding Rhetorically and Assignment 2" forum, Sharon[6] posted that she had received four peer reviews, three of which assigned her work a "5" (the highest score) while a fourth evaluated her work as a "2," and expressed confusion over the differences among the evaluations. In responding to her post, other participants offered supportive comments, reminding Sharon that "many of your reviewers are just like you…learning," "Just let go and 'keep on trucking.'" "I'm sure you doing great, [Sharon]!" or "I believe you've done good work, be patient with your readers." At the same time, such responses were also couched within a set of nativist assumptions, as one from Oleh, who wrote, "I believe you've done good work, be patient with your readers. May be some of them are trolls and most likely they are just learners and English is their if not foreign then second language." A native Ukrainian, Oleh reassures Sharon and provides supportive feedback, taking on some of the reader roles Wei Zhu outlines, including reacting ("I believe you've done good work") and justifying ("May be some of them are trolls and most likely they are just learners and English is their if not foreign then second language"). In this instance, however, Oleh does not justify his own reading of Sharon's work but uses her peer reviewer's qualities ("trolls") or language status ("learners" and speakers of English as a "foreign" or "second language") to explain the anomalous review score. Oleh's explanation, in other words, is built upon the nativist assumption that second or foreign language speakers may have provided the anomalous review: If the reviewer was not a "troll," then English must be his/her second or foreign language. Oleh's post is followed immediately by other posts from other participants.

> Marcia: I received a review from someone whose first language was obviously not English. That wasn't the problem as I read his review. I overlooked all the grammatical errors because of this, and there were many. My negative reaction to his review was in the comment that there were "grammatical errors" in my essay and that I would get better as I write more. I almost choked because there were no grammar errors in it. He obviously was using his own limited knowledge of English grammar as a reference point for evaluating my essay which would make sense to him but would not be correct in analyzing mine. After considering his comment for a few minutes, I decided not to dwell on it and let it go by commenting in this forum. By the way, none of the other reviewers made any comment regarding my use of grammar.
>
> Rana: I hear you [Marcia] :) probably a smiley is not even the correct emoticon to put here, but I'm just noticing the exact same thing that happened to me . . . can't do anything about it, so I too ma [sic] just posting here. Hope you are enjoying the course though . . . Cheerio.

The issue here is not so much that participants assumed these reviews were written by NNES peers (although those assumptions are troubling) but that writers sometimes discounted reviews because they assumed the texts were written by NNES peers when the texts did not demonstrate an acceptable level of proficiency or "fluency" marked by grammatical correctness. In this context and others characterizing this MOOC and the large group of students it involved, the instructors provided as much instruction and intervention as possible. We also recognized, however, that participants themselves needed room in the discussion forums to respond to each other without the direct intervention of instructors, practicing the attitudes toward World Englishes we encouraged.

Promoting Emergence through Optional Assignments

To bridge our emergent pedagogy with the need to evaluate participant performance, we offered an optional Level Up[8] activity based on the World Englishes content. The "World Englishes: Engaging Globally" Level Up challenge contained two parts: A recorded or written response to a prompt about World Englishes shared on the discussion forums and a brief reflection submitted as a quiz for assessment purposes. The prompt included the following four generative questions:

- Why talk about "World Englishes" rather than "Standard English"?
- What are the difficulties/challenges of learning a World English?
- What are some strategies for learning a variety of English?
- What advice do people offer about learning a variety of English?

After posting their responses to the discussion forums, participants composed short reflections in response to the following prompt:

> *Please provide a brief reflection on what you learned from completing this Level Up for Distinction Activity. Consider what you learned from the World Englishes content including the videos and discussion posts from other students in this course. Has your opinion of World Englishes changed after interacting with the content, and if so, how has your opinion changed? What do you still have questions about? How will this impact your daily life?*

To complete the first part of the Level Up activity, participants could draw on course content and their personal experiences to compose a discussion forum post or record a video response. The second part of the activity required participants to engage with their peers in the discussion forums, dip into the various threads and differing perspectives on the topic, and ultimately synthesize and reflect on how the activity impacted their own perspectives on the topic. Throughout the discussion forum posts and the reflection responses, several common themes emerged, including the personal relevance of World Englishes, the sharing of skills and knowledge based on personal experience with linguistic difference, and the importance of recognizing and embracing language variations and individuals' different positions.

As much as we wanted to embrace an emergent and collaborative pedagogy that enhanced participant learning, the individual nature of educational attainment and the need to assess and certify individuals at times took precedence. For example, although emergent pedagogy emphasizes collaboration among participants and instructors (as in the peer review process and discussion forums), Coursera emphasized credentialing opportunities for individuals, offering levels of certificates based on course completion. In such an environment, assessing collaborative learning in a manner that is fair to all participants—each of whom comes to the course with different backgrounds, experiences, learning objectives, and learning styles—can be difficult. The Level Up format, we hoped, offered participants the chance to work collaboratively and then create an individual reflection that could be assessed for individual performance.

Approximately 50 participants completed the Level Up activity for World Englishes.[9] Most surprising about these submissions were the different levels of collaboration involved. Although some of the discussion threads related to World Englishes had up to 75 posts from multiple participants, many of the threads in the Level Up activity contained only the original participant's post. We attributed this to the activity prompt itself, which failed to inspire conversation and discussion amongst diverse learners or the exchange of resources on the large scale that we expected and hoped for. Other threads, like "Disappointing Reviews on Assignment 2," which emerged from the participants' own interests and learning needs, did a better job of engaging participants in negotiating World Englishes and applying that understanding to the course content and composing generally. Participants also encountered interface difficulties that shaped some of the collaborative possibilities. The discussion forum algorithm emphasized threads that contained more posts or received more views, which encouraged even more posts and views as these same threads were easily accessible. Threads with only one post were more difficult to find and therefore less likely to receive comments.

This interface challenge may also have contributed to participants' reflections on the module, many of which summarized the material presented in the World Englishes content module rather than complicating or expanding on it. To borrow again from Chi's taxonomy, the reflections were more active than interactive. Participants who completed the Level Up activity wrote reflections based primarily upon their own personal experiences and the course content without mentioning or synthesizing other participants' perspectives on World Englishes.

Our pedagogical approach to the Rhetorical Composing MOOC also employed scaffolded activities and assignments to make learning accessible for as many participants as possible. We created small, low-stakes activities that built towards larger assignments. Ideally, we wanted participants to transfer what they learned from the low-stakes activities to more complex or even to completely new learning contexts. We hoped that by opening the course with the World Englishes content module and Level Up activity that World Englishes would serve as a framework for the entire course. We expected that participants would utilize their understanding and experiences with World Englishes in all aspects of the course, even those not specifically related to language diversity, including the discussion forums and peer review. However, almost none of the participants' reflections for the World Englishes Level Up activity mentioned the peer review process. One participant did discuss how World Englishes helped with responding to discussion forum posts, commenting,

> Initially, my focus was on the grammatical errors and then after reading the post several times, I realize that the individual was writing with English as a second language. My focus changed to the nature of the content of her post. As I encountered more posts from others of foreign dialect, I found it became easier for me to focus on content and provide constructive feedback.

The framework of World Englishes helped this participant move from an error-based approach to commenting on peers' writing to a focus on the ideas, yet this example is an outlier from most of the World Englishes Level Up reflections. Although many of the submissions discussed how a new or more complicated understanding of World Englishes helped the individual author reflect on his or her own experience with language diversity and fostered a greater sense of tolerance and diversity, only this one comment explicitly connected the World Englishes framework to the rest of the Rhetorical Composing MOOC content. As we note previously, we attribute this phenomenon in part to the reflection prompt itself. In retrospect, we consider this a missed opportunity.

The need for more explicit scaffolding in World Englishes was also apparent in other participant reflections. As one participant wrote,

> I know there is a variety of pretty much every language out there, depending on many factors, including location, situation, exposure, education, etc, but I still fully believe in there being a Standard that we ought to aspire to. Sure, the goal is to communicate, but I think it's okay to expect that we do it properly. . . . I realise the moderators made sure to tell us to read our peers' work for basically the meaning

and intention, but not to harp on errors. But . . . how can we simply accept erroneous language as "World English"?

The reflection ends with a practical question: What are participants supposed to do with the knowledge of World Englishes? Based on this reflection, the participant appears unsure of how to negotiate World Englishes and is left with the decision either to ignore or accept World Englishes. As an instructional team, we do not believe that this is simply a binary choice, but instead another way to work within a World Englishes framework is to provide feedback that balances effective rhetorical communication with additional attention to stylistic elements. This is a place for us as instructors to step in and clarify how participants can incorporate their understanding of World Englishes into course elements like the discussion forums and peer review process and their own rhetorical composing in other aspects of their lives.

Ultimately, because of our implementation decisions, the World Englishes module and its Level Up activity did not fully achieve the intended purpose of engaging participants in a language diversity framework with the goal of building a more collaborative and supportive learning community for all learners. We believe in the value of World Englishes and will continue to augment our emergent pedagogy with this framework; however, we recognize the need to make more explicit the relationship between World Englishes and other course elements. We also will work to offer more emergent opportunities for participants to engage with the content in a way that values collaboration.

Conclusion

As we reflect on our own teaching and learning in the MOOC, we are reminded of the work of Valerie Kinloch and Tim San Pedro, who in turn call on the work and words of Leona Okakok. These scholars encourage us to be open to multiple worldviews, especially those that may conflict with our own, to see those worldviews instead as "different and diverse" (Kinloch and San Pedro qtd. in Paris and Winn 27). Kinloch and San Pedro include as an epigraph the following quotation from Okakok, which articulates the insight we hoped MOOC participants would realize through their interactions with one another: "We all know that we go through life convinced that our view of the world is the only valid one. If we are interested in new perceptions, however, we need to catch a glimpse of the world through other eyes. We need to be aware of our own thoughts as well as the way life is viewed by other people" (Okakok qtd. in Kinloch and San Pedro 29). In Rhetorical Composing, the World Englishes content was one space intentionally constructed for participants and instructors to acknowledge and engage diverse perspectives. The activities associated with the World Englishes module—including the instructor-produced Level Up activities and the student-driven discussion forum threads—encouraged students and instructors to engage, negotiate, and transform their understandings of linguistic diversity through interactions with one another. In the spirit of emergent pedagogy, we invited students to share their experiences with one another, discover the points of similarity and contention, and collectively come to new understandings and knowledge that could not be anticipated by instructor design. Such dynamic collaborative engagement—what Kinloch and San Pedro term the "dialogic spiral" (30)— affords participants greater access to new information, different perspectives, lines of argument, counterarguments, challenges to conventional thinking, and "shared understanding or a 'shared mental model'" of the topic, question, or task (Chi 87).

Although we recognize moments when this collaborative engagement did occur, often in the discussion forum threads, we also recognize moments when this collaborative engagement was limited or hindered, often by our own assumptions about students and emergent pedagogy. In our practice of emergent pedagogy, we assumed that students would be able to transfer course knowledge from module to module without direct instructor intervention, taking a leap of faith and connecting the World Englishes framework to the rest of the course content. Instead, we observed that students did not necessarily apply the World Englishes framework to the rest of the course content, or they used the framework to support their previously held understandings of linguistic diversity or nativist ideologies.

In retrospect, we believe the process of dynamic collaboration would have been greatly enhanced if we, as instructors, engaged more intentionally with cultural issues throughout the course. Specifically, we needed to be more explicit about the connections between World Englishes and composing, especially with peer review. Although students were able to glimpse other worldviews through their interactions in peer reviews and discussion forums, the lack of scaffolding on our part allowed some students to use these glimpses to reinforce their own previously held notions of language diversity and "correct" writing. Additionally, although students were encouraged to engage in self-reflection about their own experiences with World Englishes, these reflections were often superficial and not informed by an understanding of how the World Englishes framework applied to the rest of the course or their identity as writers in a global setting. By engaging students with World Englishes early and often and prompting them to undertake deeper reflection throughout our courses, we can encourage them to identify and examine their own cultural values (Hofstede) and the influence that these values have on their experience of composing and collaborating in multilingual and translingual educational settings.

Notes

1. We elect to use the phrase "World Englishes" as it was the term we deployed in the MOOC. For the sake of consistency, we continue to use "World Englishes" here. At the same time, we acknowledge the work of Canagarajah on global English and translingualism (*Literacy as Translingual Practice; Translingual Practice*) in informing our pedagogical goals. In particular, we sought to create a learning context in which all writers—but especially multilingual and translingual writers—could engage strategies, infuse practices, and effect change in the "norms" of English language use in the MOOC.

2. Initial funding for the Rhetorical Composing MOOC was provided by a Bill & Melinda Gates Foundation grant in 2013, awarded to institutions proposing writing-based MOOCs that incorporated Open Education Resources (OER) in their curricula. The Rhetorical Composing MOOC was offered in Spring 2013 and Autumn 2014.

3. For a more detailed description of UDL and participatory design, as well as the creation of our "World Englishes" module for the Rhetorical Composing MOOC, see Ben McCorkle et al., "Habitus, Disposition and Disruption in MOOCs" and Kaitlin Clinnin et al., "(Re)framing Pedagogy."

4. The World Englishes page was launched prior to the formal opening of the course. This pre-launch opening of the World Englishes module strived to set a tone and climate that might encourage participants away from unexamined nativist assumptions about language, language users, and writing instruction. The module did not include scholarly work on World Englishes or global English, but materials included were informed by the work of such scholars as Kingsley Bolton and Braj Kachru (*World Englishes*), A. Suresh Canagarajah ("The Ecology of Global English;" *The Literacy of Translingual Practice; Translingual Practice*), and Braj Kachru (*Alchemy*). The module included a video introduction that alluded to the effects of colonization and the attendant spread of English across the globe as a political tool but emphasized the influences and needs of the more local and regional—family, culture, economics, and religion—that ultimately shape, reshape, and enrich English and Englishes spoken globally. The module was supplemented roughly one month into the course by an interactive Google Hangout hosted by Cynthia Selfe that featured Paul Kei Matsuda speaking with participants about second-language writing (Michaels).

5. Terry Fellner and Matthew Apple, and Wan Shun Eva Lam also demonstrate the value of class-assigned blogging to NNES learners. They found that students who blogged as part of their course requirements realized both an increase in number of words produced and use of academic vocabulary. Lam found that having an online presence positively affected a student's "identity as a competent user of English" (Warschauer and Liaw).

6. Pseudonyms have been assigned to all MOOC participants.

7. As Tita Beaven et al. argue, participatory literacy (the "ability to contribute to blogs, wikis, social networking and sharing sites, virtual worlds, and gaming environments") as well as "self-determination and motivation" are "fundamental to success in a massive open online course" (32). As much as we would have liked all partici-

pants to perform multiple acts of participatory literacy during the MOOC, we also recognize the rights of participants to choose not to engage or engage in only a few activities, assignments, and content.

8. Rhetorical Composing offered participants several optional Level Up activities as a way to earn a Certificate of Completion with Distinction, such as submitting personal literacy narratives to the Digital Archive of Literacy Narratives website, creating a remix of an artwork, or publishing one of the formal composing assignments in a public forum, among others.

9. There were a total of 53 submissions for the World Englishes Level Up activity; however, participants were able to submit multiple times to improve their score on the activity. The activity was graded pass-fail. To pass the activity, participants needed to provide a URL to their discussion post or other asset and complete an alphabetic reflection of at least 50 characters.

Works Cited

Beaven, Tita, Mirjam Hauck, Anna Comas-Quinn, Tim Lewis, and Beatriz de los Arcos. "MOOCs: Striking the Right Balance between Facilitation and Self-Determination." *Merlot Journal of Online Learning and Teaching* 10.1 (2014): 31-43. Print.

Bloch, Joel. "Abdullah's Blogging: A Generation 1.5 Student Enters the Blogosphere." *Language, Learning & Technology* 11.2 (2007): 128-41. Print.

Bolton, Kingsley, and Braj Kachru, eds. *World Englishes: Critical Concepts in Linguistics*. Vol. 4. London: Routledge, 2006. Print.

Bradley, Linda. "Peer-reviewing in an Intercultural Wiki Environment: Student Interaction and Reflection." *Computers and Composition* 34.1 (2014): 80-95. Print.

Braine, George. "ESL Students in First-year Writing Courses: ESL Versus Mainstream Classes." *Journal of Second Language Writing* 5.2 (1996): 91-107. Print.

Canagarajah, A. Suresh. "The Ecology of Global English." *International Multilingual Research Journal* 1.2 (2007): 89-100. Print.

---. *Literacy as Translingual Practice: Between Communities and Classrooms*. London: Routledge, 2013. Print.

---. *Translingual Practice: Global Englishes and Cosmopolitan Relations*. London: Routledge, 2013. Print.

Chi, Michelene T. H. "Active—Constructive—Interactive: A Conceptual Framework for Differentiating Learning Activities." *Topics in Cognitive Science* 1.1 (2009): 73-105. Print.

Clinnin, Kaitlin. "Redefining the MOOC: Examining the Multilingual and Community Potential of Massive Online Courses." *Journal of Global Literacies, Technologies, and Emerging Pedagogies* 2.3 (2014): n. pag. Web. 30 June 2015. <http://jogltep.com/index.php/JOGLTEP/article/view/24/11>.

Clinnin, Kaitlin, Kay Halasek, Susan Delagrange, Scott DeWitt, Ben McCorkle, and Cynthia Selfe. "(Re)framing Pedagogy: The Potential of Participatory Design in Writing MOOCs." 2015. TS. Ohio State University, Columbus, OH. Print.

Corbett, Steven J., Michelle LaFrance, and Teagan E. Decker, eds. *Peer Pressure, Peer Power: Theory and Practice in Peer Review and Response for the Writing Classroom.* Southlake: Fountainhead Press, forthcoming. Print.

Dalke, Anne French, Kim Cassidy, Paul Grobstein, and Doug Blank. "Emergent Pedagogy: Learning to Enjoy the Uncontrollable—and Make It Productive." *Journal of Educational Change* 8.2 (2007): 111-30. Print.

de Langen, Frank, and Herman van den Bosch, "Massive Open Online Courses: Disruptive Innovations or Disturbing Inventions?" *Open Learning: The Journal of Open, Distance, and e-Learning* 23.3 (2014): 216-27. 10 March 2014. Web. 28 June 2015. <http://www.tandfonline.com/doi/abs/10.1080/02680513.2013.870882>.

DeWitt, Scott, Michelle Cohen, Chase Bollig, Kaitlin Clinnin, Susan Delagrange, Kay Halasek, Ben McCorkle, Jennifer Michaels, and Cynthia Selfe. *The WEx Training Guide.* Unpublished training manual. Ohio State University 2014. Print.

Fellner, Terry, and Matthew Apple. "Developing Writing Fluency and Lexical Complexity with Blogs." *The JALT CALL Journal* 2.1 (2006): 15-26. Print.

Hart-Davidson, Bill. "Learning Many-to-Many: The Best Case for Writing in Digital Environments." *Invasion of the MOOCs: The Promise and Peril of Massive Open Online Courses.* Ed. Steven D. Krause and Charles Lowe. Anderson: Parlor Press, 2014. 212-22. Print.

Hesford, Wendy S. "Global Turns and Cautions in Rhetoric and Composition Studies." *PMLA* 121.3 (2006): 787-801. Print.

Hofstede, Geert. *Culture's Consequences: Comparing Values, Behaviors, Institutions, and Organizations across Nations.* 2nd ed. Thousand Oaks: Sage Publications, 2001. Print.

Horner, Bruce, Samantha NeCamp, and Christiane Donahue. "Toward a Multilingual Composition Scholarship: From English Only to a Translingual Norm." *CCC* 63.2 (2011): 269-300. Print.

Horner, Bruce, and John Trimbur. "English Only and U.S. College Composition." *CCC* 53.4 (2002): 594-630. Print.

Hu, Guangwei, and Sandra Tsui Eu Lam. "Issues of Cultural Appropriateness and Pedagogical Efficacy: Exploring Peer Review in Second Language Writing Class." *Instructional Science* 38.4 (2010): 371-94. Print.

Ihm, Hee-Jeong. "Role of Teacher Feedback in Peer Review Activities in English Composition Classes." *Foreign Languages Education* 21.3 (2014): 1-26. Print.

Jordan, Jay, ed. *Redesigning Composition for Multilingual Realities.* Carbondale: NCTE, 2012. Print.

Kachru, Braj. *The Alchemy of English: The Spread, Functions, and Models of Non-native Englishes.* Champaign: U of Illinois P, 1990. Print.

Kinloch, Valerie, and Tim San Pedro. "The Space between Listening and Storying: Foundations for Projects in Humanization." *Humanizing Research: Decolonizing Qualitative Inquiry with Youth and Communities.* Ed. Django Paris and Maisha T. Winn. Los Angeles: Sage, 2014. 21-42. Print.

Lam, Wan Shun Eva. "Second Language Literacy and the Design of the Self: A Case Study of a Teenager Writing on the Internet." *TESOL Quarterly* 34 (2000): 457-82. Print.

Lowe, Charles, and Terra Williams. "Moving to the Public: Weblogs in the Writing Classroom." *Into the Blogosphere: Rhetoric, Community, and Culture of Weblogs.* Ed. Laura Gurak, Smiljana Antonijevic, Laurie Johnson, Clancy Ratliff, and Jessica Reyman. University of Minnesota, 2004. Web. 28 June 2015. <http://blog.lib.umn.edu/blogosphere/>.

Matsuda, Paul Kei. "The Myth of Linguistic Homogeneity in U.S. College Composition." *College English* 68.6 (2006): 637-51. Print.

---. "Teaching Composition in the Multilingual World: Second Language Writing in Composition Studies." *Exploring Composition Studies: Sites, Issues, Perspectives.* Ed. Paul Kei Matsuda and Kelly Ritter. Logan: Utah State UP, 2012. 36-51. Print.

McCorkle, Ben, Cynthia Selfe, Kaitlin Clinnin, and Kay Halasek. "Habitus, Disposition and Disruption in MOOCs: Developing Responsive Pedagogy at Scale." 2015. TS. Ohio State University, Columbus, OH. Print.

McGettigan, Andrew. "Will 'Moocs' Be the Scourge or Saviour or [sic] Higher Education?" *The Guardian.* 12 May 2013. Web. 27 June 2015. <http://www.theguardian.com/commentisfree/2013/may/12/moocs-scourge-saviour-higher-education>.

Michaels, Jen. "Special Guest Paul Kei Matsuda on Second-Language Writing (Rhetorical Composing MOOC)." *YouTube.* YouTube, 20 May 2013. Web. 25 September 2015. <https://www.youtube.com/watch?v=Oh1oNnPr338>.

Min, Hui-Tzu. "The Effects of Trained Peer Review on EFL Students' Revision Types and Writing Quality." *Journal of Second Language Writing* 15 (2006): 118-41. Print.

---. "Training Students to Become Successful Peer Reviewers." *System* 33.2 (2005): 293-308. Print.

Osberg, Deborah, and Gert Biesta. "The Emergent Curriculum: Navigating a Complex Course Between Unguided Learning and Planned Enculturation." *Journal of Curriculum Studies* 40.3 (2008): 313-28. Print.

Ruecker, Todd. "Analyzing and Addressing the Effects of Native Speakerism on Linguistically Diverse Peer Review." Corbett, LaFrance, and Decker 91-105. Print.

Rysdam, Sheri, and Lisa Johnson-Shull. "From Cruel to Collegial: Developing a Professional Ethic in Peer Response to Student Writing." Corbett, LaFrance, and Decker 77-89. Print.

Springs, Gene R. "Sustaining Hype? Massive Open Online Courses (MOOCs) and Open Access Course Materials." N.p., n.d. Web. 30 April 2015. <http://kb.osu.edu/dspace/bitstream/handle/1811/68025/SpringsGeneR_ACRL2015_paper.pdf?sequence=1>.

Vardi, Moshe Y. "Will MOOCs Destroy Academia?" *Communications of the ACM* 55.11 (2012): 5. Print.

Waldrop, M. Mitchell. "Massive Open Online Courses, aka MOOCs, Transform Higher Education and Science." *Scientific American,* 13 March 2013. Web. 27 June

2015. <http://www.scientificamerican.com/article/massive-open-online-courses-transform-higher-education-and-science/>.

Warschauer, Mark, and Meei-Ling Liaw. "Emerging Technologies for Autonomous Language Learning." *Studies in Self-Access Learning Journal* 2.3 (2011): 107-18. Print.

Yuan, Li, and Stephen Powell. "MOOCs and Open Education: Implications for Higher Education." Cetis Llp Publications. N.p., March 2013. Web. 11 February 2015. <http://publications.cetis.ac.uk/2013/667>.

Zhu, Wei. "Interaction and Feedback in Mixed Peer Response Groups." *Journal of Second Language Writing* 10 (2001): 251-76. Print.

"This is a Field that's Open, not Closed": Multilingual and International Writing Faculty Respond to Composition Theory

Lisa R. Arnold

> This article reports on the results of a qualitative, interview-based study in which multilingual writing faculty based at the American University of Beirut, in Beirut, Lebanon, read and responded to "core" texts of composition scholarship primarily published in North America, for a North American audience. This study is premised on the assumption that composition researchers located in North America can learn a great deal about the culturally and linguistically specific assumptions that form the base of our discipline from listening to the responses of teachers of writing in other geographical, cultural, and linguistic contexts. Participants' responses highlight, in particular, the contemporary challenges faced by, and the values attached to, the teaching and learning of writing in multilingual, international contexts of higher education.

In the conclusion to their 1995 article, "Importing Composition: Teaching and Researching Academic Writing beyond North America," Mary Muchiri et al. warn against the uncritical importation of composition studies research into multilingual and non-U.S.-based contexts, closing with three questions for North American writing researchers. They ask,

> Imagine you could pack something of the world of composition, just enough to fit in a small box that would fit under an airline seat. It is not for foreign aid, or for trade, both of which can be exploitive; let us think of it as a barter. What would you pack in this box; what is essential in the composition enterprise? That's the fun part. Now here comes the hard part: Where would you send it? And even harder: What would you expect to get in return? (196)

Christiane Donahue followed up on these questions in her 2009 article, "'Internationalization' and Composition Studies: Reorienting the Discourse," urging compositionists to engage in research that would account for the diverse pedagogical traditions, methods of research, and values attached to literacy in non-U.S. contexts.

This article responds to the concerns and questions articulated by Donahue, Muchiri et al., and others by reporting on the results of a qualitative study in which multilingual writing faculty based at the American University of Beirut (AUB) read and responded to "core" texts of composition scholarship primarily published in North America and for a North American audience.[1] The writing faculty participating in the study also voluntarily attended a ten-session seminar in which they read and discussed the selected texts. The seminar was offered as a professional development opportunity for writing faculty, and I acted as a participant-observer throughout, following up with study participants using questionnaires and interviews during and at the conclusion of the seminar.[2] This study is premised on the assumption that composition researchers located in North America can learn a great deal about the culturally and linguistically specific assumptions that form the base of our discipline by listening to the responses of teachers of writing in other geographical, cultural, and linguistic contexts.

Participants' responses highlight the contemporary challenges faced by, and the values attached to, the teaching and learning of writing in multilingual, international contexts of higher education. These challenges—which include the high stakes of English as a language for international students and teachers, and the imagined and real power differentials at work for nonnative speakers of English who are teaching and learning (in) English—are rarely represented in composition studies scholarship. What's more, much composition scholarship tends to speak to an audience that is assumed to be monolingual and assumed to teach primarily monolingual, native speakers of English. International and multilingual students are generally represented—when they are represented at all—in composition scholarship as a population with needs that are "different" from the norm, or as a population of concern to compositionists because they are becoming a larger part of the student demographic in North American universities. In composition scholarship, teachers of writing are almost always represented as citizens of the U.S. or Canada living and working in North America.

Increasingly, rhetoric and composition scholars have urged the discipline to make turns toward international, transnational, and multilingual (sometimes framed as translingual) contexts of writing practices and pedagogy (see, for example, Arnold, Bazerman et al.; Canagarajah; Donahue; Hesford; Horner, NeCamp, and Donahue; Matsuda; Muchiri et al.; Thaiss et al.; Zawacki and Habib, among others). As we attempt to make these turns and explore related questions, we must do so in ways that are not exploitative and that do not take for granted the assumptions that we hold as educators largely trained and located in North American contexts.

Rhetoric and Composition at the American University of Beirut

Rhetoric and composition's limited cultural and linguistic purview is the result of many factors, including the fact that no institution of higher education outside of North America offers a graduate degree in rhetoric and composition, and few scholars with a doctorate in the field work in other geographical locations, even though many international institutions are involved in the teaching of writing in English (and in other languages). The context of AUB is unique, however, in this regard: the Department of English has four dedicated lines for full-time, professorial-rank faculty with doctorates in rhetoric and composition. The department also plans to offer an M.A. in rhetoric and composition in the near future. As an American-style university that is a leader in the Middle East–North Africa (MENA) region, AUB can thus be seen as a potentially rich site for research that can respond to the calls of rhetoric and composition scholars who want to make writing research outside of North America more visible within the discipline.

Like most writing programs in the U.S., AUB's writing program occupies an important, but often mischaracterized, position within the university, in that it is often seen as responsible for the writing abilities of all undergraduate students and ensuring that these students are prepared to meet the high standards for academic writing across disciplines. This writing program faces the additional challenge of addressing and negotiating the wide diversity of students' educational and linguistic backgrounds.

What's more, faculty across disciplines at AUB—the majority of whom are Lebanese—articulate a variety of standards for what constitutes "good" writing. While vague complaints about students' grammatical and syntactical problems may seem all too familiar to a North American audience, these refrains carry a different weight in the Lebanese context. For many of the multilingual faculty who studied elsewhere and returned to their home country to teach, AUB represents the best education that Lebanon—and perhaps the MENA region—has to offer. If AUB students graduate without a solid proficiency in English, then—for these faculty—the university's reputation will suffer.

At AUB, nearly all students are multilingual; most have grown up with vernacular Arabic as the language most commonly spoken at home and in the community, in combination with formal training in Modern Standard Arabic, English, and/or French at school. Some students also have proficiency in other languages, such as Armenian or German. Students may have varying levels of spoken and written fluency in one or more of these languages, and their fluency may change over time. Of course, as Donahue and others have pointed out, contexts of writing cannot be understood merely in terms of their linguistic landscapes—when considering the Lebanese context of writing practices and pedagogies, researchers must also take into consideration the complex colonial and postcolonial histories of the nation and the region that surrounds it, as well as its rich—and contentious—religious, social, and political diversity.

There are more than forty full- and part-time faculty, most at the instructor or lecturer rank, who teach in the writing program at AUB. These faculty, most of whom were educated in Lebanon and some abroad, hold a range of educational backgrounds, most commonly in English literature or linguistics, English education, teaching English as a foreign or second language (TEFL or TESL), and creative writing. Although most of the writing faculty at AUB had little to no coursework in rhetoric and composition theory prior to the seminar, their many years of practical experience teaching writing at AUB and elsewhere, as well as their ongoing engagement in professional development, positions them as experts in their own right.

The Seminar and Study

In recent years, AUB has made an explicit commitment to improving the writing abilities of its students and has recently made several strategic decisions in line with this commitment. From 2012-14, I served as the first director of the university writing program. In this role, I explored a number of avenues through which I could offer the faculty teaching within the program opportunities for professional development. In particular, I pursued activities that would improve faculty members' knowledge of the field of rhetoric and composition; foster the development of a "community of practice" within the department; and ultimately serve students, who would benefit from improved teaching and learning environments. One of these opportunities, a ten-session professional development seminar on composition theory, was offered during the 2013-14 academic year.

The purpose of the seminar was to enable writing faculty to benefit from the university's commitment to writing by providing them with an incentive to learn more about current theories of writing instruction, to encourage self-reflection about teaching practices, and to apply scholarship to the writing program context when appropriate. Seminar session topics and readings, which were chosen by the facilitators, included a general introduction to rhetoric and composition, the place of literature in the composition classroom, teaching writing as a process, writing as a social act, English as a global language, the effects of globalization on the teaching of writing, and translingual and transnational concerns in the teaching of writing. Two sessions, one at the end of each semester, were also devoted to the teaching of writing locally in Lebanon and at AUB, respectively.

In total, seventeen faculty members—some new to the department and to teaching, and some having more than thirty years of experience—participated in the seminar. Five faculty members who had previously audited a graduate course that I offered on the same topic acted as facilitators for the two-hour sessions (each facilitator planned and led two sessions), and I sat in on every session, acting as participant-observer. Throughout the seminar, in addition to in-class discussions about assigned readings, participants were offered the opportunity to reflect in writing on their pedagogical practice, responding to guiding questions online about the relevance of the readings to the context of writing instruction at AUB.

Fifteen seminar attendees also voluntarily sat for hour-long, IRB-approved interviews with me during the course of the seminar.[3] During these interviews, we discussed the seminar sessions and topics that seemed most relevant to faculty members' work as writing teachers, the difference between North American- and MENA-based contexts of writing pedagogy, and interviewees' thoughts about the effectiveness of the seminar as a professional development opportunity. My discussion of the interview data throughout this essay is informed in part by my own observations and notes taken during the seminar sessions, as well as the results of two anonymous questionnaires that were distributed via LimeSurvey to all seminar participants at the conclusion of the fall and spring semesters.

Making Sense of Rhetoric and Composition in Lebanon

Prior to attending the seminar, writing faculty at AUB had varying levels of familiarity with rhetoric and composition scholarship. Besides the graduate-level course in composition theory that I taught in Spring 2013, which had been attended by five full-time and two part-time writing faculty (the full-time faculty were invited and agreed to become seminar facilitators), a similar course had been taught two times before, albeit with minimal participation by instructors. A number of other activities within the community of instructors drew on scholarship and included readings in rhetoric and composition or second-language writing; events, however, focused primarily on pedagogy. Faculty development workshops and lectures by invited scholars addressed topics defined by instructors, such as responding to writers, using grading contracts, and understanding academic integrity in the writing classroom. For a time, instructors also facilitated their own informal reading group to discuss academic readings. A few seminar participants and facilitators had previously engaged in independent or collaborative research projects that required familiarity with, and exploration in, the discipline—and at least one participant who had been educated in the U.S. had taken a course in writing pedagogy for completion of her master's degree in creative writing.

During the interviews, I asked seminar participants and facilitators to identify and reflect on the themes or issues that we had discussed during the seminar that seemed "most relevant" to their everyday teaching practices, or to the AUB or Lebanese context more generally. In response, interviewees outlined differences that they perceived between rhetoric and composition and other disciplines that they were more familiar with, such as linguistics or literature. They also discussed the negative or positive value of becoming familiar with the history of the discipline, as well as theories of teaching practice. The interviewees' general responses to composition scholarship demonstrate that many of the grounding theories of the discipline resonate with writing faculty outside of North American borders. In particular, and perhaps because the interviewees already had so much practical experience as teachers, AUB writing faculty identified themselves as professionals through discussion of composition theory.

When characterizing rhetoric and composition in relation to other related disciplines, Anna, who holds a master's degree in comparative literature and a bachelor's degree in English language and literature, described the discipline as "a bridge between . . . the theory on language acquisition and . . . literature which would be the production or manifestation of ideas. . . . I have always felt like linguistics is very concrete, [while] literature is very abstract . . . and this bridges the two." Layla, who completed her bachelor's and master's degrees in applied linguistics and who holds a TEFL diploma, assessed the discipline as "more context-based" than linguistics, a comment that was substantiated by Rania, a facilitator with an educational background in English language (linguistics), who also said that rhetoric and composition "looks at the complexity of what the students bring . . . to the classroom—their culture, their home language, their school experiences."

Interviewees also described the field as promoting a kind of "flexibility" or "tolerance" toward students. When asked how she would summarize the rhetoric and composition perspective to someone who didn't know the field, Jenna, a facilitator with undergraduate and graduate degrees in English language (linguistics) and TEFL, said "it's in the approach towards teaching writing . . . it's in the approach towards looking at how the student evolves as a writer. Maybe [in] EFL you look at students and we see them as EFL students, but in rhetoric and composition . . . what you see is a developing writer." For Samar, too, the discipline provided a different way of thinking about students, saying: "I think that composition allows the whole world to open up. . . . [The field] allows for this broader thinking of what we are doing . . . especially with people who are sometimes second-language learners." Rasha, whose background in translation studies and literature gave her a different disciplinary perspective from those with experience in linguistics and TEFL, described her direct and indirect exposure to rhetoric and composition over time as a process of becoming more "tolerant and more understanding of students' writing."

Several interviewees said that becoming familiar with the discipline's scholarship "affirmed" their own views about writing pedagogy. Karma, for example, said that participation in the seminar "made me feel more at ease. As in, 'OK, I am not doing something completely wrong or outrageous or out of line.' It was reassuring." For Jenna, too, the seminar

> reaffirmed the idea that this is a field that's open, not closed. . . . That's the feeling that makes me feel comfortable. . . . You have to be comfortable yourself in what you are doing, that will help you give your best to your students. So [the seminar] was reaffirming.

While most of the interviewees articulated an appreciation of the discipline generally—and saw their work as a part of it—views about the specific theories forwarded in the scholarship varied. Although it was not the only debate that stood out to seminar participants and facilitators, discussion of the "translingual approach" toward writing instruction proved significant for all interviewees; the significance of this discussion was clearly tied to the specific positionalities of the teachers themselves as faculty living and working in Lebanon.

Debating Translingualism: What's at Stake

Throughout the duration of the seminar, AUB's and Lebanon's unique multilingual and multicultural context became an ongoing topic of discussion for seminar participants and facilitators. While most of the fall semester sessions were focused on topics that compositionists would consider of central importance as background to the field—including teaching writing as a process, questions about the place of literature in the writing classroom, and understanding writing as a social act—the final session of the fall semester was focused on "Teaching Writing in Lebanon." The facilitator for this session, Rania, wanted participants to transition from introductory, or "canonical," questions in composition theory to a consideration of how these questions might (or might not) apply to the local or regional context. This session also served as a bridge to the spring semester, in which topics were focused more specifically on issues of language and the teaching of writing, including English as a global language, the effects of globalization on writing pedagogy, and a session devoted to translingual-transnational concerns in rhetoric and composition.

During that final fall semester session devoted to the local context, the facilitator included among the "required" readings Bruce Horner, Min-Zhan Lu, Jacqueline Jones Royster, and John Trimbur's frequently cited "Language Difference in Writing: Toward a Translingual Approach." In this article, the authors contend that U.S.-based approaches to writing pedagogy have traditionally treated language difference as an obstacle to be overcome, rather than a resource that can be used to improve communicative competence. They argue that this "traditional" approach is problematic in that it aims to eradicate "difference" in English-language communication practices, which thus privileges monolingualism over multilingualism. Horner et al. urge compositionists to adopt a "translingual approach" toward writing pedagogy, one that "sees difference in language not as a barrier to be overcome or as a problem to manage, but as a resource for producing meaning in writing, speaking, reading, and listening" ("Language Difference" 303). They argue that this approach both takes advantage of and appreciates students' different strengths in English as well as in other languages, and it also reflects the heterogeneity of communicative practices worldwide. Scholars have both critiqued and forwarded Horner et al.'s theory since its original publication.

Of all the readings, seminar attendees spent the most time on and paid most attention to Horner et al.'s article.[4] During the discussion, attendees expressed an interest in the theory but worried about its application—one attendee asked, "Is [this approach] a free-for-all?" and another argued, "I don't think this is how language works." At the same time, attendees generally agreed that the issues raised within the article were important for the Lebanese context; one attendee remarked that language use is "always a relevant question in this part of the world. . . . In the past, Arabic has always been taboo in the English classroom . . . now [this article asks], how can it be an asset?"

These initial responses from the final fall semester session were corroborated by and developed within the individual interviews. When asked what ideas from composition theory introduced during the seminar were the "most pertinent" for the local (AUB, Lebanese, or MENA region) context, nearly all interviewees mentioned the translingual approach toward writing pedagogy. While responses to the viability of the translingual approach, at least as outlined by Horner et al., differed, all seminar participants and facilitators concurred that the complicated linguistic and educational context of Lebanon necessitated a thoughtful approach to issues of language difference and "error" in students' writing development. This consensus among seminar attendees suggests that a more flexible approach toward language difference, like the translingual approach, may be useful in the Lebanese context. What is more, this agreement seems particularly important in light of the disciplinary perspectives and pedagogical experiences held by the seminar attendees, many of whom had learned to teach writing, formally or informally, from an EFL or ESL perspective, a perspective that would presumably align with the approach toward writing pedagogy critiqued by Horner et al.

The interview responses demonstrate that scholars in composition studies would do well to consider the voices of writing faculty outside of North

America to better understand what is at stake in taking a translingual approach in a context where multilingualism is the norm for both teachers and students. The framing of Horner et al.'s article seems to target an audience comprised of primarily monolingual teachers of writing whose students are also mostly monolingual—the coauthors imagine an audience of skeptics who will ask questions such as, "How do monolingual teachers of writing teach a translingual approach? Wouldn't teachers of this approach have to be multilinguals themselves?" (310) and "My students are all monolinguals. Why would they need to learn a translingual approach to writing?" (311). For AUB writing faculty considering a translingual approach, however, the questions must evolve; faculty teaching in the Lebanese context might reframe the questions as follows: "As a multilingual teacher who has succeeded professionally because of my own mastery of standard English and whose success is measured in part on students' improved fluency in English, how can I say I am serving my students if I allow for language difference in writing or speaking?" and "My students are all multilingual but are limited in their English proficiency, particularly at the university level. Why would my students need to employ a translingual approach if their future success depends on their mastery of standard English only?"

In listening to multilingual, internationally based writing faculty, composition scholars—particularly those who live and work in North America and who are themselves monolingual—can consider from a new perspective the limits and opportunities afforded by a translingual approach to writing pedagogy, as well as what may be at stake for multilingual students as teachers take translingual approaches toward writing pedagogy. In the interviews, participants and facilitators articulated reasons for their resistance to, and also support of, the ideas forwarded by Horner et al. They also identified what they perceived to be advantages and disadvantages of being multilingual like their students, and they stressed that in the Lebanese context of AUB, taking a translingual approach in the writing classroom was less of a choice than an everyday reality. These writing faculty members' responses help provide grounded understandings for what it means to take a translingual approach in the writing classroom.

International Writing Faculty "Speak Back"

In the multilingual contexts described by Muchiri et al.—Kenya, Tanzania, and Zaire—as much as in Lebanon, where English-language universities such as AUB are highly selective and students already have considerable fluency in English, English carries a different value for its users. Indeed, in the Africa described by Muchiri et al., as in Lebanon, "everything here is not just in language (the code of thought) but is in *a* language (a particular code, among others)" (190). As such, the teaching of (English) writing in these contexts inevitably carries a different meaning for teachers and students alike. While AUB faculty may have no choice but to work within and across language difference on a daily basis, their decisions about how to do so, and for what reason, were deliberate and well considered, as the interviews attest.

During the interviews, writing faculty at AUB described their own, and their students' implied, resistance to translingualism in the writing classroom. After the spring semester had concluded, Donia, for example, said that she was

> still not very convinced [by translingualism]. . . . I understand that it is a theory . . . we cannot ignore it—there is this influence, there is this integration of mother language or other languages—but . . . as [an] instructor[], I cannot find myself accepting students using Arabic. . . . I can understand it's good for me to know it, but if I want to accept and be tolerant to the interference of the mother language, I think I am not doing my job; I still find that this should not be acceptable. I mean, you can use [your knowledge of Arabic] as a way to improve the language of the student, but not [to] give them this leeway to go on and just use it as an excuse.

Like Donia, Rania also questioned, at first, whether or not translingualism would undermine her efforts to serve students according to the standards of her profession. Rania cited perceptions of some Lebanese students who pursued higher education in the UK that British universities held higher standards for students from the UK in comparison to students from developing nations who, it was assumed, would return to their home countries after graduation. With these perceived attitudes in mind, Rania worried that allowing for multiple languages or varieties of English in the writing classroom—particularly in the Lebanese context, where students may be culturally, politically, and linguistically disadvantaged if they wish to pursue professional or educational opportunities abroad—could prove to be a new form of colonialism. She "[wondered] whether . . . this translingual approach" was a way to keep the already disadvantaged in their "place" by saying, in effect, "don't give them correct English—it's enough if you are able to understand at this level." Later, as Rania prepared to facilitate two of the seminar sessions, she began to rethink her initial resistance to translingualism and to appreciate the "fine distinctions it makes between . . . being aware that people are different and using this difference to the advantage of the learner."

Importantly, the semester before the seminar began, four writing faculty had decided to collaboratively experiment with Arabic-English translation activities in their composition classrooms; they theorized that the activities would improve students' grasp of language choice and the rhetorical possibilities that emerged from making careful decisions about language. Three of the four faculty members also attended the seminar, and during the interviews, each of the faculty members reflected on the translation exercise from the semester before in relation to translingualism. For Jahnoo and Rasha, the classroom experiment helped ground their understanding of the kind of responses that students might have to translingual work in the writing classroom. Jahnoo explained that for the students "who really liked the Arabic," the translation activities were productive. For "those who did not want the Arabic at all, they rebelled. They just hated it . . . so we had to give them a different prompt for writing because they just did not want [to do it]. They found English much easier than the Arabic." Rasha found the students' responses to the activities—even while some students were resistant—to be "more involved" than the reflections she was used to reading. In their responses, students were not saying "'Okay, Arabic helped or Arabic did not help' . . . or whether they thought it was silly." Instead, Rasha explained, the students "had a passionate, a more engaged kind of answer to why it was silly or why it was very helpful and they sort of analyzed their answers more thoroughly rather than give flat superficial answers."[5]

As the above excerpts illustrate, even in the midst of resistant attitudes on the part of teachers and students, translingualism is a reality in the Lebanese context of education. Indeed, many interviewees characterized occurrences of translingualism in their classrooms as common. Many of the writing faculty had been trained with the understanding that the use of languages other than English should be prohibited in the classroom; this became a point of discussion during the seminar itself, as some attendees asked whether or not it was okay to "allow" multiple languages in the classroom, while others noted that "the moment you turn your head [students are] going to use Arabic." Salma said,

> that wasn't even a question for me—whether they code-switch during group work or not—and I was shocked to hear [during the seminar discussion] that some people mind it. . . . To really be honest, none of them use English during group work—I can hear them, and I wouldn't go and tell them, "This is an English class, go do the group work in English."

Faculty members provided a number of examples of translingual activity in the AUB writing classroom. In one example, a student was conducting research on rental law in Lebanon, as well as local debates surrounding the law. Nearly all the articles he identified that were related to the law were written in Arabic, and some of the terminology was untranslatable, so the instructor, Jahnoo, advised the student to "try to translate them but those that are really technical, keep them in Arabic and type them in Arabic." The student also "went and followed all the demonstrations that took place in town; he interviewed people; he interviewed a lawyer and he interviewed a professor at USJ [Université Saint-Joseph de Beyrouth, a French-language university in Beirut]." Jahnoo explained that the student "was concerned about . . . grammatical structures, more than about the terminology. . . . And he came hundreds of times to the office to ask me questions about sentence structure . . . so sentence structure and style remain a concern for our students when they are negotiating meaning."

Both Jahnoo's and Rania's portrayal of translingualism as an everyday experience in their classrooms highlights the problematic assumptions behind a monolingual approach to writing pedagogy. For Rania, translingualism is necessary "to be able to deal with everyday life." She argued that "one needs to develop this ability, this versatility . . . this sensitivity to . . . what different contexts, what different audiences, what different settings require. . . . Why do we expect our students to be monolingual when in reality nobody is monolingual?" Jahnoo valued her role as a "facilitator" for her students as they developed their communicative competencies, which means using all their language resources in the process. She said:

> For me, I think that the most important thing is to enable students to have a flow in thinking and a flow in expression . . . so when ideas flow, they might flow in Arabic, they might flow in English, they might flow in French because many of our students are French educated. So, how do you make these ideas mix and match or mesh together so you can communicate more easily?

In dealing with the "everyday" occurrences of students' translingual practices, interviewees described a kind of identification with students—for better or for worse—based on their shared multilingualism. For some interviewees, their experiences of struggling with language shaped their beliefs about teaching. Malik, for example, stressed during his interview a conviction that exposing students to formal English and maintaining high expectations for English in the classroom was essential to his teaching practice. He argued that "we need exposure to the language itself in order to be able to survive as non-native speakers—survive, as in . . . to understand that there are nuances in the language—words that mean something else from the native language we come from." According to Malik, if he did not provide this kind of exposure to his own students—for their survival—he felt that he would be shirking his responsibilities as a teacher.

Like Malik, Donia maintained her doubts about the translingual approach throughout the seminar; but in contrast to Malik, she understood the potential value of working with multiple languages in the classroom. She remarked, "I have always understood my students and how they think, and I would tell them, this is what you mean, this is what you want to say in Arabic, but this is how you say it in English." While before, she "was not very comfortable with this feeling, now," after discussing scholarship on global Englishes and translingualism, she "say[s] no, it's acceptable, it is something that research [supports]. . . . Yes, I have more the courage to use [Arabic] and to admit using it" in the classroom.

Some faculty who are less fluent in Arabic because of their educational experiences abroad seemed to relate more readily with their students' use of multiple languages in the classroom. For example, Karma, who is Lebanese but whose education abroad was in English, understood her students' difficulties with English based on her own experiences with Arabic, saying "I think about my own Arabic: I consistently make the same mistakes and . . . I get the masculine and feminine completely muddled up, so I think my experience with . . . struggling with other languages . . . puts a bit of a different perspective on things." In recognizing her students' experiences as similar to her own, Karma defined her teaching approach as more open to language difference in the classroom.

Similarly, Salma and Samar, who are Lebanese but were educated abroad, highlighted in their interviews how they used their own backgrounds to help their students feel more comfortable and confident in the writing classroom. Salma, for example, explained,

> I understand where [French-educated Lebanese students] come from. I understand that they will not be able to find the words as easily as others do. . . . They would say that they were from a French background and they would say it, worried. . . . The past couple of years, I would start telling them at the beginning . . . I came from a French background and they would be shocked, [saying,] "Miss, you have an accent, where did you get it from?" and I start laughing and I say, "Here, on campus."

Samar, who was educated in English, described how she would tell her students about her own experience of learning Arabic from family visits to Lebanon when she was young. She said, "I have a perspective of learning Arabic and being embarrassed by my Arabic, and . . . a lot of students will say, 'I don't like to speak in class because I don't speak very well,' and I am like, 'How are you going to learn if you don't try?'" For Samar, who described her approach as "empathetic," it was important for her students to learn about her personal experience with Arabic because it allowed them to feel more comfortable making mistakes in class, which Samar believes is an important part of students' development in the writing classroom.

At the same time, some interviewees, while admitting that they were often generous in their openness to other languages in the classroom, worried that their first-hand identification with their students could problematically interfere with their success as teachers. Jenna, for example, said, "I am not against [the translingual approach] . . . [but] I still need to understand why we are going there; how are we going to use this to help the students move forward?" To explain her hesitation, Jenna recounted a story in which a student used a French word in an essay because he assumed Jenna would understand because of her knowledge of French. But because she was reading in English, Jenna had to explain, she did not understand his meaning. The student, according to Jenna,

> was so upset, and I see why he was upset because he thought he was using the right words. . . . He couldn't see why I could not understand. . . . So this is what I don't like about this, when they become too confident. . . . They are in for a major disappointment when people don't understand what they are saying. That's my major concern. . . . I don't mind them being confident, but I mind them being too confident. . . . They get this false perception of abilities and skills which are not there.

Whatever stance they took in relation to language difference in the writing classroom, interviewees ultimately articulated definitions for what it means to work and teach from a translingual perspective, across languages, on a daily basis. The theory that Horner et al. anticipated would be met with resistance by their presumably monolingual audience was a reality in the Lebanese context of writing instruction. Jenna exclaimed that the audience for the Horner et al. article was clearly "a group of monolingual teachers! They didn't have us in mind. So, *nehna* [we are] not just more than one reader—we have a high level of tolerance because of our ability to understand languages." Indeed, even for Donia, her multilingual capabilities allowed her to function more thoughtfully as a writing teacher; she said, "When we correct our students' papers, I think we are more able to understand what they need, though they may not be able to express it well." She theorized that "maybe globalization has played a role now; everybody is open to everybody," and she remarked that "it's interesting to know that there are people who think that this can be workable, and it's interesting to know that monolingual people have one look at language [and the] teaching of language, and others have a different [view]."

During the interviews, I asked participants and facilitators whether or not they thought being monolingual would make it difficult for a writing teacher to be open to language difference in the classroom. While most agreed that being multilingual "gives [teachers] one more resource" (Rania), none thought that having more than one language was necessary. For most interviewees, the prime requirement for writing teachers was the attitude they took. Rania put it this way: "[The translingual approach is] not really the ability to speak different languages. It's the frame of mind that you develop. The openness, the critical thinking, the not-jumping-to conclusions. . . . It tells me that I need to . . . step back a little bit and learn more about the background of the students who come into my classroom."

Violetta suggested that the best approach for monolingual teachers would be to "talk to their students, in conferences, individually." These conversations would benefit the monolingual teacher because "you see and you start to be aware"—which, for Violetta, is an especially important step when it comes to teaching writing, "because writing is not easy in itself, and they have so many things to do. . . . Even if the speakers are native speakers . . . this is challenging for the native speakers themselves. . . . So this doubles if you are teaching our students, the kind of students we have in our context, it's a double effort." Rasha, in turn, stressed the importance of being a critical reader; she argued that "the person who can do a better job [in taking a translingual approach] is the person who reads more, be that in a monolingual way or a multilingual way. I think it depends on what kind of reader you are. Some people only know Arabic or English [but] they have so many resources because they are readers."

Ultimately, faculty members' ability to understand the challenges faced by their multilingual students—based on their own experiences learning and using multiple languages —influenced their teaching practices as well as their interpretation of translingual approaches. In the interviews, participants and facilitators formulated practical definitions for what a translingual approach toward writing instruction might mean, based on their own experiences living, working, and teaching writing in a context where multilingualism is the norm. These definitions, I argue, provide teacher-scholars a different perspective about what's at stake in the teaching of (English) writing outside of North America.

Conclusions

In fall 2011, after finishing my PhD in rhetoric and composition in the U.S., I moved to Beirut, Lebanon, having never lived abroad, having no knowledge of French or Arabic, and having no personal ties to the place or culture. Although I have since moved back to the U.S., the experience of living and working outside of North America —struggling to learn a new language and culture, and working with colleagues whose perspectives on teaching both challenged and enriched my own—was invaluable. What I learned, and what my AUB colleagues have articulated so well in their discussions of rhetoric and composition scholarship, is that there is a complexity to literacy practices and pedagogies that practitioners outside of North America understand deeply, and from which those of us trained in a presumably monolingual context can learn. While much rhetoric and composition theory, including translingual theory, appears to be just as relevant and contentious outside of North America as within it, it may be so for reasons other than our own and with different stakes attached.

For those of us trained and based in North America, we must recognize our increasingly limited perspectives; at the same time, we must also recognize that our voices carry weight in the global sphere. Many of our graduate students will take their first academic positions, as I did, at universities outside of our national and cultural borders—we must prepare them to work alongside, listen to, and learn from faculty who may not have institutional power but who are experts in their own right, as they often do the hardest (and least rewarded) work of the university. Some of us will be paid to provide consultation services—to "fly in" and "fly out"—as universities outside of North America establish and develop writing programs and writing centers. We must recognize that in accepting these arrangements, we are assuming positions of disciplinary expertise and power that may override local colleagues who have significant practical expertise and personal investment in the institution (and institutional structures) that our consultations may change. Finally, we must support and seek out the voices of those colleagues who are living and working outside of North America.[6]

Notes

1. I was an assistant professor of English at AUB from 2011 until 2015 and director of the university's writing program for two-and-a-half years during that time.

2. This study was approved by AUB's Institutional Review Board and funded by a Scholarship of Teaching and Learning grant from AUB's Center for Teaching and Learning. All references to study participants are pseudonyms chosen by the participants (unless they designated me to choose on their behalf), and all participants have read this essay and were invited to offer comments on it, which I have taken into consideration.

3. Eight participants sat for two interviews each, one after the conclusion of the fall semester, and one at the conclusion of the spring semester; two participants were able to sit for one interview only. The five facilitators sat for interviews only once, after the spring semester had ended. One interview (with a facilitator) was not recorded due to technical failure.

4. Other readings during this session included Robert Tremmel's "Seeking a Balanced Discipline: Writing Teacher Education in First-Year Composition and Eng-

lish Education" and Nahla Bacha's "Developing Learners' Academic Writing Skills in Higher Education," which focuses on the development of L2 writers at the Lebanese American University.

5. A publication describing the results of the translation study described here is forthcoming. Anyone interested in the publication may contact me directly, and I will put you in touch with the authors.

6. My deepest gratitude goes to AUB's Center for Teaching and Learning for the grant that supported this project; to the faculty at AUB who agreed to be a part of this study and who made my work so enjoyable; to Yasmine Abou Taha for her research assistance in the summer of 2015; to Mary Laughlin for her editorial assistance; and to Samantha NeCamp, Connie Kendall Theado, and Brian Ray for their support and feedback.

Works Cited

Arnold, Lisa R. "'The Worst Part of the Dead Past': Language Attitudes, Policies, and Pedagogies at Syrian Protestant College, 1866-1902." *CCC* 66.2 (2014): 276-300. Print.

Bacha, Nahla. "Developing Learners' Academic Writing Skills in Higher Education." *Language and Education* 16.3 (2002): 161-77. Print.

Bazerman, Charles, Chris Dean, Jessica Early, Karen Lunsford, Suzie Null, Paul Rogers, and Amanda Stansell, eds. *International Advances in Writing Research: Cultures, Places, Measures*. Anderson: Parlor P, 2012. Print.

Canagarajah, Suresh. "The Place of World Englishes in Composition: Pluralization Continued." *CCC* 57.4 (2006): 586-619. Print.

Donahue, Christiane. "'Internationalization' and Composition Studies: Reorienting the Discourse." *CCC* 61.2 (2009): 212-43. Print.

Hesford, Wendy. "Global Turns and Cautions in Rhetoric and Composition Studies." *PMLA* 121.3 (2006): 787-801. Print.

Horner, Bruce, et al. "Language Difference in Writing: Toward a Translingual Approach." *College English* 73.3 (2011): 303-21. Print.

Horner, Bruce, Samantha NeCamp, and Christiane Donahue. "Toward a Multilingual Composition Scholarship: From English Only to a Translingual Norm." *CCC* 63.2 (2011): 269-300. Print.

Matsuda, Paul Kei. "Composition Studies and ESL Writing: A Disciplinary Division of Labor." *CCC* 50.1 (1999): 699-721. Print.

Muchiri, Mary N., et al. "Importing Composition: Teaching and Researching Academic Writing beyond North America." *CCC* 46.2 (1995): 175-98. Print.

Thaiss, Chris, Gerd Bräuer, Paula Carlino, Lisa Ganobcsik-Williams, and Aparna Sinha, eds. *Writing Programs Worldwide: Profiles of Academic Writing in Many Places*. Anderson: Parlor P, 2012. Print.

Tremmel, Robert. "Seeking a Balanced Discipline: Writing Teacher Education in First-Year Composition and English Education." *English Education* 34.1 (2001): 6-30. Print.

Zawacki, Terry, and Anna Habib. "Internationalization, English L2 Writers, and the Writing Classroom: Implications for Teaching and Learning." *CCC* 65.4 (2014): 650-58. Print.

Negotiating Languages and Cultures: Enacting Translingualism through a Translation Assignment

Julia Kiernan, Joyce Meier, and Xiqiao Wang

This collaborative project explores the affordances of a translation assignment in the context of a learner-centered pedagogy that places composition students' movement among languages and cultures as both a site for inquiry and subject of analysis. The translation assignment asks students to translate scholarly articles or culture stories from their home languages into English, and then to compare their translations and reflect on these processes. In presenting a research study of students' responses to this assignment, our goal is to highlight the important moves that students make as they examine their own linguistic attributes when translating. Our goal is to analyze these student responses within a collaborative pedagogical framework that centers on students' home languages and cultures as well as on reflective practice. The curricular shift exemplified by the translation assignment reflects a purposeful placement of value on translingual competences and mirrors a national shift toward asset-based, culturally sustaining pedagogical practices.

Introduction

This study on translation and the composing process of English Language Learners (ELLs) is a convergence of responses to two exigencies—the first local and institutional, the second theoretical and disciplinary. The first response speaks to a growing number of diverse learners, particularly international multilinguals who enroll in first-year writing courses in U.S. institutions. The second response builds on the pedagogical innovations offered by scholar-teachers such as Suresh Canagarajah ("Negotiating" 2013). Towards these ends, this study considers how theoretical inquiry into the internationalization of composition has only begun to offer practical strategies to incorporate translingual and transnational perspectives into first-year writing courses. In order to respond to the current move to engage multilingual students within U.S. composition classrooms, we offer versions of an assignment sequence that analyzes the implications of such an approach in the context of previous theoretical publications and the institutional setting of this study.

A common complaint about the intersection of composition studies and multilingual education is that there are few initiatives that develop and implement multilingual frameworks within English-medium classrooms (Hornberger and Link). Bruce Horner, Samantha NeCamp, and Christine Donahue have called for writing teachers to consider how changes can be "made at the organizational level to rethink the ways in which English is represented in U.S. composition teaching, the design of writing programs and curricula, and the preparations of (future) teachers of postsecondary writing" ("Toward" 271). In response to such calls, we devised a qualitative study, positioning us to better understand how students respond to a translation assignment. Specifically, we examined the following research questions with the aim of developing specific pedagogies informed by translingual and transnational perspectives:

- How do assignments based in translation and the translating process develop and foster high-level analytical, metalinguistic skills in ELLs?
- How does the translation of texts invite students to reflect on and explain their own writing processes and language negotiation within their lives?
- In what ways can writing about translingual and transnational experiences position students as experts—as writers with agency and authority?
- What are the affordances of the translation assignment for teaching and learning?

By positioning translation as entry to translingual and transnational writing practices, we aim to fill a pedagogical gap as we rethink and reimagine the intersections between languages. The pedagogical approaches offered in this article differ from previous work in this area, whereby translanguaging pedagogy is framed as instructors alternating their teaching from one language to another: in other words, students and instructor hear or read a lesson in one language but do their work in another (Creese and Blackledge; García and Wei; Hornberger and Link). Our practice, in contrast, introduces translation as an explicit invitation for students to use home languages and cultures as resources for learning and to incorporate these resources purposefully into their writing as students examine and reflect upon their own experiences, practices, and ideas related to crossing and/or melding multiple languages and cultures (see also Matsuda and Silva). In addition, our project builds on insights from literacy researchers, who have examined students' out-of-school translation practices as leverageable skills mirrored in school-based literacy practices (Orellana and Reynolds; Orellana, Thorne, Chee, and Lam). Adding to research accounts of how bilingual students draw on their cultural and linguistic knowledge to derive meaning and use information from translating and reading texts (Jiménez, David, Fagan, Risko, Pacheco, Pray, and Ganzáles; Medina), this study positions translation as an asset, resource, and advantageous skill for ELLs' literacy development. This notion aligns with Claire Kramsch's view that "[l]anguage competence should be measured not as capacity to perform in one language in a specific domain, but rather as 'the ability to translate, transpose and critically reflect on social, cultural and historical meanings'" (103). We position translation assignments and exercises as "a critical resource for identifying global forces, their effects on individual and collective lives, and ways of responding to and even shaping these" (Lu and Horner 118). Ultimately, making space for overt language negotiation within English-medium classrooms—namely, writing centered in strategies of translation—allows for multilingual students to compose reflective writing that self-names their own ongoing processes of negotiation between languages and between cultures.

This approach to language negotiation reflects translingual shifts in the teaching of ELLs and speaks to the 2011 MLA Ad Hoc Committee on Foreign Languages report, "Foreign Languages and Higher Education," as well as to scholars who maintain "the welcoming of translanguaging in classrooms is not only necessary, but desirable educational practice" (Hornberger and Link 239). In composition studies specifically, translingual theory and research position writing—principally English-medium writing—in constant relation to other languages, where the primary aims of translingual inquiry are the recognition of the fluidity of language and movement away from the dominant ideologies of Standardized English (Canagarajah, "Toward a Rhetoric"; Horner, Lu, Trimbur, and Royster, "Language Difference"). Canagarajah further suggests that the act of translanguaging in writing is the ability to produce texts that demonstrate successful language negotiation across diverse discourse communities, which echoes Min-Zhan Lu's earlier Living-English theories that posit the most useful language is that which works to communicate, rather than that which abides by standardized conventions. As such, assignment redesign is central to this study, particularly the implementation of useable translingual strategies that encourage students to move between, across, and within languages in their writing.

The translation assignment discussed herein is grounded in research that views the ability to move between, across, and within languages as a cognitive benefit to students (Alsheikh; Canagarajah, "Multilingual Writers"; Canagarajah, "Toward a Writing"; Creese and Blackledge; Gentil; Hornberger and Link; Lu; Mokhtari and Reichard; Mokhtari and Sheorey). Such research contends that "as school populations become increasingly linguistically diverse, refusing to acknowledge the language resources of students . . . limits the possibilities for their educational achievement" (Hornberger and Link 240). We see the practice of translanguaging within the translation assignment as a pedagogical tool offering a "possibility for teachers and learners to access academic content through the communicative repertoires they bring to the classroom while simultaneously acquiring new ones" (Hornberger and Link 245). Students also have the opportunity to reflect and learn from their ongoing processes of language negotiation and, thus, illuminate and name for themselves the nature of this process and its relationship to other literacy-based moments in their lives.

Situating the Local

The move to incorporate and negotiate between translingual and transnational perspectives in the first-year writing classroom, as discussed in the opening paragraph, is a local and institutional response to population shifts. The curricular redesign occurred in a bridge writing course at a large public Midwestern university. Like many institutions of higher education across the U.S., this university has witnessed a rapid increase of international students. As a result, most if not all of the students in the bridge course Preparation for College Writing (PCW) are international, with the majority Chinese, and others from such countries as South Korea, Saudi Arabia, and Thailand, and still others who are first-generation U.S. citizens. In response to this shifting demographic, a number of PCW instructors experimented with new approaches that paid heed to the recent call for translingual, transcultural pedagogies (Horner et al., "Toward"). Amid much departmental discussion—instructor monthly meetings, culturally sustaining pedagogy workshops, and a PCW retreat—assignments and classroom activities were redesigned to explicitly frame the students' languages and cultures as assets and sites of inquiry. Implicitly, the new course initiatives highlighted the students' ongoing negotiations of languages, cultures, and genres (Canagarajah, "Negotiating" and "Toward a Rhetoric"). The translation project outlined in this chapter represents one such assignment.

Our interests, as three teacher-researchers, stem from some similarities among our experiences with the demographic shifts and changing pedagogical imperatives associated with our teaching of PCW. Informing and shaping such interests are our own linguistic, cultural, and institutional identities that are simultaneously similar and variant. Such positionalities provide us with unique insights into the translanguaging practices of our students. Like the students who enroll in PCW, we come from diverse linguistic and cultural backgrounds. One of us is a U.S. monolingual, and the other two are internationals (one monolingual and one multilingual). We will briefly explore these backgrounds because it is important to consider the multiple dimensions of and approaches to teaching via a translingual lens, particularly because many teachers have a limited set of strategies for supporting translingual learning. Nancy Hornberger and Holly Link explain that it is not necessary for teachers to master the many languages spoken by students in order for translingualism to function as a pedagogical benefit. In other words, monolingual teachers have the ability to create learning spaces that are open to the diverse social realities of our students, and consequently to broaden the context of U.S. composition "to [that of] a discipline directly confronting, investigating, and experimenting" with language difference (Horner et al., "Toward" 291).

Researcher Backgrounds

Julia is a monolingual teacher-researcher who is a citizen of a multilingual country. While she teaches in a U.S. postsecondary institution, Julia self-identifies as international. While her own linguistic background is monolingual English, she had some grade school and undergraduate education in French. Julia currently lives in one of the most linguistically diverse cities in Canada, which has served to drive her professional interests in translingualism, which she views as a living form of language used not only by international multilinguals but also domestic multilinguals and monolinguals.

As Assistant Director of the First-Year Writing Program, Joyce added full administrative support to the translation assignment and other experimentation with a translingual, transcultural pedagogy in the PCW classroom. Though primarily monolingual and from the U.S., she grew up in a bilingual household hearing and speaking both Polish and English. Last summer, partly because so many of the ELLs in PCW are Chinese, Joyce taught at the Harbin Institute of Technology in China for the express purpose of learning more about Chinese culture and language.

Xiqiao came to the U.S. from China in her early twenties in pursuit of graduate degrees. She attended a public university in her early years of immigration. Yet, Xiqiao came from a different generation of immigrants—a time prior to China's economic boom, when students could only afford to study in America when one's studies were funded by merit scholarships offered by a U.S. university. Nonetheless, she felt, and responded to, the pressure to add academic English to her linguistic repertoire to maximize her social and academic success in the U.S.

Methodology

The translation assignment can be divided into three stages: individual translation, comparative analysis, and individual narratives reflecting on the translating process. In stage one, students who share a home language work in groups of three to four and choose a single text that is written in their home language.[1] Excerpts of texts are then distributed to each member and translated into English by each group member in isolation from other members. In stage two, group members compare translations for similiarities and differences. Here, the student considers personal experiences and feelings towards the translation process, as well as the choices they made when translating and why. In stage three, students create a final narrative that incorporates the reflective discussions of stage two. Moving between languages, the groups articulate and explain their translation process and the choices inherent in this process.

The point of the assignment is not to assess the students' writing on the basis of grammatical correctness or adherence to a fixed standard of academic English, or to evaluate the "correctness" of the translation. Instead, we might ask: Does the student's explanation of her translation process provide sufficient and compelling evidence, including examples from her home language? Did the student fully explain her process, so that it is clear to readers? Finally, did she think through the larger implications of their translation process, especially in terms of each member's own learning? Again, the assignment's emphasis, like our research, is on the student's interpretation of her translation process.

In both enacting this assignment and evaluating its impact, we use action research. As a methodology, action research is defined as comparative research based within social action, leading to recommendations for change (Lewin; McLaren). Situated within a broader program-wide initiative on pedagogical innovation, our research focuses on critical reflection upon our own pedagogical practices, with particular emphasis placed upon how theory-informed strategies and assignments can engage multilingual students with intellectual work that treats their multilingual experiences as sites of inquiry and learning.

Data for this study was collected from a broader, two-year study, where we worked to develop a research project to analyze students' evolving understandings of language differences as indicative of transnational genres, discourses, and cultures. Out of a total number of seventy-two student essays from the spring 2014 semester, nine essays—three from each section—were selected and coded, which helped us develop a coding scheme that allowed for the systematic coding of a larger corpus. The focal narratives were inductively analyzed to generate primary categories such as word equivalency, losses and gains in translation, sentence structure, and so on. We then worked to create secondary analytical constructs (e.g., audience, semantic, syntactic). The final analytical categories allowed us to describe the "invisible" translation strategies students use and to recognize the complex, dialogic relationship between languages and cultures from the students' perspectives.

Here, we report on three findings from the data: how students negotiated audience awareness, viewed language as object, and developed cultural sensitivities. These findings represent a typical sampling of student work. Audience awareness allows us to capture the moves students make when they appeal to the expectations and needs of their reader. Language as object encompasses both semantic (the meaning of words, phrases and other language structures) and syntactic concerns (matters of organization and cohesion at the word, sentence, and paragraph level). Cultural sensitivities capture instances when the writer analyzes how cultural aspects of their home language affect their translation process. However, it is important to recognize that these analytical categories are not discrete or mutually exclusive.

Discussion

Audience Awareness

In our analysis, audience awareness was reflected throughout the other coding categories: semantic, syntactical, and cultural sensitivities. Each category speaks to the writers' awareness of their readers, as defined and labeled in their reflective narratives. Whether they saw their reader as U.S., or simply, in the words of one Chinese student, a "foreigner," these student translators acknowledged how much audience awareness had affected their translation process—a fact perhaps reinforced by the multiple home languages represented by the writers in these classes. In writing for their readers, the students were essentially communicating with one another. Because attention to audience was so pervasive and interconnected to the other categories, we have chosen to discuss audience as an overarching element.

As they described their translating processes, the ELL writers recognized the necessity of making specific home culture or language traits clearer to an English or U.S. foreign reader who otherwise might not understand. Yet the students also acknowledged occasional moments when translation seemed impossible: when there seemed to be no equivalent English word or phrase for the one that appeared in their home language. In the reflective essays, this led to moments of analysis when the writer included the original word in the home language to demonstrate the very challenges of moving between, across, or within languages.

As outlined in the methodology, the assignment required students to look back at each group member's translation processes to help them better understand their own translation choices. Often, the student's own translation choices stood out most clearly when placed against the choices of their peers. Inevitably, differences in the translations emerged, and these differences invited rich small-group discussion, which led to the linguistic and cultural analyses incorporated in the students' final reflective narratives. Written individually, these papers demonstrate and explain the translation choices the student writers had made, which is the point of the assignment.

In fact, as the ELLs described their translation processes, their sharp awareness of their readers informed each of the coding categories we describe below. The ELLs also recognized how greatly issues of language are intertwined with issues of culture. The writers regularly described personal language strategies and choices for the purpose of communicating their cultures to cultural and linguistic outsiders. Rather than seeing such overlap among our categories as a concern, we view it as indicative of the complexity of the translation process itself.

The translation assignment created an exigency, whereby the student writers felt the need to explain their linguistic and rhetorical choices to their readers. In so doing, they analyzed how their audience awareness, and the need to clarify words and concepts from their home languages for their readers, drove their translation processes. These moves map onto Canagarajah's notion of how articulate and purposeful translanguaging can enable recontextualization strategies, as writers focus on the rhetorical effect their translations have on their readers ("Negotiating" 50). The student reflections are informed by audience awareness and by an underlying philosophy that the very act of translation requires careful consideration of their readers' differently constructed knowledge sets and expectations, both linguistic and cultural. Indeed, each student's fairly sophisticated explanation of her translation processes and choices might be theorized as belonging somewhere along a continuum, as illustrated in figure 1, with one end representing the translator's decision to stay as close as possible to the sense of the original, even if audience understanding might be compromised, and the other end being her choice to move away from the original, in an attempt to connect better with and move closer to an audience with different cultural and linguistic expectations.

Fig. 1. Text-to-Audience Spectrum.

The tension of negotiating across the arrow typifies the students' processes of translating or translanguaging between their home and host languages. Figure 1 represents the writer's translating negotiations, wherein she positions herself along a spectrum between a more "precise" translation that is faithful to the original (indicated by the beginning point of the arrow) and one that more thoroughly adjusts to audience expectations (indicated by the arrow's end point). Christine Tardy argues that such an act of translanguaging is an act of linguistic interpretation, definition, and understanding, which positions the individual on a continuum of self-inquiry. We saw writers taking various positions along this spectrum, often within the same translation act. That is to say, at some points in their reflective essays they discussed how closely they had stuck to the literal meaning of the original while, in other sections, they analyzed how they had to "adjust"—for example, add in new language or words that were not in the original—in order to fully explain a cultural idea or word(s) from the original work. Thus, students' reflections on translation processes demonstrate the complexity of the ongoing negotiations they continually make, both in and out of the classroom, moving from one language to another.

It is also important to note that even writers from the more literally minded side of figure 1 sometimes expressed audience consideration as an important factor in their decisions to "stick to the original." An example of such a writer would be the one who chose to retain what she felt was an important aspect of the original, by carrying over the Chinese practice of putting the family name first rather than last, thus adhering to her own customs, rather than those preferred by English speakers. Such a practice, she argued, would give her readers a "flavor" of Chinese naming culture. Other examples of student writers whose consideration of audience led them to the other side of the spectrum—that is, to add in ancillary and explanatory information that was not in the original—appear below, as does an analysis of the writer who admitted the utter impossibility of making the complicated cultural background of the original text totally clear to her "outsider" readers—or at least, without something being lost in the translation process.

Semantic Issues

As described above, some writers veered toward the right side of the spectrum, in terms of trying to choose English words and phrases that would be more identifiable to and thus friendlier for their readers, even if these might not be fully accurate or word for word to the original. One such ELL writer described the purpose of her addition of "slang" words and psychological descriptions as helping to make the sense, if not the exact wording, of the original clearer:

> To make my story more attractive and readable, I used more slang words and add a psychological description instead of academic vocabulary. For example, "而" originally means rest or get off work; however, I used the word "knock off" instead to let me readers feel more casual. Moreover, I added a psychological thought to make my story more coherent which is "I don't need to farming anymore if I could have a rabbit like this everyday."

Still another student, who chose to entitle her paper "How to Translate a Story to Foreign People," wrote of the difficulty of translating Chinese words that had no precise equivalent in English. This student explains how "American[s] might never see them before:" that is, a Chinese measuring tool that had been mentioned in the Chinese story she translated may be unfamiliar to American readers. As she put it:

> "秤," it's a kind of tools for weighing something, but only Chinese people used it. So I used "scale" represents "秤" in the translation. . . . This is the point that really challenges me because of there are no corresponding words in English. If I translate more exactly, I should use many words even another story to explain it. But it would be complex and complicated to let reader to understand the original story. So I tried to use less words or another U.S. jargon that have close meaning to explain.

This writer also supplied a second example:

> "三国时期" is a period of old Chinese ancient time. In that period, there were three kingdoms existed, so I just translated the period to "the Three Kingdoms Period." The reason why I used "Kingdom" instead of "Dynasty" is the kingdoms in China are not strong enough like "French Kingdoms" or "British Kingdoms."

This sense of choosing an English word appropriate to a U.S. readers' audience (and presumed familiarity with the notion of "kings" from European tradition) was also reflected in a different student's discussion of his choice of the word "buckaroo" rather than "shepherd," when he translated the Chinese word "牧童" into English. His point, he said, was that "buckaroo" would appeal more to U.S. readers, whom he viewed as steeped in the Western tradition of the cowboy. The exigency of adapting to their U.S. audience and readers, within this outsider's imagined cultural context, shaped these Chinese writers' linguistic and rhetorical translation choices—something they then were able to thoroughly explain in their carefully reasoned reflections on their translation processes. In positioning multilingual writers as experts, the translation assignment by nature encourages these students to consider, reflect upon, name, and elucidate the kinds of ongoing translingual and transnational negotiations that they practice in daily life.

Grammatical and Syntactic Meanings

Telling examples of translation lie in those moments when student translators cited how linguistic differences in grammar affected their translations. An example of this would be where a missing subject reference would be clear to a Chinese reader reading Mandarin but not to an English one. One student describes her translating challenge in terms of the preponderance of pronouns in Chinese as opposed to English: "The word 'it' (as the character in the original paragraph) is used so any time that usually makes the reference ambiguous to foreign readers yet troubles no Chinese readers." The student writer then showed how she had to adjust her translation beyond the literal, adding in the explanatory references that otherwise would not have been an issue for a Chinese reader: "(he's) afraid of people will catch (him) when they hear it (the sound of him breaking the bell)." Her translation thus both mixed and separated (see the parentheses she added) English and Chinese grammatical structures—a translating choice she then acknowledged and explained in her narrative reflective essay. Her ingenious solution to the problem of translating from Mandarin to English was an attempt to have it both ways: to stay both true to the original and to provide clarity for her reader. Verbs and prepositions provided a similar issue, since as one student writer said,

> In order to make sense to my English readers, I will added some English words that it actually not exist in original story. For example, the sentence I mentioned in the above paragraph "日出而作, 日落而息." don't have a verb and preposition in its Chinese version. More specific, "日出" in Chinese means "sunrise" while "日落" means "sunset". Besides, "而作" means "working" while "而息" means "knock off" or "rest". Obviously, we can't find a verb or connection word to connect those words in Chinese and audiences definitely won't understand if I translate it literally. So I added some work so that readers can understand.

Once again, linguistic differences resulted in the translingual writer "adding in" English words to their translation, to make the meaning clearer to her audience and thus demonstrating a heightened sensitivity to linguistic and grammatical differences between home and second languages.

Another example of adjusting a translation to suit English-speaking readers was evident in sentence level translation. Often, students chose to change the structure of sentences in order to create texts that were viewed as more appealing to a U.S. audience. One student explained her choice of sentence structure in this way:

> Chinese writings often use long and complex sentences to describe stuffs, and this leads me to have to consider how to cut a long sentence to short sentences. . . . For instance, the first sentence of first paragraph:

> 太阳物理学是运用现代物理学的技术，方法和理论研究太阳和太阳活动现象的结构、化学组成、物理状态和演变过程，以及各种现象的产生机制的一门学科。
>
> It explains an academic term—[sic] solar physics, and the writer used a bunch of phrase to describe it, which increase the difficulty of translation . . . in Chinese, "恒星" means a specific kind of stars . . . if I directly translate this word to star, "star" can not represent the accurate means of "恒星." In order to make the article more fluent . . . I must take into account the connection between sentences and causality.

This student's reflection on and analysis of her process of translation explains why the very structure of her sentences and paragraphs changed during translation, as well as how linguistic differences in grammar and syntax are affected by culture, language, subject matter, and personal choice. Her focus on specific words also points to the intricacy of translation and illustrates the multiplicity of our categories of analysis.

Cultural Sensitivities

In addition to managing languages as objects of analysis and performance, students often engage with broader translanguaging concerns, most tellingly illustrated through the negotiation of common sense cultural sensitivities. In the context of this article, we use *cultural sensitivities* to capture how students focus on unpacking and articulating culturally specific aesthetics, rhetorical styles, and literary devices embodied by their texts, which then, in turn, inform their semantic, syntactical, and grammatical choices. Sometimes, students admitted being somewhat "stuck" between the two ends of the spectrum, recognizing the challenge of negotiating between the original text and the English-speaking reader's understanding. They often found themselves wondering whether it was even possible for a non-Chinese reader to understand the rich cultural references that were embedded in their original texts. These students would also admit the difficulty of translating widely known and frequently referenced tropes, tales, and metaphors that informed much of the stories' meanings. Because a reader's knowledge of these literary devices is often assumed in their home culture, translating them meant decoding their "hidden meanings" and unpacking the rhetorical traditions that inform their meanings.

For example, one student explains how she uses rhetorical strategies in Chinese literature to express emotions in her writing:

> I was asked to write a sad love story once. I remember I described a scene in the beginning [of the essay], a man standing in a daze facing a loquat tree. This was a successful [strategy] to catch the reader's attention.

According to the student, her mention of the loquat tree invokes a shared cultural reference that originated in a classic essay written in Ancient Chinese. In this original essay, a famous Chinese author personified a luscious loquat tree, which had been planted by his deceased wife, to suggest the dire contrast between life and death and to provide a subtle commentary on his sorrow. The loquat tree, as a literary device, has acquired stabilized meaning and entered the cultural consciousness as a symbol of sorrow for the Chinese. This student's ability to use this trope without referencing the source becomes evidence of her erudition as a reader and intellectual capacity as a writer. When translating the story, however, she needs to adjust her assumptions and approaches according to the rhetorical traditions of her audience and her presumably limited capacity with English. In this case, translating the text results in the loss of her writing style, which is marked by tested strategies, such as using "massive adjective words to describe [one's] inner feelings" and "careful and clever uses of tropes to show off my knowledge." Operating from her assumption that U.S. academic essays are more logic-driven, she took what she called a "scientific" and "simplistic" style to make sure that she conveyed the basic facts of the story. In the meantime, she abandoned what she described as "unnecessary decorations" for fear of using the wrong words and creating entangled sentences. Also, her use of the trope without referencing its source needs to be reconsidered in light of academic expectations for citation. To the student, making herself clear and understood by an English-speaking reader overrides her desire as a Chinese writer to create artistic and sophisticated texts.

Similar losses are present in other areas of the translation process, such as cultural subtexts, humor, aesthetics, and people's way of thinking and behaving. It is through such juxtapositions and reflections that students develop a translanguaging stance. To make texts from their culture comprehensible to cultural outsiders, students learn to recognize the affordances of genres and rhetorical styles across linguistic and cultural contexts, to articulate such culturally specific expectations, and to name and strategize moves that they often already make in everyday conversations and communications. In particular, many reflect on the importance of supplying missing background information and inferential details, unpacking established assumptions and tropes (and citing them), and explaining differences among people's ways of thinking and behaving. Practicing the very negotiating strategies they then named and articulated for themselves in their analyses, the students came to recognize the kinds of translingual strategies they were using in their everyday practices of communicating with others. In other words, the process of translating, comparing, and reflecting engaged these students in metalinguistic analysis that heightened their explicit awareness of the communicative tools they needed to make their translation clear to others who did not share the same cultural or linguistic context.

Conclusion

In this article, we have drawn on our data analysis and experiences to make recommendations for reconfiguring and repurposing the act of translation as a valuable assignment across teaching contexts. We would like to stress that the translation assignment can be introduced in a number of ways. Consequently, there are some definite differences between the execution of this assignment in each of our class sections, due to differences in inflection, as well as each teacher's own perspective. For instance, in Julia's class the focus is on close reading, library research writing, and academic language. In Joyce's class, audience is primary, as students and teacher consider meaning making and knowledge sharing within and across languages, particularly in terms of fluency. And Xiqiao's class is more multimodal in scope, focusing on how transnational experiences and their implications affect the translation process. However, despite these differences in perspective, each iteration of this assignment works to place value on translingual competencies, which mirrors a national shift toward asset-based, culturally sustaining pedagogical practices.

We believe that each version of this assignment helps students to develop a repertoire of skills towards productive negotiation with linguistic codes, identities, and cultures, and moves towards research that recognizes enhanced awareness of audience and genre as central to translingual student writing. We see the primary translingual and transnational affordance of this assignment as positioning students as experts within their writing process. Specifically, this assignment features students' own languages and cultures as assets, thereby positioning student writers as experts. Using their own translations as evidence, the students produce rich analyses and theories of their translation choices, often in the context of theorizing about the complex differences and similarities between the languages and cultures involved. Consequently, the translation assignment invites keen analysis of ongoing translating choices students are already making across contexts.

Students described how the translating exercise drove their desire to aim for the accuracy of the translation itself, because as one student wrote, "during translation, we have to make sure what it really means in order to correctly translate it into English." Eventually, this exercise led to nuanced conversations for students, with both themselves and their translation partners, about the original meaning of a given word or phrase and the affordances of parallel English words and phrases, including connotation, grammatical structures, and cultural associations. In our analysis, this negotiation with classmates often appeared as a kind of productive fretting over the affordances of various English words that are close in meaning, as the writer determined which would most accurately represent to readers the meaning of the original.

Thus, the assignment also highlights the affordances of collaborative learning in supporting the development of student agency. The very act of sharing their respective translations with their classmates—a required part of the project, in between the translation and analysis parts—catalyzed them to make rich observations about how and why they had made their own translation choices, especially in the context of what the other students in their group had chosen by comparison.

On another front, this assignment allows students to test their assumptions about and theories of language developed through prior experiences. For many, the difficulty of making semantic choices mirrors the frustrations they encounter in trying to communicate and negotiate over small mundane details, including ordering food from the cafeteria or having a conversation with a roommate. Driven by their need to articulate and rationalize the choices they make, students often venture to formulate informal theories of languages, such as English being logic-driven while Chinese follows a more indirect, inference-driven theme, or English as more precise and Chinese being more ornate. The validity of such theories aside, the intellectual work itself pivots around important issues of negotiating translingual relationships.

While translation challenges remain, this writing assignment did not diminish either the students' appreciation of their home languages or their understanding of the multiple ways to translate a given passage. If anything, it reinforced the integrity and appeal of the original texts by pinpointing how difficult translating can be. In fact, the project tended to heighten students' appreciation for the daily challenges they face in negotiating between two or more languages, and for the translation enterprise all told. By placing the onus of the assignment on the reflection written afterwards, rather than the translation itself, the assignment allowed students to articulate their own rationales for the translation decisions they themselves made.

Pedagogical Recommendations

The research results position translingual and transnational practices as inherent realities of writing classrooms, in the sense that multilinguals are always negotiating across languages and cultures. Teachers can leverage this reality when they teach, which helps students articulate their often invisible experiences. In other words, we have put theory into action. As an example of action research, or research in practice, our research-informed teaching practices worked to develop a collaborative framework centered on students' home languages and cultures while providing reflective practice for both students and teachers. For the students, rich reflection occurred in their narrative writing that rigorously analyzed their translanguaging choices, partly set against the choices of their peers. For the instructors, corresponding reflection took place in our ongoing pedagogical and research meetings, where we discussed both the students' responses and our own differing responses to the assignment as teachers. From this collaborative reflective process, we have developed four recommendations in the teaching of translation in composition classrooms.

Recommendation One: Adapt to Contexts

Because the assignment has an inherent flexibility, which allows for adaptation across various instructional contexts, we recommend that instructors consider adapting the translation assignment for their own pedagogical use. In our case, for example, Xiqiao and Joyce had their students translate cultural stories, while Julia had her students work on scholarly articles. Because the assignment emphasizes the reflective component rather than the actual translation, students could thus analyze translations of more than one kind of text. The fact that students can select texts of various genres and content as the objects of analysis and translation makes it possible for students to make many critical decisions as writers themselves. Moreover, as constructed, the assignment can be taught by either monolingual or multilingual instructors, as the students' (rather than the teachers') translingual abilities are at the project's heart.

Recommendation Two: Collaborate with Other Instructors

Because the collaborative nature of this assignment can create a synergetic environment in which collective growth is enabled—that is, both instructors and students learn—we recommend that instructors experiment with the assignment in tandem with other instructors, if possible, so as to create the opportunity for cross-class and cross-teacher exploration and discussion. In the case of this project, our own learning and teaching of this specific assignment was fostered by collaborative discussions that allowed us to voice how the assignment was working and to compare and discuss assignment scaffolding and sequencing. These collaborative moves mirrored those of our students: just as they learned from sharing and comparing their respective translations, so too did we learn from sharing our teaching narratives. Finally, the interactions between instructors, monolingual and multilingual, allowed for a level of comfort when using translingual approaches in a classroom of diverse learners. Such collaboration recognized and supported linguistic diversity as a pedagogical tool in a course where the lingua franca has traditionally been U.S. English.

Recommendation Three: Legitimize Translanguaging

Because the assignment legitimizes the usage of multiple languages within academic writing, and in fact, as key in any discussion of translanguaging, especially when coupled with class discussion of the writer's credibility or "ethos," we recommend the teaching of assignments that give students the opportunity to incorporate their home languages into written texts. In these situations, the very employment of their own languages, along with information about their cultures, encourages thoughtful and analytical writing on the part of the students who are deeply invested in the reflective arguments they make.

Recommendation Four: Invite Connections

Because the assignment creates an exigency for students to interrogate and analyze the broad range of transnational experiences that inform their identities as translingual individuals, we recommend designing assignments that allow students to comment on the affective and emotional dimensions of their experiences with transnational migration and translingual practices. The narrative assignment brings into focus various points of contestation and reconciliation, compelling students to revise old assumptions and develop new strategies to ensure their own growth as efficient and critical readers and writers. In "venting" about how hard it is, celebrating small "aha" moments, and experiencing confusion and resolution, students revisit a wide array of emotional experiences with multilingualism.

To close, even though the data collected for this study does not allow us to make universal conjectures about cross-disciplinary translingual writing practices, we do see implications for students using the insights garnered from this assignment for their language learning in formal and informal contexts. For instance, a Chinese student explained,

> I still remembered that at the beginning of this semester, after I took the first couple weeks classes in here, how I strongly desired to be an "American" person. Of course, I don't really mean to change my nationality or identity, I just wanted to let myself to "forget" Chinese language temporarily and only understand English while I was studying . . . I have changed my former idea completely. Right now, I feel pleasured that I am a multilingual user because being multilingual is truly helpful in my studying. . . . To be honest, if I only knew one language, I would never make an improvement on my academic writing capacity.

Based on this quote, this assignment has provided these ELLs with new perspectives about writing in terms of linguistic negotiation. And, while these findings do not point explicitly to how these students might use what they have learned from this assignment in other academic contexts, they do illustrate that these students not only have a new appreciation for their own languages but also exemplify many intersecting dimensions of academic writing such as the development of analytical, meta-linguistic skills within texts grounded in student agency and authority.

Notes

1. There are often outlier students whose home language is not spoken by other members of the class. In these cases, students are provided with a number of options, such as translating high-level academic English texts into classroom English, translating stories written for a specific cultural audience into classroom English, etc.

Works Cited

Alsheikh, Negmeldin. "Three Readers, Three Languages, Three Texts: The Strategic Reading of Multilingual and Multiliterate Readers." *The Reading Matrix* 11.1 (2011): 34-53. Print.

Canagarajah, Suresh. "Multilingual Writers and the Academic Community: Towards a Critical Relationship." *JAC* 1.1 (2002): 29-44. Print.

---. "Negotiating Translingual Literacy: An Enactment." *RTE* 48.1 (2013): 40-67. Print.

---. "Toward a Rhetoric of Translingual Writing." *The Working Papers Series on Negotiating Differences in Language and Literacy.* U of Louisville, 2012. Web. 10 Sept. 2014. <http://louisville.edu/workingpapers/copy_of_working-papers>.

---. "Toward a Writing Pedagogy of Shuttling between Languages: Learning from Multilingual Writers." *College English* 68.6 (2006): 589-604. Print.

---. *Translingual Practice: Global Englishes and Cosmopolitan Relations.* New York: Routledge, 2013. Print.

Creese, Angela, and Adrian Blackledge. "Translanguaging in the Bilingual Classroom: A Pedagogy for Learning and Teaching?" *Modern Language Journal* 94.1 (2010): 103-15. Print.

García, Ofelia, and Li Wei. *Translanguaging: Language, Bilingualism, and Education.* Basingstoke: Palgrave Pilot, 2014. Print.

Gentil, Guillaume. "A Biliteracy Agenda for Genre Research." *Journal of Second Language Writing* 20 (2011): 6-23. Print.

Hornberger, Nancy, and Holly Link. "Translanguaging in Today's Classrooms: A Biliteracy Lens." *Theory into Practice* 51.4 (2012): 239-47. Print.

Horner, Bruce, Min-Zhan Lu, Jacqueline Jones Royster, and John Trimbur. "Language Difference in Writing: Toward a Translingual Approach." *College English* 73.3 (2011): 303-21. Print.

Horner, Bruce, Samantha NeCamp, and Christine Donahue. "Toward a Multilingual Composition Scholarship: From English Only to a Translingual Norm." *CCC* 63.2 (2011): 269-300. Print.

Jiménez, Robert T., Sam David, Keenan Fagan, Victoria Risko, Mark Pacheco, Lisa Pray, and Mark Ganzales. "Using Translation to Drive Conceptual Development for Students Becoming Literate in English as an Additional Language." *RTE* 49.3 (2015): 248-71. Print.

Kramsch, Claire. "The Traffic in Meaning." *Asia Pacific Journal of Education* 26.1 (2006): 99-104. Print.

Lewin, Kurt. "Action Research and Minority Problems." *Journal of Social Issues* 2 (1946): 34-46. Print.

Lu, Min-Zhan. "Living-English Work." *College English* 68.6 (2006): 605-19. Print.

Lu, Min-Zhan, and Bruce Horner. "Composing in a Global-Local Context: Careers, Mobility, Skills." *College English* 72.2 (2009): 113-33. Print.

Matsuda, Paul Kei, and Tony Silva. "Cross-Cultural Composition: Mediated Integration of U.S. and International Students." *Composition Studies* 27.1 (1999): 15-30. Print.

McLaren, Peter. *Life in Schools: An Introduction to Critical Pedagogy in the Foundations of Education.* 5th ed. Boston: Allyn and Bacon, 2007. Print.

Medina, Carmen. "Reading across Communities in Biliteracy Practices: Examining Translocal Discourses and Cultural Flows in Literature Discussions." *Reading Research Quarterly* 45.1 (2010): 40-60. Print.

MLA Ad Hoc Committee on Foreign Languages. "Foreign Languages and Higher Education: New Structures for a Changed World." *Modern Language Association.* Mod. Lang. Assoc. of Amer., 2011. Web. 20 Mar. 2014. <https://www.mla.org/Resources/Research/Surveys-Reports-and-Other-Documents/Teaching-Enrollments-and-Programs/Foreign-Languages-and-Higher-Education-New-Structures-for-a-Changed-World>.

Mokhtari, Kouider, and Carla Reichard. "Investigating the Strategic Reading Processes of First and Second Language Readers in Two Different Cultural Contexts." *System* 32 (2004): 379-94. Print.

Mokhtari, Kouider, and Ravi Sheorey. *Reading Strategies of First- and Second-Language Learners: See How They Read.* Norwood: Christopher-Gordon, 2008. Print.

Orellana, Marjorie Faulstich, and Jennifer F. Reynolds. "Cultural Modeling: Leveraging Bilingual Skills for School Paraphrasing Tasks." *Reading Research Quarterly* 43.1 (2008): 48-65. Print.

Orellana, Marjorie Faulstich, Barrie Thorne, Anna Chee, and Wan Shun Eva Lam. "Transnational Childhoods: The Participation of Children in Processes of Family Migration." *Social Problems* 48.4 (2001): 572-92. Print.

Pennycook, Alastair. "English as a Language Always in Translation." *European Journal of English Studies* 12.1 (2008): 33-47. Print.

Tardy, Christine. "Enacting and Transforming Local Language Policies." *CCC* 62.4 (2011): 634-61. Print.

Young, Vershawn Ashanti, and Aja Y. Martinez, eds. *Code-Meshing as World English: Pedagogy, Policy, Performance.* Urbana: NCTE, 2011. Print.

Course Design

World Rhetorics

Ghanashyam Sharma

Course Description

In light of increasing international immigration and student mobility, unprecedented redistribution of geopolitical power, and the pervasive effects of the internet on institutions and communities locally and globally, rhetoric and composition has, albeit more in theory than in practice, started responding to the multilateral flow of ideas across nations and cultures. Building on what Wendy Hesford has called the "global turn" in the discipline, World Rhetorics explores rhetorical traditions from around the world, examining texts from historical, geopolitical, and thematic perspectives. As current and future writing teachers, students in this course learn to draw on different rhetorical traditions, have conversations with a number of guest scholars using videoconferencing, and write about and present their own pedagogical models and strategies.

Institutional Context

World Rhetorics is a part of the Graduate Certificate in the Teaching of Writing program (GCTW) at Stony Brook University. The certificate was established some time after the university's Program in Writing and Rhetoric (PWR) separated from the English department in 1998. The current course is a response to the PWR's recognition that there is a need and demand for adding a global/transnational dimension to the teaching of writing in secondary and tertiary education. This section briefly describes both the certificate and the program as the contexts for World Rhetorics. I then discuss my rationale for the design and implementation of the course, followed by a reflection on its first iteration, in the fall of 2014.

Writing about the history of the PWR, Peter Khost and Pat Belanoff observe that the program is now a thriving one, after having had quite an eventful life and background of more than forty years. Although it was not until 1982 that the Department of English hired a director of composition from outside—Peter Elbow was the first—the university had first sought to do so in 1974, meaning that the writing program was a distinct entity within the English department at least as early as the 1970s. As Khost and Belanoff's history shows, the PWR has developed new pedagogical ideas, such as the writing portfolio; it has fought in favor of writing instructors and successfully doubled remuneration for adjunct faculty; and, like writing programs elsewhere, it has experienced ups and downs since its establishment.

The GCTW provides the opportunity for graduate students to acquire an increasingly important professional skill set for teaching writing. Students complete the certificate by taking five courses in the PWR. The courses are usually cross-listed with the English department, which is the major source of master's and doctoral students for the certificate. Including these and other students, roughly half of those who enroll in the certificate are current or prospective secondary school teachers, some of them pursuing professional degrees in higher education. Not much concerted institutional effort has been made so far to promote and grow the program, but the PWR has just begun discussing the growth of the certificate, for reasons including (1) increased interest from a variety of potential students; (2) relative scarcity of comparable graduate programs in the state and region; (3) potential of the certificate to be a basis for the PWR's further growth; and (4) the need for expanding curricular opportunities in the area of writing and communication at the graduate level, including through internationalization of curricula.

From a broader perspective, the needs and challenges of writing and communication among the extremely diverse student body at Stony Brook University—which reflects a similar diversity of students in New York state at large—have also prompted us to grow the certificate and diversify our course offerings. With almost half of its students coming from beyond middle-class, European-American family/social backgrounds, Stony Brook University presents its teachers with truly "global" classrooms. It is worth noting here that institutional policies, curricula, and pedagogy do not yet explicitly and deliberately foreground the knowledge, skills, and perspectives that students bring into the classroom and need to foster in order to live and succeed in a globalized world. However, there are now discussions about internationalizing the curriculum, promoting a sense of global citizenship among students, and promoting faculty work on transnational and cross-cultural subjects. Faculty members in the PWR are increasingly using pedagogical strategies to make the curricula engaging to diverse students.

World Rhetorics is a small attempt toward "internationalizing" the curriculum, drawing the attention of the institution, program, and certificate toward the need to deliberately include international perspectives in the teaching of reading, writing, and research. Especially since most students taking the course are secondary school teachers, it is also an attempt to promote, through these teachers, a sense of belonging, knowing, and knowledge-making in the world at large among their students.

Theoretical Rationale

At many universities across the U.S., there is a lack of attention to diversity in terms of curriculum, pedagogy, and student engagement programs. Fortunately, at my institution, an increasing number of faculty members across campus are taking this lack as an opportunity. Many of us draw on the cultural and epistemological heritages of our students, both domestic and international while designing and teaching courses. Whether their families have been on the continent for centuries, decades, or years, we see all students as deserving a rhetorical education that transcends a particular tradition, or set of traditions, established upon the geopolitical power and historical contingencies of one particular region of the world, namely Western Europe and North America. Even from a pragmatic point of view, we realize that students can be more successful in their personal, social, and professional lives if they have greater knowledge of different rhetorical practices and traditions and increased curiosity and desire to communicate across national and cultural borders. In the PWR in particular, we see the broadening of the rhetorical basis of writing courses in college as an important goal of education.

My own desire to develop and teach a course drawing on rhetorical traditions from around the world was prompted by an awareness that New York is characterized by what scholars have described as "superdiversity." First used by Steven Vertovec in a BBC article and elaborated best in "Super-diversity and its Implications," this term refers to precisely the kind of diversity represented by domestic and international students at my institution, a diversity that is "distinguished by a dynamic interplay of variables" in terms of culture, class, and national origin (1024). I also developed World Rhetorics with the awareness that in the field of rhetoric and composition, there has been a general lack of attention to histories, traditions, and resources of rhetoric from beyond the Western world. For a few decades now, some scholars of rhetoric in North America have—from perspectives such as feminist, postmodernist, and postcolonial—critiqued the mainstream history and theory of the discipline for being limited to a particular hemisphere and geopolitical region in the world. Scholars like Mary Muchiri, Victor Vitanza, Patricia Bizzell, Susan Jarratt, Jan Swearingen, and Damián Baca, to name a few, have also highlighted how the field's canon has been shaped and dominated by certain power structures and power groups in terms of class, race, gender, ethnicity, and culture.

While rhetoric and composition does not have the equivalent of the robust scholarship of postcolonialism that we see in English studies, scholars like Baca have shed light on the historical and political backdrops of the field. According to Baca, the profession of teaching writing in the U.S. has historically been complicit with colonization and continues to be so, both within the West and on a global scale. Pointing out that composition treats the Greco-Roman-Anglo-American rhetorical tradition as if it is a universal history of all rhetoric, instead of being *a* rhetoric among many, Baca suggests that scholars are not aware of the colonial legacy of their discipline. Indeed, even when composition scholars theoretically subscribe to the notion of "diversity," many continue to buy into the "Eurocentric myth [that links] the Western Roman alphabet to rationality, critical agency, and social equality" (230-1). In "Global Turns and Cautions in Rhetoric and Composition," Wendy Hesford also notes that alongside a global turn, "there is evidence of a nostalgic retreat to disciplinary identities and homelands and a resurgent, though not uncritical, localism" (788). As such, I start this course with an examination of how the field has generally approached or responded to calls for going beyond the Western and mainstream canons, what the educational benefits of doing so are, and how writing teachers can pedagogically realize those benefits.

Generally speaking, the official history of rhetoric that composition studies typically relies on is inadequate, and the assumption of its universality goes counter to the needs and realities of the twenty-first century. However, since it is also unproductive to focus on those limitations, I opt for a practical pedagogical approach that helps to address the challenges. LuMing Mao's article, "Reflective Encounters: Illustrating Comparative Rhetoric," provides that approach for World Rhetorics. In this article, Mao describes a strategy for studying rhetorical traditions from beyond the Western world through "reflective encounters where different rhetorical traditions can truly converse with and learn from each other" (401). As Roberta Binkley and Marissa Smith note, studying the geopolitics of rhetoric "permits a complexified spatial deconstruction of the familiar, making it unfamiliar, and therefore in its unfamiliarity, to provide a new view, and the chance to reconceptualize our own epistemological geographic spaces, to reexamine the meanings inherent in those spaces." Thus, in World Rhetorics, students read texts from or about different rhetorical traditions, first trying to understand the "social, cultural, and linguistic forces that have been in play" (Binkley and Smith), then using that understanding for critically reflecting on the local traditions. Such encounters, Mao has suggested, help us to "interrogate the familiar inside out and to pursue the unfamiliar on its own terms" (416). To borrow words from Timothy Reagan, the objective of the course is to help students recognize that "one's own tradition is simply one among many," a recognition that is necessary "if the study of the history of educational thought and practice is to be more than a parochial artifact" (11).

Furthermore, the curriculum and pedagogy used in World Rhetorics are characterized by the following features: (1) multiple axes of inquiry, rather than a historical or comparative survey; (2) focus on pedagogy and developing teaching ideas; (3) inviting authors of some of the readings for class as guest speakers, drawing on David Cormier's writings about "community as curriculum;" (4) encouraging students to use social media platforms to share ideas and join or build community around their ideas; and (5) keeping the course student-centered and adaptable to the interests of individual students. The effectiveness of the curricular design and pedagogical strategies of the course are described and assessed in the next section.

Because a course like this is bound to select only a few rhetorical traditions and only a few texts from each, the class used three different axes to read and analyze texts, as indicated in point one above: geopolitical/regional, historical/temporal, and thematic/ideational. This three-dimensional approach to reading the selected texts helps students to gain a richer understanding of the broader contexts of and issues in the texts, as well as the changes and complexities in both. First, in order to situate a text in its geopolitical context and try to understand the broader society and culture informing it, students read one or more texts representing rhetorical traditions from different parts of the world. Second, because it is easy to look at a distant sociocultural context from a previous historical time and assume that that culture or society is still characterized by the same issues and qualities, students deliberately avoid looking at texts as slices of societies and issues frozen in time. That is, they delve deeper into how rhetorical traditions and issues have changed over time in the respective societies and cultures, as well as how our understandings of them are shaped by "relations of power, discursive construction of knowledge, colonial construction of cultural dichotomies, and rhetorical plurality brought about by diaspora and cultural hybridity" (Kubota and Lehner 7). Third, to try to understand rhetorical traditions in relation to one another, students examine them in terms of particular themes, being aware that using common terms and themes could be insufficient and even problematic. Those themes include transaction and trust as seen in textual negotiations and in other rhetorical acts, knowledge and epistemology as defined and practiced in different sociocultural contexts, education and the practice of teaching and learning, and the mediation of knowledge and information by evolving technologies. Mao's approach of "reflective encounter" serves as an overarching framework for the analyses of texts while students integrate all three approaches.

In addition to the three-pronged approach to reading texts, some other features of the course are also worth noting. First, students are provided the opportunity to discuss course issues directly with scholars of different rhetorical traditions. In the 2014 iteration of the course, I invited seven scholars, all of whom were authors of course texts; students had highly engaging conversations with the guest speakers through videoconferencing. This pedagogical strategy of taking students beyond text-based class discussion and connecting them with the authors themselves is mainly based on the concept of "community as curriculum," a strategy that I adapt from David Cormier.

While connecting students to writers and established scholars in the field, the course also has them use social media platforms to share, and join or build community around, their ideas. Somewhat related to the course objective of "connectivist" learning, toward the end of the course, students also situate course themes and issues in the context of how emerging communicative media and modes are affecting rhetorical practices in and across contexts. They examine how foundational issues and forces of the rhetorical traditions are shaping, and shaped by, contemporary mediums and modes of rhetorical practice.

The course focuses on pedagogy, and it does so not only as part of a teaching of writing certificate but also as an effort to address a pedagogical gap in the discipline. As such, students write their midterm papers trying to develop arguments or positions toward their final papers; in their final papers, they are encouraged to develop and present pedagogical approaches and strategies that help address content, methods, and perspectives beyond the dominant rhetorical traditions in the teaching of writing. Pursuing this goal, students also write regular blog posts, responding to the readings and gradually developing their teaching ideas, as well as sharing teaching ideas during class discussions.

And, finally, the course is student-centered and adaptable to the interests of individual students. Not all students have a deep knowledge of or interest in the issues, so, one-on-one consultations are necessary to help all students develop their own pedagogical visions and strategies. The course also takes a deliberate approach to helping students make connections with experienced scholars in the field. These strategies provide students the needed support to develop pedagogical strategies for an academic and cultural environment that does not readily appreciate knowledge cultures and educational practices from beyond its national and cultural borders.

Critical Reflection

While developing the course, I consulted with a number of scholars, including LuMing Mao, Keith Lloyd, and Iswari Pandey, who have taught similar courses, also learning how their scholarship addresses the lack of non-Western rhetoric in writing studies in the U.S. and what pedagogical strategies they have used when teaching similar courses. In fact, the three features of the course as described above evolved over several years through reading and conversation with scholars of cross-cultural rhetoric. When I taught it for the first time in 2014, some of my strategies led to significant outcomes, while others were less successful. Here, I try to make sense of those successes and failures, highlighting what I would recommend to other colleagues teaching similar courses and how I might update the course in the future.

The greatest challenge I faced with the design of the course was that of scope. It is impossible to cover even one rhetorical tradition with sufficient breadth and depth within a single semester (Miller 70). However, my approach of using a sampling of materials from each rhetorical tradition and exploring the materials from three different axes—time/change, place/context, and theme/perspective—was, overall, quite effective. Students examined the texts and attempted to situate them in their geopolitical and material contexts, with attention paid to sociopolitical changes that occurred during the time the texts were written. One of the students, Michael Guerriero, made an astute observation about the benefit of this approach, which he presents in the form of a realization on a publicly accessible blog: "While working on the final paper for this course, I did not just learn about the various traditions of different cultures, I learned a new way to think about these cultures. . . ."

While noting that the course could only "scratch the surface," Guerriero went on to describe an epiphany he had when he realized that rhetorical traditions are always in flux and what we take for granted as characteristic of a tradition may have already disappeared. When he learned that *both* Chinese and Western rhetorical traditions highly value memory, he realized that "the Chinese emphasis on memory is not a foreign concept at all. Memory is a rhetorical component in both cultures that [is still] maximized in one, but [gradually] minimized in another." By introducing the factor of time and change, Guerriero was able to discuss the significance of understanding both place/context and time/history. Further, Guerriero identified the significance of understanding both place/context and time/history as follows:

> This has implications beyond even the important revelation that commonalities exist in cultures as vastly different as China and America. Essentially, I realized both that our rhetorical traditions have changed, and that they will continue to change. "The way we do things" is not set in stone, and even if it was, the flow of time would carve new shapes into it just as rivers carve out massive canyons. Our rhetoric will change. We have no power over this. What we do have the power to decide is how it will change. How ought we change, evolve, our rhetorical traditions?

Guerriero introduces the context of place and time, the importance of change, and the possibility of similarity across unexpected places and practices, essentially highlighting the need to focus on themes and issues instead of viewing rhetorical traditions as fundamentally and always different.

Perhaps the least effective aspect of the course was the plan to let students use social media in order join and grow the network of scholars in the profession. While students praised the more traditional mode of networking, in the form of guest speakers invited by Skype or Google Hangout, as the best aspect of the course, they were not as enthused by my suggestion that they also try to share their own ideas and join the community beyond the classroom via social and professional networks. For one thing, some of the scholars with whom I tried to connect students did not use social media platforms such as Facebook, Twitter, and blogs. Also, the idea of students "friending" teachers and scholars is not generally accepted, so a few students followed up conversations with the scholars who virtually visited our class via email. I must also note, however, that because this course feature was not fully conceptualized on my part, I may need to either better develop and implement it or drop it altogether in future iterations.

One of the reasons I think students should seek to make virtual connections is because doing so can allow them to connect to scholars of rhetoric from other parts of the country and the world. But teachers must also note limitations, such as time zone differences, an issue that required the use of prerecorded audio in lieu of a visit by an Egyptian colleague and frustrated my attempts to invite scholars from a few other countries. The only nonlocal scholar who virtually visited the class was Jay Jordan, who was teaching at his university's Korea campus in Seoul. My attempts to connect students with like-minded students and scholars were also limited by the time of day even here in the U.S. Because I taught at 7:00 p.m. EST, I was able to organize a videoconference between my students and a class taught by Iswari Pandey at the California State University at Northridge at 4:00 p.m. PST. This would not have been possible if the class had been taught later in the evening.

Another challenge, which was prominently highlighted in the course's seminal reading, Mao's "Reflective Encounters," was trying to understand the rhetorical traditions of unfamiliar cultures, contexts, and times while using the local terms of Western rhetoric. To try to tackle this challenge, students remained aware and sensitive about potential pitfalls, adopting the idea of "reflectively encountering" unfamiliar traditions and ideas in order to question what they may have assumed about local traditions and practices. While this issue was substantively discussed in class by all students, Guerriero articulated it best in a blog post titled "Approaching a New Frame of Mind:"

> The solutions to our problems in teaching writing to all students, not just minorities, can be found by looking at other cultures. We needn't replace our own methods, nor should we, but we can build on our foundations finding inspiration in the plethora of ideas and strategies that the world has already provided us with.

From my perspective, the most important takeaway for students in the course is the ability to reflect on the local while learning more about societies, traditions, and bodies of knowledge emerging from elsewhere in the world—however small the practical steps they can take as teachers may be.

Another area where I believe the course was generally effective was in its focus on pedagogy. Students regularly discussed and wrote about what they could take from the readings and discussions to their classrooms. Some students, such as Adina Raso, thought very ambitiously while writing their blogs, asking how we may be able to reshape and reframe secondary and higher education in the U.S. by broadening the scope of education's intellectual and cultural basis. Raso observed that the narrow historical foundation of education in this country likely contributes to social problems:

> Perhaps the reason why America still has issues with race, sexuality, and religion is because the "illusion of inclusion" has become an incredibly pervasive and superficial aspect of our society. While trying to include all races, sexes, and religions, we ignore important differences that ultimately put strain on local and national relationships.

She went on to suggest that these problems can only be tackled if education and social policies are more inclusive, if the intellectual bases of education are broader, and if teachers draw upon different traditions and cultures:

> We mustn't ignore our differences and try to assimilate diverse groups. We need to acknowledge one another and hold critical, nonjudgmental conversations about the state of relations in this country. . . . This needs to change if we are to negotiate our future as a nation.

At the end of the semester, when students presented their ideas to a group of faculty in the PWR during an informal social gathering, Raso reflected on the class in one of the most inspiring ways I have heard during my more than two decades as a teacher. She said that reading about different rhetorical traditions and exploring issues of rhetoric with a focus on education helped her realize that being a teacher could be a means to change the world, instead of being a job she might do along the way. By helping the next generation learn to draw from epistemologies beyond cultural and national borders, she observed, teachers of writing and rhetoric can help to change the world, and to right many wrongs within it.

Highlighting issues of teaching and learning in one of her blog posts, another student, Sara Santos, observed that teachers should not try to find solutions and fix problems but instead ask questions when necessary. Another student, David Johnson, blogged by applying the pedagogical approaches he considered in World Rhetorics to writing center work. Amy McDougal, who also made her writing public, wrote about gender equity through a rhetorical and political-cultural lens. Overall, the class was generally interested in drawing pedagogical strategies and ideas from class discussions, research, and reading. This interest was reflected at the end of the semester in an extremely rich set of practical pedagogical ideas that the class wrote collaboratively in a private Google Doc file. In this document, students described a range of practical strategies, translating more general discussions into suggestions and plans for the classroom.

Students used blogging as a fairly effective means for sharing their reading responses and responding to one another's posts; but, they essentially used blogs like discussion boards limited within the class, except when (and if) they shared their blogs in their own social networks. The students' blog posts, as evidenced by the excerpts that I cited above, were generally very thoughtful and substantive: blog entries ranged from summaries and reflections of readings for class to critiques and analyses, to applications of ideas in academic work, to discussions of their implications for education and society. In sum, relatively low-tech and traditional pedagogical approaches took precedence even where more high-tech approaches would have been desirable but were prohibitive due to logistical challenges as well as habit and comfort, for both students and myself. For instance, instead of joining conversations through the course's Twitter and Facebook accounts, students directly contacted the guest speakers to thank them for their time or to ask them follow up questions.

Perhaps the most successful aspect of the course was the involvement of seven guest speakers who spent about an hour each with my class, engaging students by presenting their ideas and responding to students' questions and observations about their work, which the students had read for class. The idea was to move students beyond texts and connect them to experts in the field. There were a few instances of technological and logistical difficulties, including one instance that required rescheduling, but students looked forward to talking to the experts and appreciated the opportunity to do so.

Looking back at the first iteration of the course more than a year after I taught it, I think it was quite a multifaceted, ambitious endeavor; I might have overdone some aspects of it. When I teach the course in future, I plan to focus more on enabling and encouraging students to draw on rhetorical traditions of their choice to develop and adapt teaching skills for their current or anticipated work in the classroom. I also intend to find alternative ways to create connections between students and scholars from beyond U.S. borders. Since students did not embrace social media—they cited privacy concerns in an end-of-semester reflection—I plan to develop strategies that might address such concerns while still engaging them in virtual, social conversations with the broader community of scholars. I also intend to pay more attention to media and multimodality, asking students "to collaborate with speakers of world languages to design and remix texts . . . targeted at a range of local and global audiences" (Fraiberg 118). I might also encourage students to seek "partnerships with international classrooms and speakers of world languages by having [them] conduct mini-ethnographies in their own local contexts and cultures and target this research toward international audiences as part of a cross-cultural exchange" (Fraiberg 118).

The gaps in the rhetorical foundations of writing pedagogy may remain as striking as they are today for some time. However, I am optimistic that increasing numbers of teachers in the field will take small steps and gradually build the momentum. As Baca notes, while "the field rethinks its role for the 21st century, perhaps we will also consider how Composition Studies might join the much larger conversation of disparate and local composing practices throughout history, across the Americas and beyond" (239). The highly positive feedback of my students from fall 2014 has left me very inspired. I hope to further improve and teach this course many more times.

Works Cited

Baca, Damián. "Rethinking Composition, Five Hundred Years Later." *JAC* 29 (2009): 229-42. Print.

Binkley, Roberta, and Marissa Smith. "Re-Composing Space: Composition's Rhetorical Geography." *Composition Forum* 15 (2006): n.pag. Web. 23 July 2014. <http://compositionforum.com/issue/15/binkleysmithspace.php>.

Bizzell, Patricia, and Susan Jarratt. "Rhetorical Traditions, Pluralized Canons, Relevant History, and Other Disputed Terms: A Report from the History of Rhetoric Discussion Groups at the ARS Conference." *Rhetoric Society Quarterly* 34.3 (2004): 19-25. Print.

Cormier, David. "Rhizomatic Education: Community as Curriculum." *Dave's Educational Blog*. Stony Brook U, 3 June 2008. Web. 1 May 2015. <http://davecormier.com/edblog/2008/06/03/rhizomatic-education-community-as-curriculum/>.

Fraiberg, Steven. "Composition 2.0: Toward a Multilingual and Multimodal Framework." *CCC* 62.1 (2010): 100-26. Print.

Guerreiro, Michael. "Approaching a New Frame of Mind." *World Rhetorics Blog*. Stony Brook U, 3 Dec. 2014. Web. 20 May 2015. <https://you.stonybrook.edu/michaelguerriero/2014/12/03/approaching-a-new-frame-of-mind/>.

Hesford, Wendy S. "Global Turns and Cautions in Rhetoric and Composition Studies." *PMLA* 121.3 (2006): 787-801. Print.

Johnson, David. *A Level Playing Field*. Stony Brook U, Oct. 2014. Web. 21 May 2015. <http:// you.stonybrook.edu/davidjohnson>.

Khost, Peter, and Pat Belanoff. "Community through Collaborative Self-Reflection: Reports on a Writing Program History and Reunion at Stony Brook University."

Composition Forum 30 (2014): n.pag. Web. 20 May 2015. <http://composition-forum.com/issue/30/stony-brook.php>.

Kubota, Ryoko, and Al Lehner. "Toward Critical Contrastive Rhetoric." *Journal of Second Language Writing* 13.1 (2004): 7–27. Print.

McDougal, Amy. *Global Rhetorics*. Stony Brook U, Oct. 2014. Web. 21 May 2015. <http:// you.stonybrook.edu/amcdougal>.

Mao, LuMing. "Reflective Encounters: Illustrating Comparative Rhetoric." *Style* 37.4 (2003): 401. Print.

Miller, Thomas P. "Teaching the Histories of Rhetoric as a Social Praxis." *Rhetoric Review* 12.1 (1993): 70-82. Print.

Raso, Adina. "Chinese Rhetoric: Memorization, Cultural Values, and Why the West Isn't the Best." *Fables*. Stony Brook U, Oct. 2014. Web. 20 May 2015. <http://you.stonybrook.edu/myblog21/>.

Reagan, Timothy. "An Introduction to the Study of Non-Western and Indigenous Educational Traditions: A Philosophical Starting Point." *Non-Western Educational Traditions: Indigenous Approaches to Educational Thought and Practice*. 3rd ed. New York: Routledge, 2004. 1-22. Print.

Santos, Sara. "Bringing Down the Lego House and Building it Back Up." *A Multicolor Brick Road: Understanding Rhetoric Across Cultures, Languages and Spaces*. Stony Brook U, 20 Nov. 2014. Web. 20 May 2015. <http://you.stonybrook.edu/smsantos/2014/11/20/i-dont-know-and-thats-okay/>.

Swearingen, C. Jan, and LuMing Mao. "Comparative Rhetorical Studies in the New Contact Zone: Chinese Rhetoric Reimagined." *CCC* 60.4 (2009): W32-W44. *Proquest*. Web. 5 May 2015.

Vertovec, Steven. "Super-diversity and Its Implications." *Ethnic and Racial Studies* 30.6 (2007): 1024-54. Print.

Course Syllabus

Stony Brook University
World Rhetorics
Topics in Composition and Writing
WRT/EGL 614
Instructor: Dr. Shyam Sharma
Email: ghanashyam.sharma@stonybrook.edu

The term "global" has become increasingly important in the research, scholarship, and pedagogy of composition and rhetoric over the last decade or so. In its broadest sense, the word subsumes globalization and global issues in their many manifestations, such as increases and changes in patterns of global immigration, the redistribution of geopolitical power, and the all-pervasive effects of the internet on local/global and transnational institutions and communities. Within the humanities at large—including English studies and rhetoric and composition—the scholarship and professional networking that cross national borders are turning from a one-way traffic of texts and ideas to a multilateral exchange of ideas, collaborative work, and hyper-connected professional communities. Academics have started paying attention to how transnational/global forces are influencing the production and use of texts, ideas, and professional practices. Hence, students pursuing careers related to the teaching and scholarship of writing and rhetoric have a range of powerful reasons to pay attention to the emergence of the global in this discipline.

This seminar focuses on the "global turn" in the study of rhetoric and writing. Students will study a number of rhetorical traditions from around the world, exploring texts along three different axes: historical/temporal, geopolitical/spatial, and ideational/thematic. They will develop two consecutive but overlapping projects, the first to explore a particular tradition or phenomenon in rhetoric and the second to develop a theoretical framework geared toward informing pedagogical practices, formulating research methods or questions, or some other academic or professional implementation of their choosing. Toward the end of the semester, the class will together explore how new media and modes of communication are affecting rhetorical practices in and across contexts, examining how the foundational forces of the major rhetorical traditions are shaping contemporary rhetorical practices. The broader goal of the course is for students to develop an understanding and appreciation of rhetorical traditions beyond the mainstream (Greco-Roman-Anglo-American) history of rhetoric, situating that understanding in their current academic engagements and future prospects in anticipated professions/disciplines. The course will feature a number of guest speakers who are specialists in different rhetorical traditions; it will also provide students the option to participate in a side conversation online with students and scholars of rhetoric and related fields from different countries/contexts around the world.

COURSE OBJECTIVES

On successfully completing this course, students should be able to
- identify and discuss a few rhetorical traditions beyond the Greco-Roman-Anglo-American tradition in some detail
- develop a personal interest and expertise in a particular historical, geopolitical, or thematic area in global rhetorics
- develop and present theoretical, research, or pedagogical projects on cross-cultural rhetoric
- conduct basic research involving primary and secondary sources
- engage in effective peer review and professional networking to enhance knowledge-building and knowledge-sharing on the subject of global rhetorics

REQUIRED TEXTS

Baca, Damián. "Rethinking Composition, Five Hundred Years Later." *JAC* 29 (2009): 229-42. Print.

Baraunik, Richard. "The Birth of Open Source Learning Revolution." *TED: Ideas Worth Spreading*. TED Conferences, Feb. 2008. Web. 10 May 2015. <https://www.ted.com/talks/richard_baraniuk_on_open_source_learning?language=en>.

Binkley, Roberta, and Marissa Smith. "Re-Composing Space: Composition's Rhetorical Geography." *Composition Forum* 15 (2006): n.pag. Web. 23 July 2014. <http://compositionforum.com/issue/15/binkleysmithspace.php>.

Bizzell, Patricia, and Susan Jarratt. "Rhetorical Traditions, Pluralized Canons, Relevant History, and Other Disputed Terms: a Report from the History of Rhetoric Discussion Groups at the Ars Conference." *Rhetoric Society Quarterly* 34.3 (2004): 19-25. Print.

Brydon, Diana. "Conference Keynote: Canadian Poetry and Poetics in a Globalizing World." Western States Rhetoric and Literacy Studies Annual Meeting. Mount Allison, Winnipeg. 20 Oct. 2012. Web keynote address. 5 May 2015. <http://publicpoetics.ca/conference-participants/>.

Campbell, Kermit E. "Rhetoric from the Ruins of Ancient Africa." *Rhetorica* 14.3 (2006): 255-74. Print.

Connor, Ulla. "New Directions in Contrastive Rhetoric." *TESOL Quarterly* 36.4 (2003): 493-510. Print.

Cormier, David. "Rhizomatic Education: Community as Curriculum." *Dave's Educational Blog*. Stony Brook U, 3 June 2008. Web. 1 May 2015. <http://davecormier.com/edblog/2008/06/03/rhizomatic-education-community-as-curriculum/>.

Craig, Elizabeth C. "Review of *Contrastive Rhetoric.*" *Linguist List.* International Linguistics Community Online, N.d. Web. 10 May 2015. <http://linguistlist.org/pubs/reviews/get-review.cfm?SubID=188428>.

Gage, John T. "A Review of *Rhetorical Traditions and the Teaching of Writing.*" *Rhetoric Review* 3.1 (1984): 100-5. Print.

Grettano, Teresa. "A Review of *Rhetoric Before and Beyond the Greeks.*" *Composition Studies* 33.2 (2005): 128-30. Print.

Hesford, Wendy S. "Global Turns and Cautions in Rhetoric and Composition Studies." *PMLA* 121.3 (2006): 787-801. Print.

Hutto, David. "Ancient Egyptian Rhetoric in the Old and Middle Kingdoms." *Rhetorica.* 20.3 (2002): 213-33. Print.

Khagram, Sanjeev, and Peggy Levitt. "Constructing Transnational Studies." *The Transnational Studies Reader: Intersections and Innovations.* Ed. Sanjeev Khagram and Peggy Levitt. New York: Routledge, 2008. 1-22. Print.

Koch, Barbara J. "Presentation As Proof: The Language of Arabic Rhetoric." *Anthropological Linguistics* 25.1 (1983): 47-60. Print.

Lloyd, Keith. "Rethinking Rhetoric from an Indian Perspective: Implications in the Nyaya Sutra." *Rhetoric Review* 26.4 (2007): 365-84. Print.

Mao, LuMing. "Reflective Encounters: Illustrating Comparative Rhetoric." *Style Fayetteville* 37.4 (2003): 401-25. Print.

Markel, Mike. "The Rhetoric of Misdirection in Corporate Privacy-Policy Statements." *Technical Communication Quarterly* 14.2 (2005): 197-214. Print.

Matalene, Carolyn. "Contrastive Rhetoric: An American Writing Teacher in China." *College English* 47.8 (1985): 789-808. Print.

Miller, Susan. *Trust in Texts: A Different History of Rhetoric.* Carbondale: SIUP, 2008. Print.

Miller, Thomas P. "Teaching the Histories of Rhetoric As a Social Praxis." *Rhetoric Review* 12.1 (1993): 70-82. Print.

Mishra, Vidya Niwas. "Sanskrit Rhetoric and Poetics." *Mahfil* 7.3/4 (1971): 1-18. Print.

Miyahara, Akira. "Toward Theorizing Japanese Interpersonal Communication Competence from a Non-Western Perspective." *Academic Communication Journal* 13.3 (2008): 279-92. Web. 2 May 2015. <http://www.acjournal/holdings/vol13/Iss3/spec/kluver.htm>.

Olid-Pena, Estefania. "The Art of Future Discourse: Rhetoric, Translation and an Interdisciplinary Pedagogy for Transglobal Literacy." Diss. Georgia State U, 2012. Web. 2 May 2015. <http://scholarworks.gsu.edu/english_diss/94/>.

Pandey, Iswari P. "Literate Lives Across the Digital Divide." *Computers and Composition* 23.2 (2006): 246-57. Print.

Porter, James E. "Recovering Delivery for Digital Rhetoric." *Computers and Composition* 26.4 (2009): 207-24. Print.

Reagan, Timothy G. *Non-western Educational Traditions: Indigenous Approaches to Educational Thought and Practice.* Mahwah: Lawrence Erlbaum, 2005. Print.

Sharma, Ghanashyam, and Maha Bali. "Bonds of Difference: Illusion of Inclusion." *Hybrid Pedagogy* (April 2014): n.pag. Web. 1 May 2015. <http://www.digitalpedagogylab.com/hybridped/bonds-difference-illusions-inclusion/>.

Sharma, Ghanashyam, and Christopher Petty. "Putting Everything on the Line?" *RhetComp @ Stony Brook*. N.p., 2 Mar. 2014. Web. 1 May 2015. <https://rhetcompatstonybrook.wordpress.com/2014/02/26/putting-everything-on-the-line/>.

Stroud, Scott R., "Argument in Ancient India: The Case of Śankara's Advaita Vedanta," *Ancient Non-Greek Rhetorics*. Ed. Carol S. Lipson and Roberta A. Binkley. New York: Parlor P, 2009. 240-64. Print.

Sung-Gi, Jon. "Towards a Rhetoric of Communication, with Special Reference to the History of Korean Rhetoric." *Rhetorica* 28.3 (2010): 313-29. Print.

Swearingen, C. Jan, and LuMing Mao. "Comparative Rhetorical Studies in the New Contact Zone: Chinese Rhetoric Reimagined." *CCC* 60.4 (2009): W32-W44. Proquest. Web. 5 May 2015.

Wang, Bo. "A Survey of Research in Asian Rhetoric." *Rhetoric Review* 23.2 (2004): 171-81. Print.

Williams, Bronwyn T. "Speak for Yourself? Power and Hybridity in the Cross-Cultural Classroom." *CCC* 54.4 (2003): 586-609. Print.

Wright, Elizabeth A. "A History of the Arts of Memory and Rhetoric." *InSight* 5.2 (2009): 1-11. Print.

Zimmer, Michael. "Zuckerberg's Theory of Privacy." *The Washington Post*, 3 Feb. 2014. Web. 5 May 2015. <https://www.washingtonpost.com/lifestyle/style/mark-zuckerbergs-theory-of-privacy/2014/02/03/2c1d780a-8cea-11e3-95dd-36ff657a4dae_story.html>.

ASSIGNMENTS

1. Reading Response (30%): To help you enhance reading, exploration of the themes, and class discussion, this assignment asks you to respond in the form of blog entries (400-1000 words). While you don't need to present finished blog posts, you are encouraged to write clearly and with a broader audience in mind. Whenever possible, connect multiple texts and focus on the theme of the week. Discuss, critique, connect, and/or build on the key terms and/or arguments in the texts; assess the uses and limitations of the theoretical frames or their underlying assumptions; and/or pose questions and directions for the class to consider in light of your reflections on the issue at hand. Cite from the readings (with page numbers) for reference during class discussion. For initiating class discussions, you will be asked to either discuss your own posts or those of other members of class. Beyond preparation for class, consider your responses as an opportunity for developing your ideas for the larger assignments. Note: in order to allow other members of class to read your response before class, post it by noon on Monday; make sure to read everyone's responses in preparation for class.

2. Midterm Paper (20%): Pick a context or culture, rhetorical tradition or practice, artifact or medium of discourse, or a theme that crosses contexts or traditions and is rhetorically significant—then write an in-depth analysis, reflection, critique, or scholarly review on it (within 7-14 pages). You can write this assignment by conducting interviews, gathering other types of data, analyzing (a) text(s), doing archival research, and/or using library research. The topic/phenomena that you choose must evolve from, draw on, or be somehow relevant to the themes and issues that the class has studied (or is planning to study) together. Your project must either situate a local issue within a transnational or global perspective or focus on an issue from beyond local (North American) contexts.

3. Final Seminar Paper (35%): This is a standard research paper assignment that asks you to present a substantive theoretical argument or a pedagogical approach that you envision using as a teacher. You can continue to explore the same theme from the midterm paper (though the same text or ideas should not dominate this assignment) or develop and write on a new topic. As in the midterm paper, you must draw on the readings for class wherever feasible, but the assignment should be driven by what is essentially your own area of expertise as it begins to evolve by the time you start working on this assignment.

4. Presentation/Teaching, Conferences, Participation (15%): As a seminar, this course heavily depends on students' active participation in class. You will be asked to sign up for and lead at least one class discussion, as well as orally share your ideas with the class at the end of semester. You must meet with the instructor to discuss your plans and get feedback, as well as support other students through peer review and contribute to class activities (including class presentations, facilitation of conversations, etc.) as assigned by the instructor.

Course Schedule

	WORK FOR CLASS	WORK IN CLASS
Week 1		Introduction, syllabus, assignments, technologies used Discussion: times, places, themes
Week 2	World Rhetorics: Introduction Read Khagram and Levitt; Hesford; Mao; Connor	Discussion of readings Pick and discuss a rhetorical issue, tradition, theme

	WORK FOR CLASS	WORK IN CLASS
Week 3	Transaction and Trust Read Williams; S. Miller	Discussion of readings Guest lecture Student presentation
Week 4	No class: Conferences Midterm Paper proposal due	Bring Midterm Paper proposals to meeting
Week 5	World Rhetorics: GRAA and its Critiques Read Binkley and Smith; T. Miller, Baca; Cormier Midterm Paper draft due	Discussion of readings Review/discuss proposals Guest lecture Student presentation Peer review paper drafts (partners must read in advance)
Week 6	World Rhetorics: South Asia Read Mishra; Lloyd; Stroud Midterm Paper revised/final draft due	Discussion of readings Guest lecture Student presentation
Week 7	Knowledge and Education Read Reagan; Olid-Pena; Canagarajah	Discussion of readings Student presentation
Week 8	World Rhetorics: East and Far East Asia Read Wang; Miyahara; Swearingen and Mao; Sung-Gi Proposal for Final Paper due	Discussion of readings Student presentation
Week 9	Teaching and Learning Read Brydon; Craig; Matalene	Discussion of readings Guest lecture Student presentation
Week 10	World Rhetorics: Africa, Middle East Read Campbell; Koch; Hutto; Wright Draft of Final Paper due	Discussion of readings Student presentation Peer review paper drafts (partners must read in advance)

	WORK FOR CLASS	WORK IN CLASS
Week 11	Mediation and Openness/Access Watch Baraunik Read Pandey; Porter; Sharma and Bali	Discussion of readings Guest lecture
Week 12	World Rhetorics: AltRhet in West Read Bizzell and Jarratt; Grettano; Gage Revised draft of Final Paper due	Discussion of readings Final presentations
Week 13	Privacy and Sharing Read Markel; Zimmer; Sharma and Petty Presentation outline due (post on Blackboard)	Discussion of readings Guest lecture Final presentations
	THANKSGIVING BREAK	
Week 14	No readings: Last class	Final presentations Reflections

Where We Are: The "Global Turn" and Its Implications for Composition

"Where We Are" highlights where we are as a field on matters current and compelling. In these invited contributions, we bring together a small group of scholars at the forefront of a particular issue or practice, who together issue a progress report of sorts in 800-1200 words. –*Editor's Note*

Moving Beyond Methodological Nationalism

Rebecca Lorimer Leonard

This section affords the opportunity to consider terminology that has flourished under a "global turn" in composition. Even more, it offers space to think through the tensions between this terminology and the design of projects taken up under the aegis of these terms. How do we make sense of researching and understanding writing instruction under such a wide terminological umbrella?

Composition studies often permits the capacious use of terminology, wherein projects (or people) are defined in terms of what I think of as the global bin, a receptacle into which all multilingual, translingual, transnational, international, global, cultural/diversity/difference specialties are thrown and often conflated. Because terminological fuzziness can be confusing and is perceived to lack rigor—and because imprecise descriptors have real consequences for hiring, funding, the use of specialists, and so forth—conversations become focused on proposing, redefining, or delimiting terminology rather than pushing teaching and research toward shared goals and pressing questions. In these few paragraphs, I do not aim to argue for right or wrong terminology per se; rather, I would like to think about how composition might orient its projects toward the real problems pressing in on writing and the teaching of writing.

One way I have started this reorientation in my own research is by considering how to move beyond methodological nationalism. Methodological nationalism is an approach to research in which questions or conclusions focus on a singular entity like the nation-state. The approach assumes that a unit of analysis, whether nation, language, culture, religion, or community, is bounded; researchers working under this approach analyze or compare within or across these boundaries (Glick Schiller). The approach's ideology tends to reify the singularity of national or cultural experiences, sometimes connecting these to singular languages under study (Shuck). Methodological nationalism also often forwards theoretical conclusions that cannot work themselves out of nationalist conclusions because they depend on and thus respond to nation-based understandings of geopolitical forces (De Genova; Grewal). Methodological nationalism is implicit in much research and teaching across the social sciences and humanities, stemming from academic training, departmental designations, and fellowships or NGO funding streams (Glick Schiller and Salazar).

For example, research on literacy and writing instruction, with roots partly in anthropology and ethnography, often maintains a focus on singular cultures, communities, languages, or locations, a focus that makes sense for deep descriptions of localities. But this may be one reason why transnational or translingual perspectives on literacy, language, and rhetoric can appear to be novel even though they have historical precedent—if the methodological assumption is static, singular units, then analysis beyond these can feel new. But these contemporary perspectives are not always wholly novel, and instead are responding to changes in communication technology, transportation, and global economies that build on preexisting flows and linkages (Glick Schiller and Salazar; Gupta and Ferguson). In other words, moving beyond methodological nationalism involves both the disruption of bounded analyses and an acknowledgement of the idiosyncrasy of such boundedness in the first place.

Moving beyond methodological nationalism also entails designing a project—questions, theoretical framework, analysis—ahead or outside of received notions of nation and culture. Several methodological approaches do this. Transnational methodology indebted to Gayatri Spivak moves beyond comparative analysis to investigate inequality and power differentials in global and postcolonial contexts (Dingo; Grewal; Hesford "Cosmopolitanism"; Kaplan). Transnational methodology informed by sociology and anthropology pursues affiliations forged in social fields across national locations, analyzing movement and stasis together "within social and economic relationships rather than in relation to geographic borders" (Glick Schiller and Salazar 194). Diasporic methodologies analyze the doubled affective and political ties created by displacement not only among host and home communities but also among host communities that share a common home (Brah; Lavie and Swedenburg; Rouse). Catherine Kell has proposed tracing trajectories of literacy meaning-making or undertaking transcontextual analysis of literacy meanings projected across contexts, while Alastair Pennycook and Emi Otsuji's "metrolingualism" takes the city as a unit of analysis and explores the superdiversity of fluid and fixed languages moving across it.

All of these methodologies move beyond the generalities that can haunt the study of difference or diversity, even as they acknowledge the occasional political utility of strategic essentialism. Importantly, they also do not ignore the borders around cultures, nations, and languages, but instead treat borders and boundaries as socially significant but historically odd, as only meaningful in relation to phenomena diffusing across them. Most of all, these methodologies model a focus on puzzles and problems that move across, or begin beyond, "global" terminology.

In my own research I follow this lead by focusing not on a singular culture, community, or language, but on how migrant writers' movement among these alters or affects their literacy. I trace literate activity as it moves or stalls across social fields or scales, looking for the "constant tension" between border breakdown and subsequent reification (Waldinger 37). I aim to understand the impact of persistent language inequalities in postcolonial contexts as well as the active habits of contemporary linguistic discrimination that affect writers everywhere. My teaching and administrative work seeks to understand multilingual writers' struggles to have their literate repertoires recognized. I attempt to teach a focus on the socioeconomic tensions that allow or disallow repertoire mobility, guiding others to ask what tracing the repertoires that move into and across contexts reveals about literacy and language values.

These goals, shaped by a methodological stance beyond nationalism, show that the terms with which "global" research and teaching are conducted can be both more precise and less restricted. Precision should come from the specific site, project, or, especially, theoretical conversation addressed. Restriction—which terms are right, wrong, accepted, new, old—should be guided by a project-based alignment of questions, goals, and theory rather than field or institutional dicta. In this way research and teaching can continue to orient toward questions that matter under a global turn without treating the terms as research itself, a shift Wendy Hesford suggested almost a decade ago in her own thinking on a global turn ("Global Turn"). I recognize that "questions that matter" differ according to person or project. In my work, my questions are after literacy's movement, context, and value. While not necessarily global terms, these terms become significant to me when understood globally. Likewise, I wonder what might be revealed by a focus on global phenomena other than languages or locales. Can a shift in terms actually change the experiences of writers deemed "global"? I hope composition studies can continue to approach global projects with the open creativity required to find out.

Works Cited

Brah, Avtar. *Cartographies of Diaspora: Contested Identities.* New York: Routledge, 1996. Print.

De Genova, Nicholas. "'We are of the Connections': Migration, Methodological Nationalism, and 'Militant Research.'" *Postcolonial Studies* 16.3 (2013): 250-58. Print.

Dingo, Rebecca. *Networking Arguments: Rhetoric, Transnationalism, and Public Policy Writing.* Pittsburgh: U of Pittsburgh P, 2012. Print.

Glick Schiller, Nina. "A Global Perspective on Transnational Migration: Theorizing Migration Without Methodological Nationalism." *Diaspora and Transnational-*

ism: Concepts, Theories and Methods. Ed. Rainer Baubock and Thomas Faist. Amsterdam: Amsterdam UP, 2010. 109-29. Print.

Glick Schiller, Nina, and Noel Salazar. "Regimes of Mobility Across the Globe." *Journal of Ethnic and Migration Studies* 39.2 (2013): 183-200. Print.

Grewal, Inderpal. *Home and Harem: Nation, Gender, Empire and the Cultures of Travel*. Durham: Duke UP, 1996. Print.

Gupta, Akhil, and Ferguson, James. "Beyond 'Culture': Space, Identity, and the Politics of Difference." *Cultural Anthropology* 7.1 (1992): 6-23. Print.

Hesford, Wendy. "Cosmopolitanism and the Geopolitics of Feminist Rhetoric." *Rhetorica in Motion: Feminist Rhetorical Methods and Methodologies*. Ed. Eileen Schell and K. J. Rawson. Pittsburgh: U of Pittsburgh P, 2010. 53-70. Print.

---. "Global Turns and Cautions in Rhetoric and Composition Studies." *PMLA* 121.3 (2006): 787-801. Print.

Kaplan, Caren. *Questions of Travel: Postmodern Discourses of Displacement*. Durham: Duke UP, 1996. Print.

Kell, Catherine. "Inequalities and Crossings: Literacy and the Spaces-in-Between." *International Journal of Educational Development* 31.6 (2011): 606-13. Print.

Lavie, Smadar, and Ted Swedenburg, eds. *Displacement, Diaspora, and Geographies of Identity*. Durham: Duke UP, 2001. Print.

Pennycook, Alastair, and Emi Otsuji. *Metrolingulaism: Language in the City*. New York: Routledge, 2015. Print.

Rouse, Richard. "Mexican Migration and the Social Space of Postmodernism" *Diaspora: A Journal of Transnational Studies* 1.1 (1991): 8-23. Print.

Shuck, Gail. "Racializing the Nonnative English Speaker." *Journal of Language, Identity, and Education* 5.4 (2006): 259-76. Print.

Waldinger, Roger. *The Cross-Border Connection: Immigrants, Emigrants, and Their Homelands*. Cambridge: Harvard UP, 2015. Print.

Across Time and Space: The Transnational Movement of Asian American Rhetoric

Morris Young

In her 2006 essay examining the "global turn" in rhetoric and composition, Wendy Hesford sought to "foster reflection about the possibilities of an imagined global geography" and to "examine the ways in which scholars imperil or safeguard disciplinary identities and methods that take for granted the nation-state and citizen-subject as units of analysis and ignore the global forces shaping individual lives and literate practices" (789). Almost a decade later we have seen scholarship that takes up the "imagined global geography" come to the forefront of the field, often gaining recognition by the Conference on College Composition and Communication with its major awards (e.g., Adsanatham; Berry, Hawisher, and Selfe; Canagarajah; You).

While my own work has focused on Asian Americans and their rhetorical and literacy practices, I have begun to consider the implications of what Hesford identifies in her second point above: how scholars may "take for granted the nation-state and citizen-subject as units of analysis and ignore the global forces shaping individual lives and literate practices." What does it mean to reframe the rhetorical work of Asian Americans as a transnational process and practice? How does challenging the nation-state and citizen-subjects as the object of analysis reveal larger networks of activity? And perhaps most central to my current research is to consider the (trans) socio-historical contexts and global forces that have shaped Asian American lives and literate practices. That is, how do we think across time and understand the implications of history in the rhetorical practices of today's Asian Americans? How do we think across space both in terms of movement across actual borders between nations or locations and movement across discursive spaces that regulate the status and activity of people?

In my earlier work, *Minor Re/Visions: Asian American Literacy Narratives as a Rhetoric of Citizenship* and in my coedited collection with LuMing Mao, *Representations: Doing Asian American Rhetoric*, my goal was to define Asian American rhetoric, theorize rhetorical concepts, and understand how Asian Americans enter into the public sphere and engage in public debates on their own terms. In my current project, I consider the spatial dimensions, both metaphorical and material, that shape the conditions for rhetorical production. This raises questions about how we study space—especially one that is created by exigency and informed by history, culture, and a variety of social dimensions—and movement where the rhetorical activity of people exists not simply in the places they originate or in the places they settle.

For example, when the U.S. government created the "Asiatic Barred Zone" in the 1917 Immigration Act, this act served as a rhetorical strategy by the nation-state to metaphorically and materially write Asians out of the U.S., functioning as a spatial trope in U.S. national policy to contain Asians by keeping them outside its borders. However, rather than simply denying people entry, the Asiatic Barred Zone provided a means for rhetorical inclusion by allowing people marked as aliens ineligible for entry to and citizenship of the U.S. to respond with their own discursive acts to be written into U.S. national and legal discourse. Similarly Angel Island is a space that both regulated Asian bodies and facilitated rhetorical action. In late-nineteenth- and early-twentieth-century America, Chinese immigrants seeking the "Gold Mountain" of America accessible by life in California were processed at Angel Island, the immigration detention center in San Francisco Bay. While in bureaucratic limbo, they carved poems into the detention center walls, capturing their anguish and anger and claiming agency and identity through their words. Angel Island acted as a specific material site of rhetorical production where these early Asians in America responded to U.S. immigration policies, racial politics, and discrimination through delivery, appeal, and metaphor and literally writing their existence into place.

Finally let me point to three scholars whose work extends the transnational/transhistorical contexts that frame Asian American rhetorical activity. In focusing on the Filipino American National Historical Society (FANHS) and its founder and executive director, Dorothy Laigo Cordova, Terese Guinsatao Monberg works to "recover" the rhetorical legacy of Cordova, who has often been hidden from traditional scholarly references to FANHS. In Cordova's work Monberg shows how rhetorical study reveals the colonial relationship between the U.S. and the Philippines and the history of discursive movement between those nations in the work of FANHS. In *Writing Against Racial Injury*, Haivan Hoang examines the rhetorical activity of Vietnamese American students whose transnational movement and history is relatively recent. Hoang develops a theory of ethos and examines the use of memory to create rhetorical situations that challenge racism and write against injury. Finally, in *Relocating Authority: Japanese Americans Writing to Redress Mass Incarceration*, Mira Shimabukuro focuses on the rhetorical activity of Japanese and Japanese Americans held in WW II internment camps. In one example, she reveals how a group of Japanese American internees collaboratively wrote, published, and distributed bulletins that explicitly refused the military draft as long as the community was still "interned" against its will. Shimabukuro's work shows how this resistant rhetoric was "co-authorized" by local and global agents of both collective "damage" and collective "sponsorship."

What is exciting about the work of these three scholars is that it crosses historical boundaries (moving from the not-too-distant past to the contemporary), examines rhetoric and writing across genres and purposes, and seeks to understand specifically the relationship between Asian Americans and their uses of rhetoric. But underlying these studies of specific communities and actors is an understanding of how the movement of people across time and space interacts with structural forces that shape conditions and experiences of their rhetorical activity.

Works Cited

Adsanatham, Chanon. "'Civilized' Manners and Bloody Splashing: Recovering Conduct Rhetoric in the Thai Rhetorical Tradition." Diss. Miami University, 2014. Web. 22 Sept. 2015.

Berry, Patrick W., Gail E. Hawisher, and Cynthia L. Selfe. *Transnational Literate Lives in Digital Times.* Logan: Computers and Composition Digital P/Utah State UP, 2012. Web. 22 Sept. 2015.

Canagarajah, A. Suresh. "The Place of World Englishes in Composition: Pluralization Continued." *CCC* 57. 4 (2006): 586-619. Print.

Hesford, Wendy. "Global Turns and Cautions in Rhetoric and Composition Studies." *PMLA* 121.3 (2006): 787-801. Print.

Hoang, Haivan. *Writing Against Racial Injury: The Politics of Asian American Student Rhetoric.* Pittsburgh: U of Pittsburgh P, 2015. Print.

Mao, LuMing, and Morris Young, eds. *Representations: Doing Asian American Rhetoric.* Logan: Utah State UP, 2008. Print.

Monberg, Terese Guinsatao. "Listening for Legacies: Or, How I Began to Hear Dorothy Laigo Cordova, the Pinay Behind the Podium Known As FANHS." Mao and Young 83-105.

Shimabukuro, Mira. *Relocating Authority: Japanese Americans Writing to Redress Mass Incarceration.* Boulder: UP of Colorado, 2015. Print.

You, Xiaoye. *Writing in the Devil's Tongue: A History of English Composition in China.* Carbondale: SIUP, 2010. Print.

Young, Morris. *Minor Re/Visions: Asian American Literacy Narratives as a Rhetoric of Citizenship.* Carbondale: SIUP, 2004. Print.

The Global Turn and the Question of "Speaking From"

Bo Wang

In the past decade, rhetoric and composition scholars have called for "globalizing" the discipline to meet the challenges of globalization (Hesford; Hesford and Schell; Royster and Kirsch). A substantial body of work has been produced in the intersecting fields of rhetoric and composition to reset scholarly visions and priorities from a globalized, transnational perspective. Scholars have used global and transnational studies to challenge the existing theoretical assumptions and redraw the parameters of analysis in feminist rhetoric, comparative rhetoric, human rights rhetoric, composition, and other areas (Baca; Dingo; Dingo, Riedner and Wingard; Lyon; Wang). These works have not only integrated global and transnational studies into the discipline's critical operations but also articulated some larger goals for the future.

The transnational literacy practices, transnational feminist pedagogies, and other critical frameworks developed thus far have surely enabled us to see how the circulation and exchange of texts and artifacts in transnational spaces can alter our assumptions about rhetorical argument, audience, and situation. They have helped us consider how we can connect localized, individual stories to global networks so as to expose, rearticulate, and transform global power relations. Yet it seems to me that turning to the global entails a reflection on the question of "speaking from" (Mignolo). We may have to ask ourselves a new set of questions: What does it mean to "globalize" our discipline? How do we develop a globalized view of rhetoric and composition? In whose terms, and in the name of what kinds of knowledge or intellectual authority, are such scholarly practices performed? From which epistemic space and location are we speaking?

In my own work, I search the historical archives of early twentieth-century Chinese intellectuals' translations of euroamerican feminist discourse for insight and inspiration. My research shows that Chinese intellectuals translated a large number of euroamerican philosophical, literary, and historical texts on women's rights, putting the translated texts in conversation with their own cultural heritage and lived experience. For instance, Mary Wollstonecraft's *A Vindication of the Rights of Woman* and Henrik Ibsen's *A Doll's House*, among numerous euroamerican texts, were translated into Chinese and recontextualized by the Chinese debates on women's rights. Meanwhile, Confucian notions of humanity, self-cultivation, and womanhood were brought in dialogue with euroamerican concepts of human rights, individualism, and feminism. This translational work, or what I call "transrhetorical practice," exemplifies the dialectical processes by which concepts, theory, and discourse are translated, recontextualized and reconceived as they *move across* cultural, geopolitical borders.

I see transrhetorical practice as both a metatheoretical framework and inventional heuristic. More specifically, transrhetorical practice describes the meaning-making process of cross-cultural translation that takes place in the interstices of two or more different worlds caught in asymmetric power relations. This dialectical process brings self and other together and subjects both to transformation in close linguistic and cultural encounters. What this means for our scholarly practices is that a globalized rhetorical perspective must bring the language and symbolic practices of the other into an open-ended dialogue with euroamerican practices and allow plural local terms to frame and reframe one another across shifting cultural and historical contexts. In such dialogic exchanges, euroamerican practices will no longer be used as the norm to generate broad conceptual categories and universalizing theories; instead, both the universal and the particular are to be historicized to reveal the limitations of each term in its historical interconnectedness with other terms.

Transrhetorical practice is inevitably metonymic. As Maria Tymoczko notes in a different context, "the metonymies of translation are a key to the construction of the representations that translations project—whether they are representations of history, culture, values, or literary form" (57). That is, when concepts pass from one language to another, they must always be differently constructed through a new set of connections and contexts. This notion of translation accentuates the strategic choices the colonized made to establish authority by responding to the political, social, aesthetic, and ideological context of the receiving culture and giving voice to the native experience. For rhetoric and composition scholars, this means an awareness of the representational function of our work in the many worlds we traverse; it also implies a focus on the negotiation and exchange through which new rhetorical concepts, genres, and strategies are brought into being across languages, cultures, times and locations.

Transrhetorical practice is a spatial-temporal concept. It involves the creation and transmission of knowledge through time across different spatial-temporal spheres and cultural sites. Its horizon is historical; it situates the multiple interpretations and utterances of certain concepts generalized from particular times and spaces within their own geohistorical locations. Through recontextualization, transrhetorical practice links cultural specificities of language practices in a local environment with larger geopolitical forces and networks. As my own research has shown, drawing on classical and vernacular Chinese as well as euroamerican languages, early twentieth-century Chinese intellectuals experimented with neologisms to rearticulate what "women's rights" might mean to them. Their translations of such concepts constitute a new locus of enunciating "feminism" in transnational spaces. Thus, transrhetorical practice is a way of border thinking that may lead to new meanings and new ways of naming.

As we continue to "globalize" our discipline, enacting transrhetorical practice means that we need to think about the question of "speaking from" and consider local, native discourses and interventions as coeval contributions to global and transnational studies of rhetoric and composition. Recovering marginalized work by rhetors and writers outside of the metropolitan centers and identifying specific terms and concepts in their work to develop new interpretive frameworks—examples of transrhetorical practice—may help us expand our analytical vocabulary and include the other in the domain of a cross-cultural dialogue. The point of departure in such a dialogue, in my view, is no longer necessarily always anchored in euroamerican terms and concepts with which we are familiar and comfortable. We may as well experiment with plural local terms and use what we have learned from other cultures to engage with critical issues of mutual concern. Then we might be able to converse with rather than speak down to the other. We might be able to model for students the kind of reflexive, dialectical meaning-making process of reading and writing in transnational spaces. As such, transrhetorical practice might offer one way of imagining a globalized discipline of rhetoric and composition in our own time.

Works Cited

Baca, Damián. *Mestiz@ Scripts, Digital Migrations, and the Territories of Writing*. New York: Palgrave, 2008. Print.

Dingo, Rebecca. *Networking Arguments: Rhetoric, Transnational Feminism, and Public Policy Writing*. Pittsburgh: U of Pittsburgh P, 2012. Print.

Dingo, Rebecca, Rachel Riedner, and Jennifer Wingard, eds. *Transnational Feminisms*. Spec. issue of *JAC* 33.3-4 (2013): 517-669. Print.

Hesford, Wendy S. "Global Turns and Cautions in Rhetoric and Composition Studies." *PMLA* 121.3 (2006): 787-801. Print.

Hesford, Wendy S., and Eileen E. Schell, eds. *Transnational Feminist Rhetorics*. Spec. issue of *College English* 70.5 (2008): 461-528. Print.

Ibsen, Henrik. *A Doll's House*. Trans. Nicholas Rudall. Chicago: Ivan R. Dee, 1999. Print.

Lyon, Arabella. *Deliberative Acts: Democracy, Rhetoric, and Rights*. University Park: The Penn State UP, 2013. Print.

Mignolo, Walter D. *Local Histories/Global Designs: Coloniality, Subaltern Knowledges, and Border Thinking*. Princeton: Princeton UP, 2000. Print.

Royster, Jacqueline Jones, and Gesa E. Kirsch. *Feminist Rhetorical Practices: New Horizons for Rhetoric, Composition, and Literacy Studies*. Carbondale: SIUP, 2012. Print.

Tymoczko, Maria. *Translation in a Postcolonial Context: Early Irish Literature in English Translation*. Manchester: St. Jerome, 1999. Print.
Wang, Bo. "Comparative Rhetoric, Postcolonial Studies, and Transnational Feminisms: A Geopolitical Approach." *Rhetoric Society Quarterly* 43.3 (2013): 226-42. Print.
Wollstonecraft, Mary. *Vindication of the Rights of Woman*. 1792. New York: Penguin Books, 1982. Print.

Doing Transnational Writing Studies: A Case for the Literacy History Interview

Kate Vieira

Neither the pervasiveness of writing in everyday life nor the movement of people across international borders is abating. Global migration has increased 33% since 2000 (UNFPA), leaving millions of people negotiating family, politics, and money across borders (Waldinger). Likewise, according to Deborah Brandt's recent book, *The Rise of Writing*, more people are writing in more aspects of their lives, with as yet unknown emotional, cognitive, and civic consequences. Driving both trends are the familiar characters of our rapidly globalizing age—state politics, changing technologies, economic neoliberalism.

But how precisely do such macrosocial forces act on both writing and migration? How do they pressure the ways these two widespread experiences act on each other? And what do these intricate relationships mean for the lives and livelihoods of ordinary people, who are increasingly moving and writing across borders? Such questions, in my view, are at the heart of transnational composition studies today.

In this piece I make a brief case for one way we might begin to answer them. Specifically, I detail the utility of a data collection method that can help researchers trace how larger historical currents are enmeshed in transnational literacy: the literacy history interview (LHI).

Adapted from life history methods used by sociologists Daniel Bertaux and Martin Kohli and popularized by Deborah Brandt (in *Literacy in American Lives*), LHIs hone in on one aspect of a life, that of literacy, to examine how it courses through people's experiences, acting in concert with historical trends. Both ethnographically specific and historically broad, the LHI has recently helped transnational writing studies researchers explore Hmong literacy history in relation to colonization, war, and refugee status (Duffy, *Writing*); the cross-border movement of language and writing among educated migrant women (Lorimer Leonard); the global spread of English in post-communist Slovakia (Prendergast); the role of the state in Filipina labor migrants' literacy training (Lagman); and documented and undocumented migrants' writing in response to immigration policies (Vieira, *American*).

To sketch out one way LHIs do such work, I offer below a bare plot outline of an LHI from my recent fieldwork in the former Soviet and new European Union state of Latvia. There, I am working with transnational families to understand the relationship between shifting communication technologies and migration in the aftermath of political upheaval (for a similar study I conducted in Brazil, see Vieira, "Writing").

Consider, then, the following excerpted LHI of Katrina, a Latvian in her late 20s:

Katrina's earliest home was in a small town in Soviet Russia, where her grandparents cared for her while her mother finished her degree in Moscow. At six, she moved to Latvia with her mother, who began a new work assignment there. In kindergarten, then, Katrina learned basic literacy in Latvian. At home, she learned basic literacy in Russian to write letters to her left-behind grandparents. Later, on the heels of the impoverished *perestroika* years, her favorite aunt migrated to Western Europe, teaching Katrina to use email to communicate with her. Still later, after Latvia gained independence and joined the European Union, Katrina, fed up with subsistence wages, left for a job in Germany. She studied German to pass her medical boards and wrote a blog in English to negotiate the migration process.

This excerpt is spare but suggestive. One can make out a line between the Soviet Union's dictatorial job placement program and a child scratching out a letter in Cyrillic; between poverty amidst political transition and a teenager tapping her first email; between the European Union's economic inequality and a young woman's efforts to learn German; between the tumult of labor migration and the desire to compose in the blogosphere. As borders moved across people and people moved across borders, Katrina learned to write in new ways, knitting together a literacy network that, rooted in the east, was shifting westward. To establish such a preliminary analysis as support of a finding or a theory would require much more methodological work. Still, the way even one person remembers how literacy happened for her offers a window into writing's relationship with the wider, shape-shifting world.

Instead of conducting an LHI, I could have observed Katrina write at her computer, tracked her keystrokes, videotaped her gestures, attended her classes, collected her blog posts, and so forth. Such observational methods would illuminate what Paul Prior calls the "party" of literacy, its in-the-moment practices. LHIs, in contrast, get not so much at the writing practices of transnationals, but instead at Writing and The Transnational, as capital-letter trends that are nonetheless subjectively experienced.[1] They get not so much at the party of literacy, but at the relationship of literacy to the Party (excuse the pun). As such, LHIs help untangle the knotted threads of literacy and history—which, for those who have lived through migration, a violently changing political regime, or both, may be one of literacy's prevailing mysteries.

Transnational writing demands examination in relation to social inequality, political change, and technological innovation. It is this big picture played out across everyday lives to which LHIs afford us access. When carried out with the right combination of journalistic pushiness and compassion, and when analyzed sensitively and rigorously, LHIs can help reveal how letters, emails, languages, and blogs orient people in the larger historical and geographic landscapes across which they are moving and writing.

Acknowledgments

I am grateful to the University of Wisconsin Research Competition for funding data collection and the Spencer Foundation for funding data analysis, to Rebecca Lorimer Leonard for feedback and Margaret Bertucci Hamper for editing assistance.

Notes

1. As John Duffy has pointed out, LHIs' reliance on subjective understandings of literacy is a strength, lending the method value for work with marginalized populations ("Recalling").

Works Cited

Bertaux, Daniel, and Martin Kohli. "The Life Story Approach: A Continental View." *Annual Review of Sociology* 10 (1984): 215-37. Print.
Brandt, Deborah. *Literacy in American Lives.* Cambridge: Cambridge UP, 2001. Print.
---. *The Rise of Writing.* Cambridge: Cambridge UP, 2015.
Duffy, John. "Recalling the Letter: The Uses of Oral Testimony in Historical Studies of Literacy." *Written Communication* 24.1 (2007): 84-107. Print.
---. *Writing From These Roots: Literacy in a Hmong-American Community.* Honolulu: U of Hawai'i P, 2007. Print.
Lagman, Eileen. "Moving Labor: Transnational Migrant Workers and Affective Literacies of Care." *Literacy in Composition Studies*, 3.3 (2015). Web. < http://licsjournal.org/OJS/index.php/LiCS/article/view/95>.
Lorimer Leonard, Rebecca. "Traveling Literacies: Multilingual Writing on the Move." *RTE* 48.1 (2013): 13-39. Print.
Prendergast, Cathy. *Buying into English: Language and Investment in the New Capitalist World.* Pittsburgh: U of Pittsburgh P, 2008. Print.
Prior, Paul. "Combining Phenomenonological and Sociohistoric Frameworks for Studying Literate Practices: Some Implications of Deborah Brandt's methodological trajectory." *Literacy, Economy, and Power: Writing and Research after Literacy in American Lives.* Ed. John Duffy et al. Carbondale: SIUP, 2014. 166-84. Print.
UNFPA. "International Migration 2013 (wall Chart)." *United Nations Population Fund.* N.p., 2013. Web. 6 Sept. 2015. <http://www.unfpa.org/resources/international-migration-2013-wall-chart>.
Vieira, Kate. *American by Paper: How Documents Matter in Immigrant Literacy.* Minneapolis: U of Minnesota P, 2016. Print.
---. "Writing Remittances: Migration-Driven Literacy Learning in a Brazilian Homeland." *RTE*, 50.4 (2016). Print.
Waldinger, Roger. *The Cross-Border Connection: Immigrants, Emigrants, and their Homelands.* Cambridge: Harvard UP, 2015. Print.

Localizing Transnational Composition Research and Program Design

Amy Zenger

I am interested not only in how we embrace globalized, transnational, and international perspectives on research and teaching, but also how we theorize locality. Rhetoric and composition values research, program design, and teaching that "imaginatively address[es] the needs and opportunities of its students, instructors, institution, and locale" ("CCCC"). As the field has expanded in geographical scope, strong efforts have been made to valorize difference at the local level; the expansion of the field has also disclosed the ultimately local character of their work to U. S. compositionists (Muchiri, Mulamba, Myers, and Ndoloi).

My thinking about locality has been prompted by the ongoing project of reconstructing downtown Beirut after the 1975-90 civil war in Lebanon, which destroyed the downtown area, leaving empty and ravaged streets and buildings. The rebuilding project forced planners, architects, and governments to define what "Beirut" meant as a locality. Today, some critique the elegantly rebuilt city center on the grounds that they got it wrong, saying that the new urban core is "not really Beiruti."

Transnationalist theories offer a purchase on understanding the local not simply as "what is there" but in terms of the contestations that shape a place. Michael Peter Smith, an urban design theorist, writes that "even the most material elements of any locality are subject to diverse readings and given different symbolic significance by differently situated social groups and their corresponding discursive networks" (121). As a result, he argues, locality is "a highly politicized social space where representations of place are constructed and contested" (121). In *Modernity at Large*, Arjun Appadurai argues that localities are not simply there—a preexisting reality to which people adapt themselves; rather, localities are "inherently fragile social achievement[s]" (179). In social terms, becoming a local (for children or outsiders, for example) means learning how to engage in locality-producing practices (185).

As an American-trained compositionist working in the Middle East, I have questioned the ways I and others in my position conduct research or construct, revise, or administer composition programs outside of the U.S., particularly when these programs purport to adhere to American models of liberal arts education. Universities and programs have sprung up at an astonishing rate in this region, including programs replicated whole cloth from U.S. universities.

As we make choices that shape composition programs in these contexts, how should we understand what is local about these locales? All too often, the local—the "other" of transnational, international, global—is regarded in composition theory and practice as a naturalized space, "pure," and not demanding theorization. The problem with this commonsense definition is that it pushes us to accept the binarization of space (as global/local) reified in globalization discourses, and thus fails to provide us with a meaningful basis for making decisions. Research that does not account for the complexity of localization may only bring knowledge back to the "center" and reinforce North/South divisions, doing little to benefit the research locale. In terms of program design, one approach is to import practices, assignments, terminologies, entire curricula, administrative structures and even teachers and implement them directly, making adjustments in response to experiences on the ground. At another extreme is *localism,* a response Wendy Hesford (2006) cautioned against: a retreat behind rigidified boundaries, rejecting connections and ties across borders. Neither of these approaches engages with locale in optimal ways.

In composition, we have developed a good understanding of how to study the specificity of programs in comparison to each other (see Thaiss, Bräuer, Carlino, Ganobscik-Williams, and Sinha), but this does not give us a strong way to understand how each program becomes localized in the first place. Chris Thaiss offers *terroir* as a metaphor, suggesting an organic evolution, shaped by myriad natural conditions, to account for particularity in each of the programs documented in the study (6). Nedra Reynolds draws on social-constructionist theories of space to consider how metaphors of space shape the ways composition is imagined and practiced, and to explore how material spaces of writing are experienced, without, however, moving to transnational scales.

To put my question in more general terms, how is it that we define, construct, or rebuild *any* composition program or approach in relation to its locale? In my current research, I turn to theorists and practitioners in architecture, urban planning, and landscape design to see how they go about defining locality as a basis for design practice. My contention is that rhetoric and composition can benefit from identifying its own repertoire of planning tools and processes that would allow us to conceptualize locality for research and program design.

Transnational theories avoid representing global and local as intrinsically different forces that exist in binary opposition. Smith aims to intervene at the level of theory to show that the transnational, the national and the local work together in complex ways at different scales to shape the specificities of an urban space. He argues that "global and transnational networks are constituted by their interrelations with, and thus their groundedness *inside,* the local" (122, emphasis in original). According to him, transnational theory allows us to perceive the material and everyday "not as a sedentary, nostalgic site of 'local culture' but as a dynamic crossroads of local, national, and transnational place-making practices" (185). By insisting on the constructedness of place, transnational theorists offer compositionists approaches for meaningful local action in terms of research and program design. Envisioning localities as functioning simultaneously on local, national, and transnational scales allows us to avoid the global/local impasse imposed by globalization discourses. Some urban theorists also suggest approaching analysis and design in terms of values and strategies, rather than in terms of pre-conceived models or comprehensive plans. For example, Nan Ellin defines qualities of places "in flow" as *connectivity, porosity, hybridity, authenticity,* and *vulnerability*. Imagining program design and teaching in terms of values and strategies, rather than in terms of models to adopt, offers more flexible possibilities for defining our work in transnational contexts—which are, in effect, all contexts.

Works Cited

Appadurai, Arjun. *Modernity at Large: Cultural Dimensions of Globalization*. Minneapolis: U Minneapolis P, 1996. Print.

"CCCC Writing Program Certificate of Excellence." *Conference on College Composition and Communication*. N.p., n.d. Web. 20 Feb. 2015. <http://www.ncte.org/cccc/awards/writingprogramcert>.

Ellin, Nan. *Integral Urbanism*. New York: Routledge, 2006. Print.

Hesford, Wendy. "Global Turns and Cautions in Rhetoric and Composition Studies." *PMLA* 121. 3 (2006): 787-801. Print.

Muchiri, Mary N., Mulamba, Nshindi G., Myers, Greg, and Ndoloi, Deoscorous B. "Importing Composition: Teaching and Researching Academic Writing beyond North America." *CCC* 46.2 (1995): 175-98. Print.

Reynolds, Nedra. *Geographies of Writing: Inhabiting Places and Encountering Difference*. Carbondale: SIUP, 2004. Print.

Smith, Michael Peter. *Transnational Urbanism: Locating Globalization*. Oxford: Blackwell, 2001. Print.

Thaiss, Chris. "Origins, Aims, and Uses of Writing Programs Worldwide: Profiles of Academic Writing in Many Places." Thaiss, Bräuer, Carlino, Ganobscik-Williams, and Sinha 5-22.

Thaiss, Chris, Gerd Bräuer, Paula Carlino, Lisa Ganobscik-Williams, and Aparna Sinha, eds. *Writing Programs Worldwide: Profiles of Academic Writing in Many Places*. Fort Collins: WAC Clearinghouse and Parlor Press, 2012. Print.

Fast Movements, Slow Processes

Jay Jordan

This semester, for the second time in the last couple of years, I am leading a graduate seminar on histories of rhetoric. Little scholarship traces the development of multilingual composition in antiquity (with Brian Ray's article as a clear and excellent exception), so I typically feel like students and I hit a rich but untapped archival vein when we read Quintilian on early language acquisition and "Asiatic" styles, or when we confront Isocrates' simultaneous welcome of those we would now call "international students" and his proud defense of Athenian hegemony. Such encounters remind me and, I hope, my students that the "global turn," like many other turns, is not new. Thinking about the role that cultural and linguistic diversity play in rhetorical education has a history that significantly predates current discussions of "translingualism" or older discussions of "multiculturalism" or longstanding scholarship on "second language" writing. Such encounters also give me an opportunity to discuss global and international considerations in a broad context of rhetorical studies. So much has been made of the "division of labor" (Matsuda, "Composition Studies") between rhetoric and composition on one side and multilingual composition on the other that I feel compelled to wear away at the divide by calling attention to how rhetorical education itself has, perhaps always, tried to account for diverse nations, cultures, languages.

However, the global turn does productively collect a variety of ways in which rhetoric and composition scholars are attending to trends that, if not new, do seem especially intense now. In several ways, rhetoricians and compositionists are especially sensitive to the effects that immigration, international capital, terrorism, and projections of military force have on students' trajectories: perhaps no unit in a U.S. tertiary institution is as affected by shifts in enrollment numbers and demographics as is a writing program. So it makes a lot of sense, for example, to discuss ethnographic research, historiography, and homeland security alongside one another as Wendy Hesford does, or to think about interactions among neoliberalism, language education, and research as Christiane Donahue does and as Bruce Horner and John Trimbur do. The global turn, instead of naming a discrete phenomenon, can instead name a helpful heuristic that synthesizes work across parts of the field and even from other fields that may otherwise seem disparate.

But paths opened by this kind of broad heuristic can encourage fast-paced, even breathless excursions. If a goal of synthetic work is, as I take it to be, to broaden our initial scholarly focus to account for different terms, concepts, theories, and pedagogies, then a further and related goal should be to pay close attention to histories and theories of different scholarly and pedagogical traditions while avoiding both uncritical uptake and dismissal. One key and personally significant example is relevant. Since 2011, an emerging and at times heated scholarly conversation has taken up the term "translingualism." Indeed, I have contributed to that conversation myself (Jordan). I have also signed documents that take nuanced positions about what the term means, might mean, and/or should mean (Atkinson, Tardy, Crusan, Matsuda, Ortmeier-Hooper, Ruecker, and Simpson; Horner, Lu, Royster, and Trimbur). I have listened to, participated in, and helped mediate conversations that have become further published statements (Canagarajah, "The End"; Canagarajah, *Translingual*; Matsuda, "It's the Wild West"; Matsuda, "The Lure"). While I do not have space here to rehearse claims, I will write that I have felt myself pulled by both "sides" of a debate about what role translingual approaches can play in view of the long history of the field of second language writing. I appreciate translingualist colleagues' impatient questions about "language" as a category—questions that do not always lead immediately to teaching programs but that nonetheless must be asked. I also appreciate second language writing colleagues' concerns that a rush to claim credit for doing translingual work risks leaving behind a robust tradition of empirical research and pedagogical rigor related to the hard work of learning additional languages.

How, then, can a scholar-teacher energized by critical approaches to language research and pedagogy, and eager to learn reliable strategies for working with multilingual students, balance innovation, inquiry, and groundedness? I am still working on my own answer, but my experience in a test bed for international education is helping me think about it. I taught last year in South Korea for my home institution's international campus in a multi-university experiment in a new city. Encouraging and disturbing evidence of the global turn was everywhere—gleaming new towers built on spec, ubiquitous data infrastructures, flags representing pan-Asian student backgrounds, ecologically damaging land reclamation. The fast pace of those developments, though, was belied at times by the careful, even painstaking, work our students were doing across their courses. In the middle of evident and quick "transcultural flows" (Pennycook) were students who were continuing the long, slow process of language acquisition at the same time they were beginning the long, slow process of learning to write for a fairly typical U.S. university curriculum. As the one-person "writing center," I engaged students with questions that focused on their rhetorical innovations. And I asked those questions along with others that acknowledged their struggle with differences between English prepositions and Korean postpositions. In other words, I was compelled by my own position on the globe and in a global flow to pay attention both to fast movements (i.e., often-novel responses to English-Korean language contact) and slow processes (i.e., language correction). My ongoing challenge—and I think one for the field as well—is to find ways to maintain such disparate focuses. Language learners are also rhetorically adept students, and they always have been both. A WPA's pressing need to staff a "multilingual" section is also an opportunity to innovate pedagogically. Language teaching involves linguistics and political economies. The global turn is not new, but it is, as it has always been, a contradictory and important opportunity.

Works Cited

Atkinson, Dwight, Christine Tardy, Deborah Crusan, Paul Kei Matsuda, Christina Ortmeier-Hooper, Todd Ruecker, and Steve Simpson. "Clarifying the Relationship Between L2 and Translingual Writing: An Open Letter to Writing Studies Editors and Organization Leaders." *College English* 77.4 (2015): 383-86. Print.

Canagarajah, A. Suresh. "The End of Second Language Writing?" *Journal of Second Language Writing* 22.4 (2013): 440-1. Print.

---. *Translingual Practice: Global Englishes and Cosmopolitan Relations.* New York: Routledge, 2012. Print.

Donahue, Christiane. "'Internationalization' and Composition Studies: Reorienting the Discourse." *CCC* 61.2 (2009): 212-43. Print.

Hesford, Wendy S. "Global Turns and Cautions in Rhetoric and Composition Studies." *PMLA* 121.3 (2006): 787-801. Print.

Horner, Bruce, and John Trimbur. "English Only and U.S. College Composition." *CCC* 53.4 (2002): 594-630. Print.

Horner, Bruce, Min-Zhan Lu, Jacqueline Jones Royster, and John Trimbur. "OPINION: Language Difference in Writing: Toward a Translingual Approach." *College English* 73.3 (2011): 303-21. Print.

Jordan, Jay. "Material Translingual Ecologies." *College English* 77.4 (2015): 364-82. Print.

Matsuda, Paul Kei. "Composition Studies and ESL Writing: A Disciplinary Division of Labor." *CCC* 50.4 (1999): 699-721. Print.

---. "It's the Wild West Out There: A New Linguistic Frontier in U.S. College Composition." *Literacy as Translingual Practice: Between Communities and Classrooms.* Ed. A. Suresh Canagarajah. New York: Routledge, 2013. 128-38. Print.

---. "The Lure of Translingual Writing." *PMLA* 129.3 (2014): 478-83. Print.

Pennycook, Alastair. *Global Englishes and Transcultural Flows.* London: Routledge, 2006. Print.

Ray, Brian. "A Progymnasmata for Our Time: Adapting Classical Exercises to Teach Translingual Style." *Rhetoric Review* 32.2 (2013): 191-209. Print.

The "Trans" in Transnational-Translingual: Rhetorical and Linguistic Flexibility as New Norms

Christiane Donahue

I have lived transnationally and translingually as a student and a scholar for some years now. My experiences studying, as a PhD candidate, and then working—as a scholar, a member of multi-country European research projects and university research laboratories, and an invited professor in multiple institutions—have transformed my life and my approach to writing research.

Human instinct when encountering the new, the different, the "other," seems to tend towards the "compare" instead of the "trans." When I began my PhD work in France in 1992, I had designed a study that analyzed student writing in the U.S. and France, at the transition point between high school and college (see Donahue, *Ecrire à l'Université*). I wanted to explore systematically what might be different in these two populations' writing. But, using analytic approaches from French linguistics that were new to me, I learned that, if I worked past surface linguistic differences, the students in both contexts negotiated, appropriated, resisted, and adapted their way into college writing using quite similar rhetorical moves.

This was my first inkling that flexibility—rhetorical flexibility—is what matters, and a "trans" understanding of language, rhetoric, teaching, and learning is essential to *any* future we imagine or have already begun, whether within the U.S. or in dialogue with other global contexts.

Globalization's forces and flows should foster a spirit of constant questioning of assumptions, a flexible openness to linguistic and rhetorical difference, and a resistance to the urge to compare. While language is only one aspect of the global/international context we are in, it is indexical of the complex multilayered meaning-making dynamic that defines writing research today. How we—all writing scholars everywhere—choose to encounter its challenges and promises makes all the difference.

For decades, scholars around the world have been observing and studying the shifting complexity of our student populations and the diversity of linguistic experiences students bring with them. The research suggests that every context is multilingual, even ones that appear monolingual; we are moving beyond diversity and multiplicity to what Steven Vertovec has called *super*diversity.

Superdiversity is a social, economic, and linguistic phenomenon that provokes the development of translingual activity via "new experiences of space and 'contact'; new forms of cosmopolitanism and creolisation (including codeswitching and multilingualism); transnationalism and integration…" (Vertovec 1044). Superdiversity also underscores the way distinctions such as "first" or "second" language do not meet the realities on the ground in this complex context of *contact* (Blommaert and Rampton 15).

Such global change cannot *not* affect language and writing. Global interconnectedness affects flows of language, language ability, texts (print and otherwise), and academic participation in multiple pathways; almost no one works in isolation. Such sweeping change certainly affords some significant shifting in composition's understanding of what writers might need and why, though affordance alone does not produce change. In a translingual model, every writer, in a superdiverse world, needs to *design* communication and meaning-making—utterances—using linguistic resources and make linguistic decisions that figure alongside the decisions the writer makes about mode or genre. That is, "in a translingual frame [...] adaptability in *language* joins the adaptability we already know writers must have across modes and media, genres and contexts" (Donahue, "Writing, English"). We might think about the ability to "re-language" much as we have carefully thought through "re-mediation."

A translingual model—as an orientation, a set of attitudes and perspectives (Canagarajah)—assumes that, as Mary Louise Pratt noted in 1991, linguistic negotiation is always part of the construction of meaning, no matter the language or combination of languages. Linguist Carol Myers-Scotton posits negotiation, in the frame of what linguists call "contact linguistics" (analyzing the linguistic outcomes of people, groups, and societies coming into contact with each other), as a key to achieving a co-construction of meaning (21). For Vertovec, individuals who successfully negotiate, picking and choosing among their various cultural and linguistic "belongings," achieve mobility (80). Pratt suggests even marginalized members of a contact interaction can achieve dialogue and power via what she has called transculturation.

The translingual model foregrounds prioritizing "what the writers are doing with language and why" over whether language use is standard (Horner, Lu, Royster and Trimbur 305), considers all languages in the presence of other languages and internally heterogeneous (Pennycook), and explains "communicative competence" as the transformative ability to merge language resources (Molina 1245), a mixed, meshed, negotiating reuse accompanied by a mindset of flexibility and decentering (Canagarajah).

The translingual model has been discussed frequently in relation to L2 writing research and teaching models. But the discipline of L2 writing and the translingual model do not so much intersect as run parallel; to entwine L2 writing in oppositional translingual discussions or vice versa is to misunderstand both L2 work and the translingual model, which I believe is a rhetorical model important to the work of composition broadly speaking, rather than a model destined to supersede L2 writing (its "next phase") or to redirect current transformative, essential models of L2 writing instruction.

While translingualism is the most widespread term currently, other terms seek to represent the same language dynamic in slightly different ways. Adrian Blackledge, Angela Creese, and Jaspreet Takhi review several terms, including Creese et al.'s flexible bilingualism, J. Normann Joergensen's and L.M. Madsen's polylingual languaging, Ben Rampton's contemporary urban vernaculars, Emi Otsuji and Alistair Pennycook's metrolingualism, and Creese and Blackledge's and Ofellia Garcia's "translanguaging" (192). Paul Kei Matsuda and others have suggested that "diglossia" might be a stronger linguistic term for side-by-side language uses (133). Blackledge, Creese, and Takhi argue forcefully for Bakhtinian-inspired *hetero*glossia (or polyphony, in European writing scholarship) as the most flexible model for the kind of literate-linguistic action in play, as it accounts for multivoicedness, intralingual diversity, and intralangue variation (194).

These ongoing discussions about ways to name and understand translingual activity suggest that it is dynamic and interdisciplinary, and that composition should build from and move beyond the focus on "pluri" or "multi" or "trans" or "inter" or "cross," as all of these prefixes imply an *a priori* distinct separate set of linguistic codes and cultural or identity units (see also Horner, Lu, Royster, and Trimbur).

The flexibility in writers' language use this model encourages and embraces is the same flexibility we need in approaching and understanding writing research outside our usual contexts. In a transnational and translingual context, how we choose to encounter international research, grounded in different histories, populations, or local contexts, is vital to how we can make progress in the world. Often, the difference in research is a difference in discipline just as easily encountered here in the U.S. (say, between education or sociology and writing studies), or a difference in time—regarding when, in its research arc, a particular community moves to a particular approach. An approach like textual analysis, considered warily these days in writing studies unless the text is studied embedded in its context, could be reconsidered in light of alternative approaches such as keystroke logging or eye tracking to better understand the back-and-forth of its production, or Bakhtinian-Volosinovian analysis of each word as a permeable capsule of socially-saturated meaning.

What if we "trans-d" rather than "compared"? Our research landscape and how we interact with other research traditions and other approaches to writing research and writing instruction is changing. Here, our instinct to compare is the most front and center. We encounter new educational-institutional contexts, new ways of thinking about writing and writing instruction, and we are quick to note differences or even "lack."

My point is not, I want to emphasize, aimed towards U.S. scholars only. My European colleagues often have the same tendency to compare rather than to "trans." A transnational-translingual model offers a way for us to move *into* the conversation differently. Claims being made world-wide about the massive shift to publishing in English should not lead us to believe all scholarly exchanges will be *transparent* but rather that they will be trans*lingual* and trans*national*. Rhetorical and linguistic flexibility are new norms as we unavoidably become international and global, as superdiversity and contact become the natural context for us all. They are norms for every writer, speaker, student, scholar, mono- (if we can still imagine mono-) or multi-lingual. They are, like the flexibility to work consciously and effectively across modes and genres, a necessary part of the fabric of our meaning-making work today.

Works Cited

Blackledge, Adrian, Angela Creese, and Jaspreet Takhi. "Beyond Multilingualism: Heteroglossia in Practice." *The Multilingual Turn: Implications for SLA, TESOL and Bilingual Education*. Ed. Stephen May. New York: Routledge, 2013. 191-215. Print.

Blommaert, Jan, and Ben Rampton. "Language and Superdiversity." *Diversities* 13.2 (2011): 1-22. Print.

Canagarajah, A. Suresh, *Translingual Practice: Global Englishes and Cosmopolitan Relations*. New York: Routledge, 2013. Print.

Donahue, Christiane. *Écrire À L'université: Analyse Comparée, France-États-Unis*. Villeneuve-d'Asq: Presses Universitaires Du Septentrion, 2008. Print.

---. "Writing, English, and a Translingual Model for Composition." *Composition, Rhetoric, and Disciplinarity: Traces of the Past, Issues of the Moment, and Prospects for the Future*. Ed. Kathleen Yancey, Susan Miller-Cochran, Elizabeth Wardle, and Rita Malenczyk. Forthcoming. Print.

Horner, Bruce, Min Zhan Lu, Jacqueline Jones Royster, and John Trimbur. "Language Difference in Writing: Toward a Translingual Approach." *College English* 73.3 (2011): 303-21. Print.

Matsuda, Paul Kei. "It's the Wild West Out There: A New Linguistic Frontier in U.S. College Composition." *Literacy as Translingual Practice*. Ed A. Suresh Canagarajah. New York: Routledge, 2013. 128-38. Print.

Molina, Clara. "Curricular Insights into Translingualism as a Communicative Competence." *Journal of Language Teaching and Research JLTR* 2.6 (2011): 1244-251. Print.

Myers-Scotton, Carol. *Duelling Languages: Grammatical Structure in Codeswitching*. New York: Clarendon, 1993. Print.

Pennycook, Alastair. "English As A Language Always In Translation." *European Journal of English Studies* 12.1 (2008): 33-47. Print.

Pratt, Mary Louise. "Arts of the Contact Zone". *Profession* (1991): 33-40. Print.

Vertovec, Steven. "Super-diversity and Its Implications." *Ethnic and Racial Studies* 30.6 (2007): 1024-054. Print.

Book Reviews

The Translanguaging Conversation: A Dialogic Review

Reworking English in Rhetoric and Composition: Global Interrogations, Local Interventions, edited by Bruce Horner and Karen Kopelson. Carbondale: SIUP, 2014. 260 pp.

Literacy as Translingual Practice: Between Communities and Classrooms, edited by Suresh Canagarajah. New York: Routledge: 2013. 247 pp.

Reviewed by Mark Brantner, National University of Singapore, Alanna Frost, University of Alabama-Huntsville, and Suzanne Blum Malley, Columbia College Chicago

> There has been a disconnect between scholarship and everyday communicative practices.
>
> —Suresh Canagarajah, *Translingual Practice* (2013)

In this dialogic review, we explore the constructs of translanguaging and a translingual orientation to language and literacy practices as they are directly and indirectly referenced in *Reworking English in Rhetoric and Composition: Global Interrogations, Local Interventions,* edited by Bruce Horner and Karen Kopelson and *Literacy as Translingual Practice: Between Communities and Classrooms* edited by Suresh Canagarajah. As the title of Canagarajah's volume indicates, his edited collection most directly addresses the translingual, but, in both texts, contributors address translanguaging as a necessary paradigm shift for our discipline and beyond. The call for that shift to a translingual orientation, approach, perspective, construct, and/or practice is both complex and compelling. Translingual practices in our collective communicative realities, according to these texts, have a longer historical and practical presence than modern, institutionally embedded, and politically expedient monolingual views of languages as discrete and additive systems with clearly defined "native-speaker" standards that "nonnative" speakers must strive to achieve. A translingual orientation, in contrast, makes room for the agency of speakers and the full repertoire of their multimodal communicative resources. In other words, and as is stressed throughout both of these edited collections, translanguaging is the communicative reality of global citizens and, as such, is essential to the investigative and pedagogical choices of composition scholars.

Both edited collections reflect the developing and often contested state of the translanguaging conversation in our field. Thus, both collections are, essentially, divided into sections that theorize "languaging;" offer contextualized, local cases of translanguaging practice; and, finally, make the pedagogical turn to consider activity in specific institutions and classrooms. Koppelson and Horner's first section "Reworking Language" does similar work to Canagarajah's part I, "Premises." In both, contributors carve out space for translanguaging conversations by interrogating language research and teaching and by demonstrating that negotiations of language difference are already a part of the communicative practices of communities. We argue that Canagarajah's, collection, which is divided into five sections, also does this work in part III, where contributors critique rhetoric and composition's translanguaging conversations. The second section of both texts, "Location and Migrations" (Horner and Kopelson) and "Community Practices" (Canagarajah), are the most specific in regards to conducting the empirical work of identifying translanguaging practices. Again, Canagarajah also offers this research in his collection's part IV, "Research Directions." Finally, each collection ends with sections that offer the ubiquitous pedagogical turn, offering classroom cases and specific instructional practices.

We approach this review from our own experiences with a translingual orientation to literacy practices in distinct institutional and social contexts, and each of us is keenly aware that we, like other scholars in rhetoric and composition, as well as researchers in second language writing, literacy studies, sociolinguistics, applied linguistics, and language education, currently have an uneasy relationship with translanguaging as a paradigm-shifting construct. In her afterword to *Reworking English,* Karen Kopelson addresses the complicated interplay of sociopolitical factors and the statist and modernist narratives of English dominance that undergird that unease, often framed as resistance or inattention, making room for a translingual orientation to writing. Kopelson highlights key tensions present across the collection, noting that "regardless of how we choose to treat attachments to language, it is necessary to remember that they are *experienced as fixed* [emphasis original], and this affective attachment is affixed further by powerful ideological supports" (212). Chipping away at those ideological supports to create an opening for a translingual disposition is difficult work and it is important to note that neither *Reworking English* nor *Literacy as Translingual Practice* does so by offering a definitive statement on translingual literacy. As Canagarajah points out explicitly in his introductory remarks, "It is too early for that kind of book" (8). Instead, these collections offer investigations of and arguments for the perceived value of a translingual orientation to communication and to writing, and contributing authors lay the groundwork for further productive development of the theories, histories, and pedagogies that bridge the disconnect between communicative realities and our classrooms.

As reviewers, we have a shared sense of the value of expanding our notions of language and literacy to encompass translingual practices, as well as somewhat different levels of appreciation for the arguments made by each of the contributors to *Reworking English* and *Literacy as Translingual Practice*. Mark approaches these texts as a rhetorician and teacher-scholar at the National University of Singapore in a first-year writing program modeled on the Harvard College Writing Program, situated in the Asian context of the larger internationalization of higher education. Alanna comes to her stance as a reviewer through her role as a WPA at University of Alabama–Huntsville and as a rhetoric and composition teacher-scholar with a social justice perspective grounded in her ethnographic work with First Nations Dakelh women in British Columbia, Canada. Suzanne is informed by her position as rhetoric and composition teacher-scholar with a long history of heading up the English as an Additional Language Program at Columbia College Chicago and a background in Spanish applied linguistics and foreign language teaching. In what follows, we engage in a conversation about how specific ideas and specific chapters in the edited collections we are reviewing further and/or challenge our developing notions of translingual practices and translingual writing.

Suzanne: All three of us believe that a translingual orientation to language invites a paradigm shift for writing studies in ways that mirror the process and post-process movements that developed over the course of several decades (the late 1960s into the early 2000s). Engaging the work of shifting our notion of language, a construct that undergirds our entire discipline, causes, necessarily, a great deal of angst, a great deal of questioning, and a great deal of struggling to define just what "it" is that we are trying to get our heads around and what we will do with "it" when we get there. Both of these edited collections include that type of foundational work, which is so important but also ends up being a bit amorphous and messy. As a result, I am struck by what seems to be our collective desire to simultaneously name and not name what we mean by translanguaging and/or translingual literacy. Horner notes the multiplicity of terms used for the newly developing ideological framework for understanding linguistic difference in the introduction to *Reworking English*, pointing out "this emerging perspective has been "variously identified as 'plurilingual,' 'translingual,' 'transcultural'—and that heralds ideals of créolité, interculturalité, diversalité (in contrast to multiculturalism and diversité)" (3). Moreover, the terms multilingual, code-meshing, and code-switching, among others, are also used throughout both collections. While Paul Kei Matsuda makes an excellent case for an understanding of the language acquisition and language education scholarship that informs both the ideological framework and the terms we are using (Canagarajah 136), I am convinced by Canagarajah's argument that we need the neologism translingual "to treat cross-language interactions and contact relationships as fundamental to all acts of communication and relevant for all of us. In this sense, the shift in literacy is not relevant for traditionally multilingual students/subjects alone, but for 'native' speakers of English and 'monolinguals' as well" (2). I agree that naming a translingual orientation to language and to communication pushes us to see languaging competencies as integrated, as comprised of all of the languages and registers we have at our disposal and, with the "it" named, we can take a deeper dive into why the new paradigm is relevant to composition and rhetoric and how we, as teacher-scholars, can productively engage with it.

Alanna: Indeed, the question of why a new paradigm is relevant to composition and rhetoric engages the scholars in both texts. In Canagarajah's collection, understanding the relevance of the translingual paradigm means turning to community practices to bolster evidence of the "everyday" of translingual practice. It is most obviously evidenced in the "Community Practices" section of the text, where contributors offer cases of translingual communicative work, from Asian American (Morris Young), indigenous (Ellen Cushman; Jon Reyhner), Lebanese (Nancy Bou Ayash), and Kenyan contexts (Esther Milu), but the premise (and argument embedded in much of Canagarajah's work) is that translanguaging has been, for quite some time, nowhere more evident than in communal private and public spaces. In the "Research Directions" section, for example, Christiane Donahue carefully describes her research on French and English students' writing to demonstrate both the ways that students are already "translingually disposed" and to argue for further cross-disciplinary analysis of student discourse. Similarly, Rebecca Lorimer's argument, and productive case studies of immigrants' rhetorical attunement, documents the existing strategies and dynamic attention of communicative choices.

Mark: I think Marilyn M. Cooper does useful theoretical work towards the *why* of translanguaging. Cooper's thinking of language in terms of practices and her commitment to their ethical dimensions is a step in the right direction (Horner and Kopelson). What might happen when we think of language in terms of its use, and are we willing to take responsibility for those uses? For example, higher education writing instruction in Singapore has traditionally been tied to British or Australian traditions, but recently it has drawn more directly from American writing programs and theories—as I mentioned earlier, our program was modeled on Harvard's. And in a larger, Asian context, I see the internationalization of (American) higher education, which is clearly expanding and intensifying. More U.S. universities are partnering with universities and opening branch campuses in other countries. In Singapore, Yale and Duke partnered with my university; State University of New York–Buffalo, University of Nevada Las Vegas, and New York University opened (and closed) satellite campuses; and several European and Australian universities offer degrees. Singapore illustrates larger trends across Asia. The internationalization of higher education creates an educational landscape that imports and exports—students, labor, pedagogies, histories—but rarely combines different linguistic theories, cultural histories, and pedagogical traditions. Schools from around the world may operate in the same city, yet they tend to operate in silos. But as students progress from primary through graduate education, they may move among these institutions with divergent expectations of writing.

Alanna: Both texts rely on the work of Alastair Pennycook, who, amongst his important studies of communication in communities, critiques the export of English via English Language Teaching, in part for obliviousness to local language practice. But I am also concerned with how it imports. As the recently former WPA and the newly appointed department chair, I have engaged directly with administrative concerns relating to multilingual students. Most recently, I attended a meeting at which participants voiced concerns about new agreements between our university's administrators and Chinese universities for "2 plus 2" transfers. Students from the Chinese schools are to be given credit for the first two years of their degrees, completed at home, and the junior and senior years completed at our school; concerns involve the students' English proficiency. The conversations in the meeting began with the ubiquitous worry about the students' ability to produce standard written English (SWE) before moving on to the specific bureaucratic issue about how to count courses that only loosely resemble our general education requirements.

What the chapters of both collections offer, for the most part, are pragmatic, historical, and theoretical arguments that I can present to my colleagues. The chapters I find most compelling are those that speak to my own felt-sense of the injustice of English-only policy, begun in my own work with indigenous people and fed through advocacy of the interests of international and multilingual students at my own institution, who can get caught in cycles of remediation because they check the "limited" box on their applications, indicating that their first languages are not English.

Mark: Alanna, you talk about your strategies for making arguments to your colleagues. In Maria Jerskey's chapter, she describes the Literacy Brokers Program that she developed to support multilingual faculty at LaGuardia Community College (Canagarajah). Touted as a "safe house," the writing circle's goal was to support multilingual faculty's writing. But she finds that working with faculty produced unanticipated responses and created surprising collaborations among faculty and administrators. I think her article reminds us that such programs (as well as discussions like you're having) are messy, filled with challenges but also opportunities for surprises.

Alanna: And both edited collections, I think, offer suggestions for opportunities. Like Mark, I found compelling Marilyn M. Cooper's careful review of scholars who argue (essentially and often) for an ecological view of language production that is dependent on the communicative act between communicators, particularly as she situates this ecological view as combating the "linguistic misbehaviors" that result from SWE propagation. Similarly, I am convinced by Brice Nordquist's assertion that English handbooks are also a culprit in the propagation of SWE. In Canagarajah's collection, I am drawn to Ellen Cushman's consideration of the Cherokee writing system as an example of "the evolution of indigenous writing technologies" which developed alongside and in spite of SWE (92).

Mark: Yeah, I was really struck by Scenters-Zapico's piece (Horner and Kopelson). I really appreciated his discussions of indirect and direct literacy sponsors. I hear about these kinds of sponsorships all the time from people who migrate across national borders in Southeast Asia. Many people who migrate to Singapore tell me stories about how friends or relatives made their language learning possible by providing technological access, especially cell phones.

Alanna: In Canagarajah's text, Scott Wible describes responsible practice as evidenced by the multilingual work that went into the creation of the "World Social Forum." Wible cites the Forum's policy of supporting "multilingual meetings" by supplying translators to all participants, so that their contributions in their native language are valued (43). Similarly LuMing Mao's articulation of "indigenous rhetorics" speaks to the efficacy of local and iconic discourses of communicative power (Canagarajah 47; Horner and Kopelson 77). Mao's essays in both collections help us rethink the idea of an indigenous rhetoric in relation to globalization. He complicates the role of origin in indigenous rhetorics and expands it by considering the contingent historical encounters of competing discourses within those spaces that link back in various ways to this "origin." Mao's use of "interdependence-in-difference" will become, I think, a crucial idea for thinking about how, as he says, "discourses travel" (Canagarajah 53).

Mark: Right—Nancy Bou Ayash also addresses this issue directly as she traces the specific history of language instruction in Singapore and Lebanon (Horner and Kopelson). Her piece cautions that American writing pedagogies could be at odds with local policy. I agree. When American writing pedagogies come to Singapore, they encounter not only Mandarin, Malay, Tamil, and (mostly British) English, but a history filled with rich language differences. These three contributions give us pause to consider the forces that are at play in any context. I worry that as we dismantle our own dominant, monolithic conception of English, we will forget that other languages are shaped by historical forces as well.

Suzanne: Mark, I think you voice here precisely some of the concerns that undergird the resistance to translanguaging as a construct—that we will forget that languages (all of them) are shaped by historical and socio-political forces and social interaction. For me, the opening to a translingual approach invites us to always remember that all communicative practice is shaped by and constantly being reshaped by historical, social, political, and contact forces. The power dynamics that are easily hidden by ideologies of native and dominant languages might be more effectively revealed with a translingual orientation to languaging.

Mark: Geographic forces are at play, too. As Charles Bazerman's sketch of writing instruction around the world shows, our research-based writing pedagogies also differ from those in other places (Canagarajah 13). Our history of qualitative research is strong, vibrant, and important, but other locations around the world have adopted more social scientific approaches to studying writing. Again, I think that Cooper's call to think of language as a practice can be a way to bridge these approaches, as theories of practice exist in many social science fields. And practices can help us delineate the specific locations and objects of study for us. In fact, as I read both of these books, I thought a more developed theory of practices may be useful to many of the articles. It would, I think, help pin down the concrete and specific situations of writing.

Suzanne: I agree that we need a more developed understanding the definition, theory, and practices relating to translanguaging, and I think that in essence, these collections in juxtaposition offer very good starting points for exploring what we are developing and what we are pinning down. If, however, we do adopt translingual/translanguaging as the name for that work, for me it is absolutely essential that we pay very close attention to the scholarship that has influenced our arrival at this naming. In *Literacy as Translingual Practice* Matsuda, Donahue, and Dorothy Worden all caution against considering only the scholarship and methods of composition and rhetoric and provide excellent suggestions for how we might be thoughtful about and careful in developing theory and examining translingual practices by utilizing cross-disciplinary and cross-cultural perspectives. Matsuda reminds us that rhetoric and composition's valorization of language difference is often guilty of ignoring much earlier recognitions of multilingual practices and research in fields such as applied linguistics and language education. Moreover, he notes that a deeper understanding of language scholarship, not to mention actually learning other languages, is necessary for critiques of translanguaging trends, specifically in relation to the celebration of difference to the detriment of the material necessity in global-citizen's lives of the acquisition of global English. Donahue echoes that call and argues that our research is strengthened when we look outside of our U.S. and disciplinary contexts for tools and methods of analysis. Donahue, further, reminds readers that our work currently depends on designating English as the second language (L2), which ignores rich research from traditions for which a student's L2 is not that. Finally, in the closing chapter of *Literacy as Translingual Practice*, Worden identifies what is, for me, the clearest danger in applying translingual labels, in a potentially trendy fashion, without further understanding both cross-disciplinary research and how a writer's translingual orientation and practices play out as they approach a rhetorical situation. Worden says, "this research must not revert to simple tallies of the languages used in an instance of communication" (238), and my response is, really, to shout "Yes!" and to jump up and give her a high five.

The contributors to *Reworking English* and *Literacy as Translingual Practice* provide both thought-provoking explorations of how a translingual orientation to writing affects our approach to investigations and understandings of the work of rhetoric, composition, and literacy studies. In tandem, these two collections lay significant groundwork for further refining what we mean by translanguaging and a translingual orientation to writing, offering examples of fruitful exploration, compelling questions, and critical directions. Moreover, these investigations help us understand the draw, or "lure" (Matsuda 478), of the translanguaging conversation, and help us to recognize the reality of individuals' fluid language(s) negotiation(s). The concept and attendant investigative focus of translanguaging offers composition instructors a powerful means of acknowledging and understanding the agentive communicative choices students make. It is the agency, we would argue, that composition instructors are drawn to, that composition has always recognized, and thus, despite Matsuda's cautions, that rhetoric and composition scholars are so prepared to adopt as theory and practice in writing studies. But we also must heed the thoughtful critiques of jumping into new waters without attending to the disciplinary trajectories and knowledge in second language writing, applied linguistics, sociolinguistics, and language teaching as a necessary step in our pedagogical and investigative interventions. As the afterwords in both edited collections assert, socio-political forces must also be interrogated; indeed, despite the attraction of attending to difference in this way, external forces (the "linguistic discrimination" cited by Worden) and internal forces (citizens "fixed" attachments to linguistic identity and ideology cited by Kopelson) are not going anywhere anytime soon. There is much more careful work to be done and these two collections offer rhetoric and composition teachers-scholars a wide range of provocative points of departure for that continued work.

Singapore, Chicago, Illinois, and Huntsville, Alabama

Works Cited

Canagarajah, Suresh. *Translingual Practice: Global Englishes and Cosmopolitan Relations*. New York: Routledge, 2013. Print.

Matsuda, Paul Kei. "The Lure of Translingual Writing." *PMLA* 129.3 (2014): 478-83. Print.

Pennycook, Alastair. "English as a Language Always in Translation." *European Journal of English Studies*. 12.1 (2008): 33-47. Print.

Race, Language Policy, and Silence in Composition Studies

Vernacular Insurrections: Race, Black Protest, and the New Century in Composition Studies, by Carmen Kynard. Albany: SUNY P, 2013. 322 pp.

Shaping Language Policy in the U.S.: The Role of Composition Studies, by Scott Wible. Carbondale: SIUP, 2013. 232 pp.

A Search Past Silence: The Literacy of Young Men, by David E. Kirkland. New York: Columbia UP, 2013. 187 pp.

Reviewed by David F. Green, Jr., Howard University

I recall a conversation I had with a few grad students last semester about reimagining the roles of race and power in academe from a position of possibility instead of precedent. At the heart of our conversation was my desire to apply pressure to their expectations of what English studies entails, and more specifically their ways of thinking about the standard-nonstandard English dichotomy. Our conversation reached a stalemate as they voiced their view that learning the language of power remains at the center of English studies and I my view that critical language awareness requires educators of the language arts to think differently about the circumstances that may shape a given language performance or view of communication. In many ways the students were right, as standardized written English still remains revered as the language of power within academe among many professors and still serves as a gate-keeping mechanism students must be mindful of or risk exclusion. But as many now recognize, this is not solely the case. Concepts such as code-meshing, code-mixing, translingualism, and transcultural literacies represent ways of thinking about the nuanced languages and dialects that intersperse with and enhance the prose of writers. Linguistic diversity has become a central concept in thinking about the possibilities embedded in the ways people make and understand meaning. I think my conversation with the grad students would have benefited considerably from an engagement with a trio of recent texts dealing with this very issue. Though these works were not included in the course reading list, their attention to language, race, and power provide fertile ground for graduate students and professionals seeking to enhance their understanding of composition history and culturally relevant language pedagogy. More specifically, I would argue that these texts make a clear case for the importance of critical language awareness and transcultural literacy for twenty-first-century writing instruction. As each text illustrates, composition histories, linguistic identities, and social justice legacies are not only central to composition studies as a field, but to the very lives and livelihoods shaped by what this field has come to mean both within and beyond academe.

Of these works, Carmen Kynard's *Vernacular Insurrections* provides the most extensive and comprehensive analysis and is the work with which I begin. Kynard makes a strikingly refreshing case for the relevance of Black freedom struggles to composition histories. Her work is an ambitious compendium of historical critique, teacher narrative, and critical literacy research. Kynard proves herself a deft historian, and the connections she is able to make between the Black freedom struggle tradition and the field of composition and rhetoric are imaginative, insightful, and sharp. Her narrative voice exemplifies a critical and flexible relationship with Black English from which current research on language and writing could benefit. She employs tropes, testimonials, and critical language that identify her as a quintessential "script-flipper" working in the intellectual traditions of Geneva Smitherman, Jacqueline Royster, and many others. By script-flipper, I am referring to her use of African American English, which flows seamlessly with and against the critical prose used to ground the main ideas of the text. Her text does not always mesh academic and nonacademic language varieties, which in some cases is refreshing, as her multivocality highlights her disagreement with some of the histories and scholarship she engages. *Vernacular Insurrections* marries the Black freedom struggle to composition literacies in ways that place the Black social protest tradition at the center of critical literacy and composition studies. Kynard defines composition literacies as the ongoing analysis of ways that student bodies are validated or invalidated by the ways they choose to move through higher education curricula and by the types of composing practices they bring with them to this space (8-9). The text takes its title from a term coined by Kynard, "vernacular insurrections." She describes the concept as selective interventions in the oppressive conditions of institutions and the dominant culture (11). These interventions are vernacular in the sense that they occur through the production of disruptive discourses that affirm identities, cultures, and histories outside of the dominant discourse. As Kynard understands, the Black protest tradition, like Black America, is variegated, complex, and influenced by a variety of ideologies and theories that produce different dispositions toward the dominant culture.

In terms of influences, Kynard's work owes much to Robin D. G. Kelley and Geneva Smitherman. The feel, language, and flow of the text combines a black vernacular approach with a historiographic examination of progressive Black freedom struggles and composition history. Kynard's project takes flight through its discussion of critical language pedagogy and marginalized student identities. These subjects, often relegated to the fringes of composition histories, inform Kynard's vision of the modern university and modern composition studies, which in turn provides the exigence for the study. As she notes of her project,

> At its heart, I am attempting to write a self-conscious and personal black vernacular history as a compositionist and critical literacies educator who works hard to think and teach from the vantage point of Black Radical traditions as more than just curricular content delivered in Eurocentric modes. (18)

It is here that I see this work as the progressive vision for language research many have advocated for in this journal and other spaces. Contemporary language pedagogies of any pluralistic variety benefit from considerations of language that sidestep the privileging of purely Eurocentric modes and decades-old ways of thinking on language education. For Kynard that begins by reasserting the relevance of Black protest traditions to language policy research within CCCC, open admissions and basic writing histories, and critical pedagogy.

Kynard's book is organized into five main chapters bookended by a formal introduction and an outerlude, with five teacherludes interspersed between the formal chapters. While I have often used "mixtape" as a way of getting students to think differently about the texts they read and write about in class, Kynard presents, by my account, the first intellectual mixtape monograph. In hip-hop music the mixtape has historically served as an unconventional collection of remixed, unreleased, or original music. Unlike commercially released albums, mixtapes usually target audiences invested in experimentation and playful and critical thought. Similar to the variety of music offered on mixtapes, Kynard uses the teacherludes to provide "a kind of parallel-story to the impact of the histories" presented in the work (13). I found many of the narratives intriguing and compelling, as well as more suggestive and introspective than the main chapters. In many instances I was reminded of my own experiences teaching linguistically diverse students in my former position in a Norfolk, Virginia middle school. More than anything, each teacherlude highlights the type of reflective analysis found in much of the critical race work of Derrick Bell and other critical race theorists. Her ability to mesh a narrative approach with insights into how this might apply to composition pedagogy writ large added another layer and flavor to the entire work.

The five main chapters explore a number of topics related to the Black freedom struggle and composition studies. Kynard begins with a review of the Black student protests at HBCUs beginning in the 1920s and occurring well into the 1960s. She connects this tradition of protest to the "Students' Right to Their Own Language" (SRTOL) document and implies that the study of such history can be vital to understanding the document and redressing the roots of deficit pedagogies. As she argues, the inability to see SRTOL and other critical statements on language as connected to a Black protest tradition reinforces troubling assumptions about the spirit of these documents. These statements began with the idea of empowering students who spoke a number of language varieties and of acknowledging the resistance teachers might encounter from students who value the intellectual traditions of their cultures and neighborhoods. In other words, these statements were written for the very working-class and minority students often written out of the dominant histories of composition.

Later in her work, Kynard contends that the Black Power movement informed many of the concerns, interests, and works of black scholars in the field of composition. She does this by tracing the history of the NCTE/CCCC black Caucus and the work that came from members of the caucus. In the chapter "I Want to Be African," Kynard further elaborates on the connection between the black Caucus and the Black Arts Movement (BAM) by challenging Steve Parks' critique of Smitherman in *Class Politics*. According to Kynard, Parks critiques Smitherman's work with Black English and its relationship to the radical class critique of the Black Power movement (83). For Parks, Smitherman's works favor an ethnic-centered paradigm instead of a radical leftist paradigm. While critiques of Parks' misreading of Smitherman's work can also be found in essays such as Keith Gilyard's "Holdin it Down," Kynard provides a nuanced, at times comical, but more than fair analysis of the strengths and missteps of Parks' reading of the Black protest movement and Smitherman's work with Black English. As Kynard notes, several of Smitherman's writings spoke directly to the Black aesthetic movement, the sister movement of the Black Power movement that examined aesthetic production as a vehicle and resource for political action (83).

Kynard concludes the main body of her book with a close look at the role of the black freedom struggles in basic writing histories. Acutely aware of Mina Shaughnessy's legacy, Kynard goes to great lengths to highlight some ways the foundational *Errors and Expectations* has contributed to a misguided focus on the errors of urban minority students at the expense of much more critical views of the legacies and circumstances shaping these students' entrance into academe. For Kynard, Shaughnessy's *Errors* does provide an important analysis of the patterns and reasoning of student writing examined in her classes, and because it represents a foundational text (in fact, one used to introduce Kynard to teaching composition at an open admissions college), its politics become very important to consider in what it conveys about teaching large minority student populations. The thrust of Kynard's rereading of *Errors* is to suggest that there are alternative visions that express a more radical vision of teaching for social justice with large urban minority populations. She presses for a more expansive vision of composition studies, one that eschews centers and margins in favor of social change and empowerment. For her this begins with newer (or rather, older) history lessons in language, protest, and composition instruction.

Scott Wible's *Shaping Language Policy in the U.S.* is an interesting and compelling companion to Kynard's text, though it is less ambitious in scope and less experimental in form. His work is particularly interesting given the recent rise of research interrogating code-switching, code-meshing, and translingualism as practical responses to the increased presence of linguistic diversity in composition classrooms. Wible's text focuses on language policy statements and the troubling conversations surrounding them.

More specifically, *Shaping Language Policy in the U.S.* takes as its focus the history and development of three language policy statements and their larger influence on national perspectives about language. Wible frames his project around the rise of linguistic conservatism and its dominating influence on the reception of language concerns within education during and after the Ronald Reagan administration. As Wible notes, the Reagan era of politics brought with it a sweeping resistance to multicultural educational programs and a misguided conception of nationalism linked uncritically to language education. In this interesting examination of the SRTOL resolution, the NCTE/CCCC National Language Policy (NLP), and the Department of Defense's National Security Language Policy (NSLP), Wible brings together archival research, textual analysis, and personal interviews to "illuminate how beliefs and attitudes toward language influence public demand for or resistance to various language policy texts" (15). He draws on the SRTOL resolution and the NLP as touchstones for the push-pull relationship that continues to define attitudes toward linguistic diversity within the U.S.

With clear and balanced prose, Wible makes the case for recognizing linguistic diversity as both a political and intellectual concern, one that continues to shape how the American public and American educational organizations such as CCCC interpret, address, and engage linguistic diversity. The body chapters are developed around the SRTOL, NLP, and the Department of Defense's NSLP documents. In the first body chapter, Wible complicates perspectives on the SRTOL resolution by presenting a nuanced review of the Language Curriculum Research Group's (LCRG) attempt to develop curricula and practices based on SRTOL recommendations. Wible uses the case of LCRG's failed attempt to publish a textbook developed around linguistically diverse principles as evidence of the growing English-only movement and of the conflicted views in the field of composition as a whole on linguistic diversity. He goes to great lengths to present the LCRG as a transformative group working to provide concrete classroom practices built on the SRTOL. His strongest evidence of this stems from a grant awarded to the LCRG by the Ford Foundation to complete a textbook manuscript that blends sociolinguistic research with composition practice and focuses on making Black English Vernacular legible to composition teachers working in the CUNY system. Yet, the book would never see publication, derailed by the public animus toward bilingual and multilingual language instruction.

Wible's project gathers force through its exploration of policy, public opinion, and CCCC's vested interest in making political and intellectual statements about language and cultural difference. As Wible shows, for many within the organization, linguistic diversity came to represent either a harbinger of impending loss of standards or a central vehicle for democratic education. Wible explains, "the National Language Policy asked compositionists to see themselves not only as scholars and teachers but also as citizens who could provide greater leadership in public debates about language policy and linguistic diversity" (71). Wible then moves on to review the NSLP, which he carefully explores as a conservative response to the tragic reality of 9/11 and broadening concerns about national security. As he aptly notes, the NSLP defines the need for multilingualism very narrowly, preserving an English-only position toward language education, unless the acquisition of a particular language can enhance one's ability to communicate with communities that pose threats to national security. As noted, such a position reinforces American jingoism at its worst and undermines progressive visions of composition studies. Wible concludes his work with a request for response statements from the rhetoric and composition communities that outline the importance of linguistic diversity to education, particularly within an increasingly global culture and economy.

Much like his central argument—that language policies matter because they identify the political and public positions groups and individuals take regarding education and teaching—Wible's text oscillates evenly between historical context and rhetorical analysis, and this is what I found to be both the strength and weakness of the text. For those interested in language diversity and research on SRTOL and other language policies, the book adds another resource to that history. However, at times, *Shaping Language Policy* is too careful in its analysis of particular case studies. Wible takes care to present, organize, and situate the particular policy statements he examines, yet he retreats from suggesting too forcefully how these statements might be reinterpreted for our modern concerns. I understand this was not the focus of his project, but given the detailed and meticulous way he delivers his research, I found myself looking for more vigorous conclusions or comments about the historical work provided.

One might also expect a more robust discussion of later statements such as the "CCCC Statement on Ebonics" or the "CCCC Statement on Second Language Writing and Writers," but these statements remain absent for the most part. Still, Wible's work is impressive in its nuance and detail, balanced in its analysis and prose style, and should be required reading for anyone seriously invested in language policy or critical language studies in composition.

Although Kynard and Wible highlight missing elements of language analysis in traditional composition histories, their interests and arguments remain largely conceptual and focused on sharpening alternate histories of composition. Kynard provides glimpses of the student identities most affected by oppressive attitudes toward language, David Kirkland's *A Search Past Silence* provides a passionate and empathetic defense of these identities. A moving and powerful ethnographic study of four black male students in Lansing, Michigan and the literacies that shaped their lives and relationships, Kirkland's study explores what rights to one's own language means for people whose identities often are dismissed before they utter one word. In his composition literacies study, Kirkland seeks to move beyond the narrow labeling of these four male students to gather a holistic and deeper understanding of the language and meaning making practices that shape their lives, as well as the systematic academic and nonacademic institutions that impede their progress. He, like Kynard, assumes that awareness of the sociocultural literacy practices of these students will yield a more sophisticated understanding for teachers of language and literacy.

Kirkland's work is organized into sixteen short chapters, written in an engaging third-person narrative style. The chapters fit within three larger units entitled language, silence, and identity. Each chapter is organized around a linguistic or cultural concept—such as syntax, cypha, or poverty—and these concepts serve as backdrops to the narratives told in the chapters. The chapters cycle between individual narratives featuring one of the four young men and their experiences writing poetry, developing raps, getting into fist fights, and negotiating the complex dynamics of poverty and family. Many of the chapters include the voices and perspectives of all four young men, but the focus usually revolves around an event relevant to one of them. Kirkland also takes us into the classroom with the young men, capturing the sentiments of a teacher who has given up on him.

Kirkland makes a concerted effort to place the experiences of these young men and their language, music, and families in conversation with scholarly research. However, he remains careful to let the young men lead this conversation, subordinating the scholarship to their experiences. For example, the concept of the cypha, a literal circle of voices, serves as a dominant framing metaphor throughout the book, highlighting the interactions between the young men and the collaborative function of their meaning making activities. Kirkland draws on H. Samy Alim—a noted hip-hop language scholar—but only to define and explain the concept before ushering him out the way and allowing the young men's interactions to illustrate this concept.

As the title denotes and as Kirkland is careful to illustrate, these young men tend to be silenced by institutions, teachers, and law enforcement in ways Kirkland does not seek to duplicate. In the silencing process, the literate abilities and brilliant potential of these young men are written over in ways that rewrite them as criminal, delinquent, illiterate, and dropouts. As the study shows, these young men are constantly composing raps, journal entries, or artistic drawings that help them make sense of the world they occupy and reveal to readers their brilliant young minds. Ironically, very little of this writing is acknowledged in school or out. For example, one of the young men is viciously assaulted and arrested for disorderly conduct after refusing to leave school grounds when prompted by hyper-vigilant police officers. The officers interrupted a rap cypha the young men were participating in, which demonstrates their own lack of understanding of the positive attributes of hip-hop literacy. The inability of the officers to see what the young men were doing as meaningful created a series of events that contributed as much to the young man's assault and arrest as his decision not to move on quietly. One might read this as an example of the young men's inability to negotiate the codes of power shaping their experience. Yet, it is clear the young men understand very well the literate practices of institutions, state agents, teachers, and many others. They are well aware of their vulnerability, invisibility, and powerlessness, and this is why their literacy practices should be valued: as Kirkland so poignantly shows us, such practices provide them with a means of resistance and cultural empowerment in response to their troubled experiences. Kirkland's book does a beautiful job demonstrating the type of work and literate practices that can make these young men and others like them visible. One can only imagine how different approaches to teaching writing might look if body art, dance compositions, and raps were much more readily incorporated into mainstream composition pedagogy.

A Search Past Silence is a striking monograph-length literacy narrative featuring four young men from Michigan. Kirkland's work in form and theory posits interesting possibilities for language and difference within composition studies. Our field would greatly benefit from more work willing to subordinate traditional academic literacies for more culturally nuanced narratives of composition literacy.

Taken together, *Vernacular Insurrections, Shaping Language Policy in the U.S.,* and *A Search Past Silence* add a political edge to recent discussions of language and the rising global interest in transcultural composition studies. At a fundamental level each text asks the question "what can be gained by thinking differently about what political, racialized discourses can offer the teaching of writing?" As each text resoundingly notes, much can be gained if we broaden our view of the past and of our students' literate assets. As newer studies press for newer insights into linguistic pluralism—conceptions that move away from a center-periphery model of language use—it becomes equally important to remember that linguistic swagger is a central component of rhetorical sophistication and cross-cultural communication. As each text presses, let us not forget that expressive resources like hip-hop spread Black English across the globe because they serve a rhetorical role in illustrating particular injustices, not simply because they are provocative. Thus, Black English does not serve simply as cultural affirmation, but as a model for how different language practices can be mobilized and used to rethink assumptions about links between writing and social change. Collectively, these authors provide important interventions in the dominant discourses that silence substantive discussion of linguistic and cultural difference in the teaching of writing. While conversations about translingualism, language diversity, and academic culture will continue to grow moving us toward greater global critical language awareness, for Kynard, Wible, and Kirkland their monographs already meet this demand with much swagger and flow.

Washington, D.C.

Works Cited

Bell, Derrick. *Faces at the Bottom of the Well: The Permanence of Racism*. New York: Basic Books, 1992. Print.

Gilyard, Keith. "Holdin it Down: Students' Right and the Struggle Over Language Diversity." *Rhetoric and Composition as Intellectual Work*. Ed. Gary A. Olson. Carbondale: SIUP, 2002. 115-27. Print.

Parks, Steve. *Class Politics: the Movement for the Students' Right to Their Own Language*. Urbana: NCTE, 2000. Print.

Shaughnessy, Mina. *Errors and Expectations: A Guide for the Teacher of Basic Writing*. New York: Oxford UP, 1977. Print.

Smitherman, Geneva. "English Teacher, Why You Be Doing the Thangs You Don't Do?" *English Journal* 61.1 (1972): 59-65. Print.

The Committee on the CCCC Language Statement. "The Students' Right to Their Own Language." *CCC* 25.3 (1974): 1-18. Print.

Writing as Language in Use: On the Growing Engagement between Sociolinguistics and Writing Studies

The Sociolinguistics of Writing, by Theresa Lillis. Edinburgh: Edinburgh UP, 2013. 200 pp.

Writing and Society, by Florian Coulmas. Cambridge: Cambridge UP, 2013. 192 pp.

Reviewed by Joel Heng Hartse, Simon Fraser University

Several years ago, while searching for a quote from a Singaporean film, I came across a blog that astounded me. The author wrote in a mixed code the likes of which I had never seen in actual use, though I am trained in approaches to writing as a socially situated, multimodal, and even potentially multilingual practice. The author wrote her blog in a flowing, florid mixture of standard written English, Singlish, Mandarin, and other Chinese dialects, represented by both the Latin alphabet and Chinese characters; her registers moved between more or less formal written English and informal registers used in personal diaries, social media, texting, and face-to-face communication; her blog made meaningful use of pictures, video, music, and changes in font style, color, and size. As a text, it was a researcher's dream.

I was equally astounded, then, when I met a Singaporean linguist at a conference not long after I discovered the blog. In his presentation, he discussed the use of mixed codes, registers, and varieties of English in the Singaporean context. I asked him about multilingual writing in Singapore and he replied that this was something Singaporeans never did, since writing was always for formal purposes. I brought up the blog and told him I had recently seen a Singaporean write in a creative mix of English, Chinese, and other varieties on a blog.

"But blogging is not really writing," he said.

When is writing not writing? This puzzling question goes back to some fundamental assumptions of linguistics and sociolinguistics regarding the differences between form and function in written and spoken language. And while many of the arguments for these differences have been carefully made—Walter Ong's reasoned distinction between literacy and orality springs to mind—they have also shut down many potentially revelatory avenues of research.

Two important new books highlight this paradox. Theresa Lillis's *The Sociolinguistics of Writing* and Florian Coulmas's *Writing and Society* make persuasive arguments that writing, like speech, is an everyday language practice whose use can be studied in its social context just as speech has traditionally been, from a sociolinguistic perspective. These books compellingly point the way toward the need for greater engagement between sociolinguistics and writing research, particularly when it comes to what Lillis calls "uptake" (which she defines as how writing will be read; that is, how readers react to texts) and its social consequences. Writing is said to be a highly standardized form of language, but variation in both usage and uptake surrounds us. Even at the sentence or word level, enormous variation can be seen online and in print, in formal and informal spaces, and in how people react to a range of variation, from acceptance to tolerance to hostility. There is, for example, little agreement among editors, readers, and teachers about what constitutes error and what is merely an acceptable variation.

The ideas expressed in these books are complementary, though they do not directly address each other. Lillis and Coulmas both recognize the need for more engagement between sociolinguistics and writing, but Lillis is primarily a writing specialist calling for greater engagement with sociolinguistics, while Coulmas is a (socio)linguist arguing for more engagement with writing. Taken together, the two books make a convincing argument for cross-pollination between the two approaches: a sociolinguistics of writing, or a writing-influence approach to sociolinguistics. Both should be of interest to composition scholars who are attuned to social and linguistic issues in writing.

The primary goal of Lilllis' book is to show that although sociolinguistic theory has been biased toward the study of speech, writing—an everyday language practice—is a worthy and indeed necessary object of sociolinguistic study. In the first chapter of this meticulously organized book, "Writing in Sociolinguistics," Lillis explains the aims of each chapter in bullet points at its outset. This is helpful, as she marshals evidence and arguments from many different quarters to bolster her arguments and lays out three points that form the basis of her argument: theoretically, "writing cannot and should not be viewed as separate from contexts of use and users[;]" empirically, "texts, uses, and users need to be the subject" of empirical research; and ideologically, "power, identity, participation and access" need to be considered in how writing is conceptualized (16). Lillis announces her intention to draw on numerous sociolinguistics-influenced areas of study (e.g., new literacy studies, multimodality, discourse studies, new rhetoric, and academic literacies, among many others), which is borne out by the rest of the book.

The next few chapters deal with conceptualizations of writing. In the second chapter, "The Question of Mode," rather than viewing writing as transcription of speech (as linguists sometimes do), Lillis characterizes writing as verbal, material, technological, visual, and spatial. She ends her consideration of writing's modalities with an excerpt of research participants' evaluations of a shop sign in Hong Kong—they had only to read the four characters on the sign—which showed that people of different backgrounds considered a number of factors, including aesthetics, political history, business and economics, and geopolitical relations and attitudes when they read and evaluated the effectiveness of the text. Having established the highly contextual nature of writing in society, Lillis devotes chapters three and four, respectively, to "Writing as Verbal" (which is how it is most traditionally understood by linguistic analysts) and "Writing as Everyday Practice." She makes the case that writing is as "ordinary" as speech and should thus have a more prominent place in sociolinguistic research that seeks to understand language as a social practice. Of particular note is Lillis's assertion that an enormous amount of writing takes place in most people's everyday lives and is ignored by researchers (and language users themselves) because texts like YouTube comments, homemade banners, Wikipedia edits, or reports made for work supervisors usually go unrecognized as "writing." Lillis introduces a variety of tools for the empirical study of everyday writing, and its participants, artifacts, and practices.

The next two chapters look at studies of various contextual aspects of writing, including "Resources, Networks and Trajectories" (chapter five) and "Identity, Inscription and Voice" (chapter six). Chapter five highlights the dynamic social nature of writing in terms of how it is constructed from existing semiotic resources and how writing moves through time and space via social networks. Lillis uses several examples—including a genre typically seen as static, the academic research article—to show that the way writing is conceived, shaped, and taken up by readers depends on social relationships. Chapter six describes recent research on the relationship between language and identity and argues for "the importance of writing as identity work" by discussing material on blogs, YouTube, fanfiction websites, and in writing classrooms (147).

The seventh chapter, "Theorising Writing-Reading-Texts: Domains and Frames," contrasts the approach to writing advanced by Lillis—writing as a social practice—with other prominent perspectives on writing in various disciplines. This invaluable "cheat sheet" outlines eight different approaches to understanding writing, writers, texts, and a host of other concerns in writing studies. This chapter has the potential to yield deep insights as it delineates the many possible approaches to composing and analyzing texts and encourages their cross-pollination: why not a critical discourse analysis of a text composed in an expressionist writing course, for example, or a rhetorical perspective on a poet's *oeuvre*? The book ends with Lillis proposing possible future research questions. She particularly encourages researchers to think carefully about what aspects of writing we wish to analyze and what theoretical tools we have at our disposal, in part influenced by the approaches outlined in chapter seven with which we align ourselves.

The Sociolinguistics of Writing draws on work that will be familiar to compositionists, particularly new literacy studies (itself a more sociocultural, if not sociolinguistic, approach to writing and reading). Lillis's book will probably be more accessible to teachers and scholars of composition, while Coulmas's is grounded in disciplines like history and linguistics. This may make *Writing and Society* less familiar territory for writing scholars, but it is readable and welcome as an overview of the importance of writing across eras and cultures.

While it covers less familiar ground, Coulmas's short book helpfully provides a broad historical scope. He begins with a chapter called "The Tyranny of Writing and the Dominance of Vernacular Speech," a detailed and fascinating account of why linguistics resisted "the tyranny of writing" when establishing itself as a field. Coulmas looks at work by Ferdinand de Saussure, who felt an emphasis on writing obscured knowledge about language in general, and Leonard Bloomfield, who argued that because writing tends not to reflect the changes that spoken languages undergo, written texts are imperfect as language data. The second chapter, "The Past in the Present and the Seeds of the Public Sphere," deals with writing in public domains, showing that even such feted historical texts as the Code of Hammurabi and the Rosetta Stone are ultimately communicative. He links these texts to modern-day urban linguistic landscapes (not unlike Lillis's example of Hong Kong signage) and argues that this form of public writing is an historical development unique to urban settings. Coulmas situates writing as a social act in human history dating back to eighth-century Greece, showing that the public forms of writing we see as innovative today (like Facebook) are perhaps simply the latest manifestations of writing as a public, social practice.

The next two chapters look at the consequences of the development of writing as a communicative practice in human societies: chapter three, "Written and Unwritten Language," deals with the differentiation between writing and speech, showing that each offers unique linguistic resources and has different social characteristics. Coulmas points out that the historical division of labor between writing and speech has had real effects on both language and society in Arabic, Sinhala, Greek, and many other cultures. The fourth chapter, "Literacy and Inequality," looks in more detail at the material consequences of widespread literacy and how the social significance of writing has led to literacy reinforcing social inequalities of class, gender, race, and ethnicity. Coulmas draws on examples involving suffrage and education to show that, paradoxically, the sheer importance of writing in society has allowed a "higher level of participation and equality" but has been complicit in maintaining and even introducing new inequalities (79).

Chapter five, "The Society of Letters," looks further at the role of social institutions—government, religious bodies, and schooling—in the promotion and preservation of written language. Coulmas uses examples from the language of legal statutes, the translation of scriptures, and the use of literacy and spelling in schools, further illustrating the division of labor between speaking and writing and showing the mutually constitutive nature of formal writing and powerful social institutions. Chapter six, "Writing Reform," looks specifically at the issue of writing reform as a way of showing the mutual influences of writing and society—connecting writing systems research in linguistics to more sociocultural concerns involving language, power, and politics. In the final chapter, "Writing and Literacy in the Digitalized World," Coulmas deals with writing and literacy in digital contexts, in which he sees "a profound culture change" that must be taken seriously by scholars (128). He connects technological developments back to issues of public writing raised at the beginning of the book, using Facebook, Wikipedia, and WikiLeaks as examples, and concludes by addressing unique challenges of the digital age, including the speed at which written communication can now occur and the overwhelming virtual flood of information that modern readers sometimes struggle to keep up with.

Writing and Society is valuable for anyone interested in expanding the conversation about the role of writing in society and how it should be understood. The book does seem to alternate between a theoretical exploration of the problems and complexities that emerge from linguists' division of writing from speech on the one hand and a catalogue of innovative examples of writing in society on the other, but this is not a weakness. In fact, the book is made more readable by the author's apparent indifference to winning an academic argument and desiring, instead, to introduce readers to a broader perspective on writing. Lillis's book more obviously introduces a research agenda, but at their core the two books suggest a very similar way forward: we have to start with writing *as language*—not as a technology or recorded speech—if we are going to make progress in the sociolinguistics of writing.

Read side by side (and alongside recent work in applied linguistics and composition), Lillis's and Coulmas's books seem to signal a kind of inevitable coming together of writing and sociolinguistics. Composition studies itself may be in the midst of a sociolinguistic moment. As I write, Suresh Canagarajah has just been awarded the Mina P. Shaughnessy Prize by the Modern Language Association for his 2013 book on translingual practices in writing, a work whose intellectual trajectory is similar to those reviewed here. Indeed if we, like sociolinguists, simply take writing and speech to be two different channels, or two ways of doing language, there is no reason to avoid using the tools developed for studying one to study the other. Why not apply sociolinguistic approaches to the variation of English in writing?

Both Coulmas and Lillis use wide-ranging examples of writing from across the globe in their analyses, and their work has important implications for how we view academic writing in a globalized context. The growing interest in written English as a Lingua Franca (ELF)— an emerging function and/or variety of English developing among worldwide users of the language, as distinct from so-called native Englishes, perhaps better known in composition circles as Lingua Franca English—is instructive here. In the past, ELF has been treated as a wholly spoken phenomenon emerging between two nonnative English speakers (NNES) in conversation. Usage has been seen as highly contextual and less dependent on rules of correctness (or ideologies of correctness) than on the goal of communication.

This is where writing studies speaks back to sociolinguistics: we know from years of theory and research that writing, too, is socially and contextually bound. Thus, written ELF is a legitimate and growing area of study, even if it does not involve the face-to-face communication of two NNES (Bruce Horner, for example, introduced this idea in his 2011 chapter, and the University of Helsinki is currently engaged in large-scale empirical research on written ELF). The sheer number of NNES involved in roles that require written English make written ELF worth investigating, and the fact that we can identify ELF features in the written academic English of NNES academics proves that an appeal to the supposedly more standardized or fixed written code has no more a factual or linguistic basis than the same prescriptive appeals many language scholars condemn when applied to speech.

The preliminary investigations into written ELF make it clear that variation in writing is real and is happening: the traditionally uncountable noun "research," for example, is rapidly becoming "researches" to many writers and readers; changes in preposition usage is making it increasingly as possible to "discuss about" things as it is to "discuss" them; articles like "the" are beginning to show up in places they were not previously, and to disappear in places where conventional usage would have them. Lillis's book is itself replete with samples of "nonstandard" writing, academic and otherwise, which is shown to exist in a kind of dynamic interrelationship with standard writing and the language ideologies of those who interact with texts.

These usages are "wrong" according to standard language ideology, which, as James and Lesley Milroy argue in their classic text *Authority in Language*, has the primary goal of suppressing optional variety in language use. But just because standard language ideology has not been particularly successful in regulating speech does not mean that written language is permanently fixed. Language change may be slower in writing, but it does occur. There is strong evidence to suggest that nonstandard ELF writing usage is beginning to be accepted, albeit slowly (for example, the editorial policies of the *Journal of English as a Lingua Franca* do not require a native speaker standard and discourage "polishing" by copyeditors).

Our understanding of standard written English is based on the ideologically monolingual contexts of Great Britain and the United States. The "authority" that complainants against nonstandard language usually invoke come from the written norms of these two countries (especially associated with great national literary traditions). As English continues its worldwide dominance in academic circles, one might expect that its standard written forms also would continue to dominate, since, as Coulmas argues in his third chapter, standardized, written, national languages tend to offer more functional possibilities than minority languages or dialects. But people in countries in which written ELF is emerging do not come to English as a "national" language. Because of the transnational movement and embrace of English, speakers (and writers) of the language are now less likely to see themselves as the continuers and upholders of a grand literary tradition dating back to Shakespeare, Chaucer, Swift, and Dickens. This may still happen with trained language professionals who were educated in humanities-oriented, British-based English education settings, but an enormous number of NNES write in English today, for a number of purposes. There are simply not likely to be the same type of complaints in these societies, and standard English—not only spoken, but very significantly, written English—is not likely to be maintained in the same way.

The challenge that the globalization of English presents to sociolinguistic understandings of how standardization in writing is maintained is also a challenge for teachers and researchers of writing in this Brave New World that has such variation in it. "Foreign" writing in English is hardly the only place where shifting standards occur; one need only to look at the multilingual, multimodal discourse worlds so many of our students live in. Writing studies needs to pay more attention than ever to the influence of social factors on writers and texts that Lillis and Coulmas draw our attention to, not only at the macro level (in terms of social positioning, rhetoric, and discourse styles), but at the micro level as well: syntax, grammar, and diction are all ripe areas of research when we consider—to recontextualize an aphorism about speech from sociolinguist William Labov—why anyone writes anything. Recent approaches to writing influenced by the globalization of English have begun to make these arguments, but the full toolbox of sociolinguistic theory has not been brought to bear on writing yet.

Writing and sociolinguistics have many opportunities to move closer together, not only through the more tolerant approaches to language difference in writing as proposed by the translingual camp—who are certainly influenced by sociolinguistics—but also by importing the important concepts of variation and style from sociolinguistics as an alternative to a focus on errors, especially since composition studies has been successful in showing that the notion of error itself can be an ideologically inflected construct.

It is time, I think, that writing scholars look more closely at sociolinguistic approaches. Lillis and Coulmas have proven that writing—in every possible sense of the word, from graffiti to poetry to academic essays to Facebook to novels—is as embedded in social context as spoken language is, and that it is worth studying in a way analogous to speech. And while the internationalization of academic writing in English is only one reason for doing so, it remains compelling. Questions like "Whose standard? Which variations?" take on a new, more complex sheen when comparing the published English of academic journals in India and Canada, or China and Singapore, to say nothing of essays, blogs, tweets, texts, and diaries written in those contexts. Not only can we start to see that so-called "errors" in writing may not be—they can be markers of identity, features of other Englishes, purposeful transgressions of a hegemonic standard English—but also we can begin to more broadly investigate ideologies, looking at the uptake of texts by readers, teachers, editors, and other authorities in a variety of contexts. Sociolinguistics and writing studies need each other and need the insights and approaches that the other has developed in order to bring forth deeper, richer areas of inquiry about what writing is, what it does, and the infinitely many ways in which it is done.

Burnaby, British Columbia

Works Cited

Canagarajah, A. Suresh. *Translingual Practice: Global Englishes and Cosmopolitan Relations.* New York: Routledge, 2013. Print.

Horner, Bruce. "Writing English as a Lingua Franca." *Latest Trends in ELF Research.* Ed. Alasdair Archibald, Alessia Cogo, and Jennifer Jenkins. Cambridge: Cambridge Scholars P, 2011. 299-311. Print.

Milroy, James, and Leslie Milroy. *Authority in Language: Investigating Standard English.* 4th ed. New York: Routledge, 2012. Print.

Ong, Walter. *Orality and Literacy: The Technologizing of the Word.* New York: Routledge, 1982. Print.

Del Otro Lado: Literacy and Migration across the U.S.-Mexico Border, by Susan V. Meyers. Carbondale: SIUP, 2014. 208 pp.

Reviewed by Rubén Casas, University of Wisconsin-Madison

Like goods, labor, and bodies, literacy—including the assumptions people hold about reading, writing, and how these are taught—travels across and through borders. In the U.S., where people move across the U.S.-Mexico border routinely, teachers and scholars are affected by more than just how well students can read and write in English, they are also affected by the different literacy values students bring to classrooms; likewise, students are affected by the varying ways literacy is situated in their home contexts and in their new ones. This is the origin point for Susan V. Meyers' *Del Otro Lado: Literacy and Migration across the U.S.-Mexico Border*, which seeks to explore the complexities of literacy in a transnational context, as well as to give voice to those who, coming from the other side of the border, value literacy differently than many teachers, scholars, and students do in the U.S.

The core of Meyers' argument in *Del Otro Lado* is that for Mexican-origin students and their families, literacy is valued differently, not less. This is a significant claim to make, as Mexican American and Mexican-origin students have long been accused of not caring about education. *Del Otro Lado* goes a long way to explode this assumption by examining literacy attitudes in rural Mexico and other migrant communities, the places where many Mexican-origin students first acquire a sense of what literacy is and what it can do for them. It is in rural Mexico where Meyers finds evidence of people caring about education and literacy even as they remain skeptical of what Meyers calls the "literacy contract," which is to say the vague and idealistic promises made to students about the value of traditional education. This concept is reminiscent of Victor Villanueva's critique of the "bootstraps" mentality so prevalent in the United States: just as U.S. culture teaches that hard work can pull any student out of poverty, the Mexican system makes a similar promise about formal education and how it leads to upward mobility. To demonstrate the prevalence of the literacy contract across borders, Meyers analyzes the historical crises of education that have long motivated literacy studies and posits that while traditional literacy education may yield positive upward mobility for some, students who come from Mexico have legitimate reason to be skeptical of its overall value. *Del Otro Lado* unpacks this skepticism, and just as importantly, points out the valid alternative ways Mexican-origin students value literacy in relationship to their personal happiness and economic wellbeing.

Meyers' examination of educational skepticism first plays out in the introduction, "'So You Can Buy a Taco over the Internet,'" where she argues that literacy scholars and teachers should recognize Mexican-origin literacy as a complex transnational phenomenon. Here we are introduced to Jacqueline, a "bright, driven young woman" whose college aspirations are the first within her family (1). But as Meyers reports, these aspirations are threatened when, at twelve years old, Jacqueline moves from the U.S. back to Mexico to be closer to her extended family. There she enrolls in middle school, where she struggles to perform as well as she did in the U.S. Some of her struggle is due to the inefficiencies of the Mexican system, but some of it is also due to Jacqueline's U.S.-learned literacy skills. As she relates, "I don't really understand some words [in Spanish. . . .] But [in the U.S.], I understand everything" (1). Jacqueline's example highlights not only the difficult experiences of students who move across borders, but also the gaps in extant literacy scholarship: as Meyers points out, whereas existing literature has illuminated the challenges students face when they transition from Mexico to the the U.S., little has been written about the reverse. Students such as Jacqueline are nonetheless being educated on both sides of the border, and those of us who teach writing, composition, and literacy would do well to attend to and learn from their experiences.

The three chapters following the introduction comprise the first section of the book, and in this section Meyers situates her study in the general scholarship on literacy and its perceived crises (see Brandt; Connors; Gee; Trimbur), as well as in studies that more specifically engage connections among literacy, migration, and economic development (see Kalman; McAslan). Meyers then goes on to show how the contract mentality holds sway in studies by Gerald Graff, Linda King, and Brian Street, which she argues uncritically embrace the assumption that students who "subscribe to the demands of public education" reap the benefits of social and economic capital (16). Working through these three studies, Meyers seeks to explode this myth, and then moves into a reconsideration of how people travelling across the U.S.-Mexico border position themselves in relation to institutionally sponsored forms of literacy.

In the second chapter, "'Aren't You Scared?': The Changing Face of Oppression in Rural, Migrant-Sending Mexico," Meyers offers a political and economic profile of her research site, Villachuato, Michoacán. This profile seeks to give voice to people who lack forms of traditional schooling and—because they have managed to lead meaningful and successful lives nonetheless—do not see the same value in formal education as many in the U.S. do. Said another way, Meyers gives space for research participants to speak about their educational experience and finds that what they have to say "flies in the face of official beliefs and expectations about literacy" (12), particularly in regards to how literacy is the path to upward mobility. In this same vein, chapter three, "'They Make a lot of Sacrifices': Foundational Rhetorics of the Mexican Education System," focuses on Mexico's educational system and its effects on the people of Villachuato. Although Meyers shows how the Mexican curriculum has historically emphasized the dignity of work and of rurality, she ultimately concludes that the promise of upward mobility implicit in formal education does not typically materialize—especially in rural communities. In reality, the discrepancy between literacy's promise and the lack of opportunity in Mexico leads many students to resist the state-sanctioned curricula imposed on them and to abandon formal schooling altogether. This chapter also demonstrates why many U.S. educators believe that Mexican-origin students and families do not care about literacy and—importantly—asks literacy workers to rethink this facile assumption.

Indeed, rather than not valuing literacy, Meyers shows how the residents of Villachuato resist institutional curricula for pragmatic rewards: to put it succinctly, Villachuato residents who dismiss formal literacy efforts do so because such education has little effect on their livelihood. We see lived examples of this reality in the second half of *Del Otro Lado*, where Meyers presents the case studies that make up her ethnography. In the fourth chapter, "'They Didn't Tell Me Anything': Community Literacy and Resistance in Rural Mexico," Meyers presents a chronological snapshot of women's educational experiences spanning from the Mexican Revolution to the post-NAFTA era. This chapter demonstrates how women found success in life through alternative literacies and by investing in interpersonal relationships—all in spite of persistent state-sanctioned efforts to educate them in ways that privilege the interests of the state over those of rural Mexicans. In chapter five, "'So You Don't Get Tricked': Counternarratives of Literacy in a Mexican Town," Meyers delves deeper into the conflict between rural Mexican schools and the students they are meant to serve, finding that even as teachers try to instill the abstract value of formal education, the economic realities of rural life make migration a more promising alternative. Meyers does not shy away from evidence of students' willingness to embrace what is useful in formal schooling, but she also emphasizes how they are more attracted to pragmatic, transferable skills that will help them navigate institutional bureaucracies and find employment. As the chapter not-so-subtly implies, educators on the U.S. side of the border would benefit from recognizing that, for some students, the value of education lies in the ways it leads to immediate work, rather than achieving (often unrealistic) social mobility.

The final chapter takes Meyers to Marshalltown, Iowa, a so-called receiving community where many migrants from Michoacán, Mexico relocate in the U.S. Perhaps more than any other, this chapter evinces the complexities of literacy education within a transnational setting. Meyers deftly describes the nonlinear nature of reading and writing for these students, and her cataloguing of student and teacher experiences makes a compelling case for revising teacher preparation so that it is responsive to transnational literacy contexts. Such pedagogical implications are also carried into the conclusion, where Meyers makes a final case for replacing the contract mentality with an understanding of literacy that acknowledges that people have alternative ways of achieving meaningful lives, alternative reasons for being and not being in school. Although the scope of Meyers' book doesn't offer explicit strategies for teaching in transnational contexts, it does suggest a practical philosophy for teachers to adopt. In short, we will have to rely less on educational and economic conceptions of literacy particular to the U.S. and more on complex, transnational conceptions of literacy.

Literacy in a transnational context deserves more critical attention like that which Meyers pays in *Del Otro Lado*. All told, the book is a useful reminder that literacy—the cultural practices and assumptions people hold about reading, writing, and learning—is an indelible part of the movement across borders that characterizes the twenty-first century. By paying attention to the values of the people most affected by the ebbs and flows of migration, we stand to develop meaningful educational strategies that will help Mexican-origin and other border-crossing students succeed in a transnational world. And on their own terms.

Madison, Wisconsin

Works Cited

Brandt, Deborah. *Literacy in American Lives*. Cambridge: Cambridge UP, 2001. Print.

Connors, Robert. "Crisis and Panacea in Composition Studies: A History." *Composition in Context: Essays in Honor of Donald C. Stewart*. Ed. W. Ross Wintertowd and Vincent Gillespie. Carbondale: SIUP, 1994. 86-106. Print.

Gee, James. *Social Linguistics and Literacies: Ideology in Discourse*. London: Falmer, 1990. Print.

Kalman, Judy. *Writing on the Plaza: Mediated Literacy Practices Among Scribes and Clients in Mexico City*. Cresskill: Hampton, 1999. Print.

McAslan, Erika. "Social Development." *The Companion to Development Studies*. Ed. Vandanna Desai and Rob B. Potter. London: Arnold, 2002. 139-42. Print.

Trimbur, John. "Literacy and the Discourse of Crisis." *The Politics of Writing Instruction: Postsecondary*. Ed. Richard Bullock and John Trimbur. Portsmouth: Boynton/Cook, 1991. 277-95. Print.

Villanueva, Victor, Jr. *Bootstraps: From an American Academic of Color*. Urbana: NCTE, 1993. Print.

WAC and Second Language Writers: Research towards Linguistically and Culturally Inclusive Programs and Practices, edited by Terry Myers Zawacki and Michelle Cox. Anderson and Fort Collins: Parlor and WAC Clearinghouse, 2014. 482 pp.

Reviewed by Shirley K Rose, Arizona State University

This book is part of the Parlor Press *Perspectives on Writing Series* edited by Susan H. McLeod and Rich Rice and jointly published with the WAC Clearinghouse. Given the backgrounds and reputations of the collection's editors and contributors and its placement in a book series edited by one of the founders of the writing across the curriculum/writing in the disciplines (WAC/WID) movement, it is difficult to imagine a collective effort that could promise greater credibility or authority, salience or significance for WAC/WID and second language writing (SLW) scholars who are seeking effective ways to work together for the benefit of multilingual students. The outcome of their effort has delivered on that promise.

An outgrowth of an earlier collaboration between its two editors, who coedited a special issue of *Across the Disciplines* on "WAC and Second Language Writing: Cross-field Research, Theory, and Program Development," this collection builds on arguments for the need for WAC/WID work to be informed by SLW scholarship, given issues raised by the presence of L2 writers in writing-intensive courses. The benefits of scholarship at this intersection work in the opposition direction as well, with SLW pedagogies being informed by insights from decades of work in WAC programs and research on writing in the disciplines. Contributors to the collection represent a range of institutional types, from community colleges to research universities, located in the U.S. and abroad. While providing summaries of the eighteen chapters would be impractical for me in the space of this review, the foreword, editors' introduction, and afterword do this work of summarizing particularly well.

Jonathan Hall's "Foreword: Multilinguality Across the Curriculum" sets the project in a professional context, explaining that the collection continues the argument advanced in the journal's special issue—"the concerns of multilingual writers are not in any way peripheral to or unusual in the way that our profession will evolve, but rather are rapidly assuming a central position in the discussion of the future of WAC" (5)—and applies it to the stakeholders and participants of contemporary WAC programs. Hall observes that the issue of the relation between WAC and multilingual writing was raised in the 1990s by SLW scholars such as Paul Kei Matsuda, Ann Johns, and Ilona Leki, but only recently have WAC scholars been taking the initiative to study this relationship. Hall locates the issues addressed in the contents of the collection, as well as other work at the intersection of SLW and WAC/WID, along three axes: "local and global, student experience and faculty expectations, and traditional WAC pedagogy for all students and differentiated instruction for multilingual learners" (6). He notes that these issues and tensions are always inherent in WAC/WID work, but they take on new significance in "the age of the multilingual majority" (6). Regarding the local/global axis, Hall observes that WAC has always been locally situated in specific institutional contexts and that "in today's interconnected world, the relation between the global and the local takes on added complexity as well as urgency" (6). On the persistent issue of assessment, where the desire to value student experience and adherence to a standard of performance can clash for many faculty, he articulates: "How can we insist on complexity, critical thinking, and subtle attention to the nuances of language while also opening ourselves up to new insights that may arise from translingual processes in student writing?" (9). Hall calls for "new methods, models, and technologies," but acknowledges that changing WAC/WID faculty members' pedagogies may be more challenging than changing faculty attitudes about multilinguality (11). His work to relate the project to central concerns of the WAC community and to articulate the stakes for the future of WAC/WID make the foreword an invaluable entry point for readers.

Following Hall's foreword, the editors' introduction explains that their overarching goal for the collection is to expand WAC research and practice to "include and 'embrace' . . . the differing perspectives, educational experiences, and written voices of second language writers" (16). Cox and Zawacki do not simply survey the landscape of existing, relevant WAC/WID and L2 scholarship, they also make arguments for how it might be shaped to meet future needs. They explain that while the chapters that comprise the collection are focused on research, they also wanted the collection to offer "a wealth of pedagogical, curricular, and programmatic practices" and a "range of perspectives and institutional locations" and, with the aid of the references at the end of each chapter, "an abundance of resources for further research and practice" (16). Cox and Zawacki identify familiar landmarks for readers by articulating three central principles that ground work in WAC/WID: (1) student writers' and teachers' goals for writing require a range of approaches to writing and teaching; (2) writing varies across contexts and differences must be respected and taught; (3) WAC programs' emphasis on writing can help to transform an institution's culture of teaching and learning.

They argue that these principles must be extended to include three sets of "awarenesses and practices" around which they organize their review of relevant L2 literature for WAC/WID scholars (17): (1) respecting differences in Englishes, including World Englishes, dialects of English, varieties of English, and interlanguage; (2) constructing curricula in ways that allow multilingual students to draw on their cross-linguistic and cross-cultural resources in order to be as successful as L1 students; and (3) promoting an academic writing culture that values difference as a resource rather than identifying assimilation to Western culture and command of standard written English as the goal. They use these same three "WAC/L2 writing-inclusive principles" to organize the eighteen chapters of the collection into three sections, one focused on students as writers, one on institutional contexts, and one on program-level practices.

The editors close their introduction with two more sets of three. They identify three distinct contexts for future WAC/L2 research work: (1) increasing populations of U.S. resident L2 writers; (2) increasing numbers of international L2 students on U.S. campuses; and (3) increasing globalization of U.S. colleges and universities through establishing branch campuses and forming partnerships with higher education institutions abroad. They then offer three sets of suggestions for research corresponding to their organizational categories: (1) research on "L2 students' experiences," (2) research on "faculty perceptions and teaching practices around L2 writing," and (3) research "related to a focus on courses, curriculum, and programs" (34-35).

Finally, Chris Thaiss' afterword invokes an audience of WAC/WID program faculty across the disciplines. Opening with a brief reverie in which he reflects on what he observes from his window in northern California after finishing an email to a fellow researcher in Greece, Thaiss notes how little we worry, in such exchanges, about the "fine points of our discourses—nuances of parallel construction, commas, 'who or whom?'—because if these delicacies of verbal etiquette really bothered us, we'd be driven so crazy by the unpredictability of individual readers' tastes across this busy world that we'd never have the courage to put our messages out there" (465). Starting from this observation about our "multiple communications within simultaneous contexts in our increasingly global consciousness" (466), Thaiss discusses the contribution the collection makes to building an argument against a singular focus on error and expecting or attempting to teach student writers native-speaker fluency. Echoing contributors to the collection, Thaiss contrasts the "difference as deficit," "difference as accommodation," and "difference as resource" models for conceptualizing work with multilingual writers and synthesizes recommendations for "difference as resource" teaching practices from multiple chapters in the collection. Here and elsewhere in his afterword he deftly synthesizes the research findings and arguments of the collection's individual chapters and sets them in the context of the goals and concerns of WAC/WID programs and faculty. His essay will serve as an excellent resource for WAC/WID faculty across the disciplines who want an introduction to research and theory that will inform their work with multilingual writers.

This collection can serve as a handbook of approaches to research on multilingual writing across the curriculum and in the disciplines, given the range of research approaches including surveys, focus groups, textual analysis, analysis of institutional data, and mixed methods that are represented. The inclusion of methodological discussions and careful accounts of research methods help to insure that readers from a range of epistemological orientations and disciplinary backgrounds will be able to appreciate the validity of the research presented. The collection is an obvious choice for graduate seminars in WAC/WID and SLW, especially given that the Parlor Press/WAC Clearinghouse *Perspectives on Writing Series* is available in both low-cost print and free digital forms. (These arrangements also allow for longer books, such as this one, which is nearly twice the length of many collections in the field.) Many of the chapters could also serve as readings for WAC/WID faculty workshops focused on working with multilingual student writers. *WAC and Second Language Writers* can become a guidebook for collaborations between WAC and SLW professionals.

Tempe, Arizona

Works Cited

Zawacki, Terry Myers, and Michelle Cox. "Introduction to WAC and Second Language Writing." *WAC and Second Language Writing: Cross-field Research, Theory, and Program Development*. Spec. issue of *Across the Disciplines* 8.4 (2011): n. pag. Web. 22 February 2016. <http://wac.colostate.edu/atd/ell/zawacki-cox.cfm>.

Zawacki, Terry Myers, and Michelle Cox, eds. *WAC and Second Language Writing: Cross-field Research, Theory, and Program Development*. Spec. issue of *Across the Disciplines* 8.4 (2011): n. pag. Web. 22 February 2016. < http://wac.colostate.edu/atd/ell/index.cfm >.

Transnational Writing Program Administration, edited by David Martins. Logan: Utah State UP, 2015. 348 pp.

Reviewed by Chris Thaiss, University of California, Davis

"Transnational" and "translingual" are terms increasingly heard in writing studies conversations, but what these terms might mean in the actual teaching of writing—and in the design and management of writing programs—is gradually evolving. The important collection of essays under review here addresses aspects of program design and management that all WPAs will consider vital. Reading this collection of thoughtful and incisive essays will provide readers much food for thought.

However, current WPAs and others looking for models or confident advice on building "transnational" writing-centered initiatives will be hard pressed to find them here. Except for parts of some chapters and the entire essay by Doreen Starke-Meyerring, which describes several successful Globally-Networked Learning Environments (GNLEs), the overwhelming tone of the collection is pessimistic. The essayists tend to be much more emphatic on what to avoid than on what to do.

Coming in for stern attack throughout the collection are U.S. universities that have expanded across borders with programs that try to replicate what has been successful in their home environments in the U.S. The juxtaposed chapters by Danielle Zawodny Wetzel and Dudley W. Reynolds (Carnegie Mellon University) and by Alan S. Weber et al. (Weill Medical College at Cornell) provide detailed narratives of how assumptions behind writing curricula and expectations about students that fit the home campuses failed, as part of the Education City initiative in Qatar. Wetzel and Reynolds give a frank appraisal of how courses, methods, and expectations had to evolve in Qatar in order to fit the language and cultural backgrounds of the students—while also attempting to "protect the brand" of Carnegie Mellon. In the chapter by Weber et al., the segments written by Ian Miller, Rodney Sharkey, and Autumn Watts, all of whom taught at the Doha campus, describe why the original model failed and how all aspects of design and approach had to change to be of service to students.

The chapter by Shanti Bruce is particularly striking in this regard, as it is the only essay in the collection that offers a first-hand account by a WPA of how vital it is for U.S. writing program managers to teach in the cross-borders programs they coordinate. Realizing that she could not know what instructors and students were facing in the five-weekend Bahamian courses being offered by Florida's Nova Southeastern University until she taught those courses (in business writing and world literature), Bruce proceeded to learn from her students and from fellow faculty, and the results were a revelation to her as both teacher and WPA.

Closing the collection (save for the Afterword by Bruce Horner), Doreen Starke-Meyerring's chapter on GNLEs provides a refreshing alternative to what most of the essays attack as the "expansionist" and "export" assumptions of much transnational U.S. higher education. As coeditor of the 2008 *Designing Globally Networked Learning Environments: Visionary Partnerships, Policies, and Pedagogies*, she speaks from deep experience in both designing and carrying out what she terms "true" partnerships between universities in "negotiating" and continually refining courses and mutual learning opportunities. In her descriptions of a number of GNLEs in different subject areas, countries, and cross-university partnerships, we see how far the GNLE model of mutual learning by students in different locales travels from the notion of a prefabricated course being "taught" in a different cultural context to students with varied and distinctive goals, strengths, and perceived needs.

Editor David Martins was careful to recognize that, for U.S. WPAs like himself, the concept of "transnational" encompasses not only explicitly country-to-country initiatives such as those described in the essays cited thus far, or in the chapter by Alyssa O'Brien and Christine Alfano that focuses on technological challenges and affordances in country-to-country online and hybrid teaching. Martins also includes a chapter by Chris Anson and Christiane Donahue that illustrates the diversity of the concept of "program," which the authors demonstrate through widely contrasting descriptions of entities in Saudi Arabia, Belgium, and France.

Several of the chapters illuminate a different, but much more widespread definition of "transnational": the sense that U.S. college and university home campuses increasingly serve students who were born outside the U.S. or whose parents emigrated from other countries. The companion concept of "translingual" is especially pertinent in this context, as it describes the highly varied relationships that we teachers and our students experience among the languages that we encounter in different parts of our lives and of which we have varying levels of knowledge. Several chapters of the collection explore this nexus between "transnational" and "translingual" in writing programs occurring largely on U.S. campuses.

For example, two juxtaposed chapters consider a specific transnational/translingual environment, the Mexico-U.S. border region that includes both the University of Texas–El Paso and New Mexico State University. The chapter by Barry Thatcher, Omar Montoya, and Kelly Medina-López describes six cultural groups of persons living in the border region of El Paso–Ciudad Juarez in order to show significant cultural differences that might affect performance and perspectives in writing courses at UTEP and NMSU. The chapter by Beth

Brunk-Chavez et al. is an honest appraisal of how university placement and admissions procedures operate on student models that do not fully recognize this diversity and how writing programs and student affairs offices that on the one hand intend to bring necessary services to diverse students may on the other operate without cross-communication among service units. In both chapters, the writers want their courses and teaching methods, as well as university administrative policies, to avoid the commonplace assumption in the U.S. that speaking and writing like a "monolingual" native speaker of English is the goal of a writing course.

Avoidance of the "monolingual English" assumption in writing programs is a major theme in other chapters, as is the basically flawed idea—critiqued in the chapters listed below—that writing courses can be "standard" and noncontextualized:

- Wendy Olson's "mapping" of twenty-four community college programs in Washington state that advertise ESL courses as autonomous "commodities";
- Christine Tardy's review of twenty-eight college and university websites that proclaim how they "embrace diversity," while their writing program websites portray language diversity as a reason for extra course requirements;
- Rebecca Dingo, Rachel Riedner, and Jennifer Wingard's stringent critique of the outsourcing by a University of Houston business law professor of her students' papers to an online "feedback" service;
- Nancy Bou Ayash's critique of U.S. assumptions of monolingualism in contrast to multi- and translingual assumptions in Lebanon and Singapore.

Perhaps the most incisive analysis of possible meanings of "translingual" in the collection is Hem Paudel's close comparison of the similar terms "multilingual" and "plurilingual." He suggests "mesodiscursivity" as an alternative, a kind of middle space that respects both the local and the larger discursive world. In offering suggestions for WPAs and teachers, Paudel recommends mainstreaming, rather than separate ESL sections, because mainstreaming offers the chance for students to learn "mesodiscursively" from one another's language journeys and negotiations.

David Martins and the contributing authors deserve congratulations for an engaging, provocative first attempt at helping to establish priorities for transnational writing program administration. As always, such pioneering efforts lead to thoughts of what still needs to be done. I have several thoughts in this regard.

First, for an anthology that takes U.S. higher education to task for its U.S. centrism, this is a very U.S.-centered collection. Almost all of the contributors are associated in some capacity with U.S. writing programs and/or English departments, or with transnational programs run by those universities. To some extent, scholars from other countries are cited in the chapters, but the U.S.-based writers are choosing citations and interpreting them.

Second, the dominant voices in the collection are heard as theoretical commentators and reviewers of theory on the situations they describe. There are almost no teacher voices; hence, teacher voices stand out the few times they occur. Equally important, although every chapter in this collection makes assumptions and draws conclusions about students, student voices are almost completely silent. On occasion, statistics on student enrollment or student pass rates are given, but we do not hear from students themselves.

Third, this is in most chapters a polemical collection. It relies almost exclusively on citations from other writers as evidence. The rich tradition of qualitative and mixed methods research in writing studies and applied linguistics is largely missing, except for the two studies (Tardy's and Olson's) based on their analysis of websites.

Why are these omissions and silences important to correct in future work on this subject? The polemic of the collection contends that the expansionist, export model of U.S. higher education is basically flawed, as it disregards the actual needs and strengths of the people it purportedly serves. As part of this "commodity" model, the assumption of a "standard English" is also basically flawed, holding students to a performance model no longer viable (if it ever was) in a translingual, unceasingly dynamic world. But convincing those who set policies and financial agendas will take more than polemics from insiders. It will require research that includes systematic observation of classrooms, testimony from teachers, the considered arguments of partners in transnational projects, analysis of student texts, interviews with students and teachers, and other forms of research that respect the people our programs purport to serve.

Davis, California

Work Cited

Starke-Meyerring, Doreen, and Melanie Wilson, eds. *Designing Globally Networked Learning Environments: Visionary Partnerships, Policies, and Pedagogies*. Rotterdam: Sense, 2008. Print.

Transiciones: Pathways of Latinas and Latinos Writing in High School and College, by Todd Ruecker. Logan: Utah State UP, 2015. 219 pages.

Reviewed by Kat Williams, University of Wyoming

I picked up Todd Ruecker's *Transiciones: Pathways of Latinas and Latinos Writing in High School and College* because two years ago I served an AmeriCorps term as a college access counselor, and several of my language minority students were struggling with writing in ways that their language majority peers were not. As a cohort of access counselors, we were provided with myriad trainings and materials on the education gap, including the particular needs of the student population we were trying to reach. But for some reason, these Spanish-speaking students were overlooked in the pamphlets and PowerPoint presentations. In many situations, I resorted to re-explaining content to these students in Spanish (which I speak as a second language), or just overlooked egregiously poor English syntax or style despite worrying that the ACT writing graders would not be as accommodating.

In *Transiciones*, Ruecker undertakes a two-year ethnographic study of nine students entering their senior year at Samson High School, a public school in El Paso where Spanish-speaking language minority students dominate. Ruecker's pool of subjects winnows to seven as the students matriculate at Borderlands Community College and Borderlands University in El Paso, and he then thoroughly catalogues each student's writing tasks, noting triumphs, tribulations, developments, and regressions along the way. Ruecker provides a framework for understanding the challenges that Latina and Latino students face when transitioning from high school to postsecondary education, while also emphasizing the sources of their success in this transition, especially when it comes to developing college-level writing skills. This intentional focus on capital, rather than deficit, is what makes Ruecker's two-year study particularly compelling.

The book begins with methods and study design and then quickly moves into descriptive data of each of the seven students' background and living situation, as well as each student's writing experiences from their senior year of high school and first year in college, with an emphasis on writing in first-year composition. These in-depth descriptions are broken into chapters based on the success of the students' transitions: "Struggling Transitions" (Daniel and Joanne), "Difficult but Successful Transitions" (Bianca and Yesenia), "Smooth Transitions" (Carolina and Mauricio), and "An Unexpected Transition" (Paola).

In his summaries and evaluations, Ruecker emphasizes the aspects of life in which students hold advantages and capital, and Tara Yosso's critical race theory of community cultural wealth strongly influences his study design.

Yosso rejects the deficit view of students of color, and outlines forms of capital nurtured through cultural wealth, including aspirational, navigational, social, linguistic, familial, and resistant capital. In *Transiciones*, Ruecker's diagrams of each student's sources of capital at the end of each chapter serve as accessible, if necessarily simplified, summaries of whole lives, and make for easy comparison between each individual's assets and challenges. Ruecker strives to highlight the varied and ample sources of capital in the lives of students who face significant economic and cultural challenges, offering a counter-narrative to the standard assumption that Mexican and immigrant families act as barriers to college success by encouraging or forcing children to continue living at home, or work minimum-wage jobs to take up economic slack. In the case of Carolina, for instance, her stereotypically large, single mother-led family proves to be an invaluable asset to her first-year college experience, and Ruecker breaks down all the ways in which nonmonetary wealth added to her success.

Ruecker eventually provides the practical advice I could have used when working with my Latina/o students, but he first balances in-depth accounts of the students' curricular writing experiences with observations of their extracurricular lives. With access to drafts of almost all of his subjects' assignments, Ruecker is able to reproduce sentences and paragraphs as exemplars of style, skill, and expression, adding color and dimension to student writing in an educational climate that too often focuses on student deficit.

That certain students' more profound struggles were not dramatized or fetishized as the sole indicators of failure is a strength of his writing—Joanne's pregnancy, for example, is given less discussion space than her concrete struggles in first-year composition. There are times when outside circumstances beg more explanation, however. We are told that Mauricio's grandfather *and* girlfriend died in separate car crashes midsemester, but it is unclear what support network or personal characteristics of resilience allowed him to finish that semester with an improbably impressive 4.0 GPA.

Ruecker's methodological approach to his research is closely tied to the way he frames his results. In keeping with Brenton Faber's theory of ethical ethnography as described in *Community Action and Organizational Change*, Ruecker does not just observe the students at work in their high school English classes, but involves himself as a classroom assistant of sorts, providing one-on-one and group help to all students (not just the study's subjects). When the students transition to college, he communicates and meets with them frequently, falling into the simultaneous roles of advisor, counselor, tutor, and even editor.

Ruecker acknowledges the impact he has on the students' outcomes and succeeds in his effort to provide quality research while interacting closely and compassionately with his subjects. While reading *Transiciones*, I was reminded of a very different approach taken by the makers of the critically acclaimed

2011 documentary, *First Generation* (Fenderson and Fenderson). In this film, documentarians record the lives of four high school students as they apply for college and attempt to become the first in their families with postsecondary degrees. As they film, however, the producers and crew strive not to influence the students' decisions or knowledge in any way, and this approach leaves in its wake some major, potentially avoidable student failures, including a late Free Application for Federal Student Aid submission that amounts to thousands of dollars in unclaimed grant money. At first for me as a viewer, these were simply cringe-worthy screen moments: upon reflection, however, I began to question the filmmaker's methods. Fortunately, Ruecker leaves readers with no such foul taste in their mouths and is careful to note when and how his influence shaped a student's trajectory, even in small ways.

Yesenia, for example, struggled with a professor who penalized heavily for mechanical errors and a shaky grasp of closed-form features. Yesenia was in the habit of using Ruecker as a resource, and he was inclined to help her in ways that writing centers might not. About one of Yesenia's procrastinated papers he writes, "When she came to me a few hours before the final was due, she still needed help with drafting an introduction, for which I provided ideas. In addition, so that she would not be penalized excessively for grammar and mechanical issues, which were still numerous, I quickly copyedited the final draft" (91). Ruecker admits that such copyediting might have been taking his involvement a bit too far, but he stands by his choices to aid the study's subjects when he believes they are being evaluated unfairly.

After presenting several chapters of comprehensive and compelling data, Ruecker uses his research to formulate plans and solutions for teachers, institutions, and communities who support language minority students in pursuit of postsecondary education. I appreciate that he dedicates two chapters to concrete solutions and achieves a depth of analysis that ethnographies sometimes lack. Though his proposals to recenter Spanish as a language of instruction may seem radical to some, I found his calls to action to be refreshingly aligned with the needs of the Latino and Latina students I have worked with.

Ruecker proposes modifications to first-year composition curricula that would support language minority students *and* push language majority students to learn a second language, including rhetorical analysis prompts that ask students to compare and contrast English-language coverage of an issue in the U.S. with Spanish articles on the same subject across the border. More radically, he recommends a complete overhaul of postsecondary education into the established two-way bilingual structure used commonly in K-8 schools. His most immediately feasible proposal is to have administrators and directors of first-year composition programs rethink and redesign their training modules for new teachers, making the implementation of an inclusive pedagogy the main goal of teacher preparation. Programs should require composition teachers to take at least an entire class focused on multicultural praxis, he writes, instead of offering a single unit or chapter on reaching language minorities and other underserved students.

Ruecker succeeds in painting vivid portraits of students graduating from an underfunded border high school with an almost 100% Spanish-speaking demographic, and gives them the credit they are due for their triumphs while describing their deficits in constructive ways. His results may not be entirely applicable to students located elsewhere in the U.S, but many of his recommendations could (and should) be adopted by university, community colleges, and writing programs everywhere.

Laramie, Wyoming

Works Cited

Faber, Brenton. *Community Action and Organizational Change*. Carbondale: SIUP, 2002. Print.

Fenderson, Adam, and Jaye Fenderson, dirs. *First Generation*. Market Street, 2011. Film.

Yosso, Tara J. "Whose Culture Has Capital? A Critical Race Theory Discussion of Community Cultural Wealth." *Race, Ethnicity and Education* 8.1 (2005): 69-91. Print.

Contributors

Lisa R. Arnold, Director of First-Year Writing and Assistant Professor of English at North Dakota State University, has published in *College Composition and Communication*, *College English* (forthcoming), *JAC*, and *Pedagogy*. Arnold is coeditor of a forthcoming collection, titled *Emerging Writing Research from the Middle East–North Africa Region*.

Mark Brantner is a senior lecturer in the University Scholars Programme (USP) at the National University of Singapore. His research includes ePortfolios, literacy, and rhetorical theory. Before USP, he was Interim Director of First-Year Writing and Visiting Assistant Professor at Binghamton University, State University of New York.

Rubén Casas is a PhD candidate in the composition and rhetoric program in the English department at the University of Wisconsin–Madison.

Kaitlin Clinnin is a PhD candidate in rhetoric, composition, and literacy studies and digital media studies at Ohio State University. Her research focuses on community in higher education and writing studies. Her work has been published in *Technoculture* and the *Journal of Global Literacies, Technologies, and Emerging Pedagogies*.

Michelle Cox is the inaugural director of the English Language Support Office at Cornell University. She co-chairs the International Board of Writing Across the Curriculum Consultants and the Consortium on Graduate Communication. Her scholarship focuses on second language writing pedagogy, writing program administration, and graduate student writing.

Rebecca Dingo is an associate professor at the University of Massachusetts, Amherst. Her books and essays seek to bring a transnational feminist lens to rhetorical and composition studies. Her book *Networking Arguments: Rhetoric, Transnational Feminism, and Public Policy Writing* won the 2013 W. Ross Winterowd Award for the best book in composition studies.

Christiane Donahue is Associate Professor of Linguistics at Dartmouth, Hanover, NH, USA, where she teaches writing and focuses on research about writing, translingualism, cross-cultural comparisons, and research methods. She works with the French research library THEODILE (Théorie-Didactique de la Lecture-Ecriture) at l'Université de Lille and participates in multiple European research projects, networks, conferences, and collaborations that inform her understanding of writing instruction, research, and program development in European contexts.

Alanna Frost is an associate professor at the University of Alabama Huntsville. Her work is invested in the intersections of students' communicative realities, English-education practice, and English language policy.

David F. Green, Jr., is an assistant professor of English at Howard University. He is also the Director of First-Year Writing, and his research interests include rhetorics of race, hip hop, and critical language awareness and composition pedagogy.

Kay Halasek is an associate professor and director of the Second-year Writing Program in the English department at Ohio State University. She is author of *A Pedagogy of Possibility: Bakhtinian Perspectives on Composition Studies* (SIU Press 1999). Her recent work focuses on writing program administration and online and distance writing pedagogies.

Joel Heng Hartse is a lecturer in the Faculty of Education at Simon Fraser University. His work has appeared in the *Journal of Second Language Writing*, *Asian Englishes*, and *English Today*. He is coauthor of *Perspectives on Teaching English at Colleges and Universities in China* (TESOL Press 2015).

Bruce Horner teaches composition, composition theory and pedagogy, and literacy studies at the University of Louisville. His recent books include *Rewriting Composition: Terms of Exchange, Reworking English in Rhetoric and Composition*, coedited with Karen Kopelson, and *Economies of Writing*, coedited with Brice Nordquist and Susan Ryan.

Jay Jordan is associate professor and chair of the Department of Writing & Rhetoric Studies at the University of Utah. He is author of *Redesigning Composition for Multilingual Realities* and of several other articles and book chapters, and he is coeditor of two volumes on L2 writing.

Connie Kendall Theado is an associate professor in the School of Education at the University of Cincinnati, where she also serves as Director of Graduate Studies. Her research interests include the history and politics of literacy testing, particularly in high-stakes contexts, transnational partnerships and teacher preparation.

Julia Kiernan is an assistant professor at Michigan State University. Through focusing on transcultural and translingual pedagogies, she strives to create learning spaces where students are encouraged to recognize the globalization of audience and the range of cultures and languages that writing must be able to engage with.

Rebecca Lorimer Leonard holds a PhD in English from the program in composition and rhetoric at the University of Wisconsin–Madison. She specializes in literacy studies, language ideologies, multilingual writing, and comparative rhetoric. Her research examines how transnational literacy practices are valued according to shifting language ideologies.

Suzanne Blum Malley is Senior Associate Provost and associate professor of English at Columbia College Chicago. Her areas of research include multilingual and digital literacies. She is a founding executive board member and secretary of the Literacy Studies–Rhetoric, Composition, and Writing Studies (RCWS) Forum for the Modern Language Association.

Ben McCorkle teaches courses in composition, rhetoric, and digital media studies at The Ohio State University's Marion campus. He is the author of *Rhetorical Delivery as Technological Discourse: A Cross-Historical Study* and serves as the codirector of the Digital Archive of Literacy Narratives (DALN).

Joyce Meier is assistant director and assistant professor in the First-Year Writing Program at Michigan State University, where she has co-led teams of scholar-teachers incorporating culturally sustaining pedagogies in their Preparation for College Writing courses. In summer 2014, she taught at the Harbin Institute of Technology in China.

Brian Ray is an assistant professor in the Department of Rhetoric and Writing at the University of Arkansas at Little Rock, currently serving as Director of Composition. His research focuses on languages issues, linguistic diversity and style, and writing program administration.

Shirley Rose is professor of English and director of writing programs in the English Department at Arizona State University. She is a Past-President of the Council of Writing Program Administrators and the current Director of the WPA Consultant-Evaluator Service. Her research is focused on writing program administration as intellectual work.

Cynthia L. Selfe, Ohio State University, has received the EDUCOM Medal (1996), the Outstanding Technology Innovator award by the Conference on College Composition and Communication (CCCC) Committee on Computers (2000), and the "Rhetorician of the Year" award by the Young Rhetoricians Conference (2013). With long-time collaborator Gail Hawisher, Selfe has also received the CCCC Exemplar Award, the CCCC Research Impact Award and the CCCC Knowledge Advancement Award (with Patrick Berry, 2013).

Shawna Shapiro is assistant professor in the Writing and Linguistics Programs at Middlebury College. Her research focuses on college transitions and curricular innovation for multilingual/L2 writers. She has written numerous articles for peer-reviewed journals and also coauthored the book *Fostering International Student Success in Higher Education* (TESOL Press 2014).

Ghanashyam (Shyam) Sharma teaches writing and rhetoric at Stony Brook University (State University of New York). His research focuses on writing in the disciplines, cross-cultural rhetoric, multilingualism/translingualism, and multimodality in composition. He has published on these subjects in a variety of venues including *CCC* and *JAC*.

Gail Shuck is associate professor of English and coordinator of English Language Support Programs at Boise State University, where she has directed the first-year ESL writing sequence, taught courses in applied linguistics and second-language writing, and developed resources and programs for multilingual Boise State students since 2001.

Emily Simnitt is an instructor in the compostion program at the University of Oregon where she also supports writing instructors working with multilingual students. Her scholarship focuses on second language writing pedagogy, writing in digital spaces, and writing program administration.

Laura Tetreault is a doctoral candidate and university fellow in rhetoric and composition at the University of Louisville.

Chris Thaiss is Clark Kerr Presidential Chair and professor of writing studies at UC Davis. His most recent book, which he coedited with an international team, is *Writing Programs Worldwide: Profiles of Academic Writing in Many Places*. He is principal investigator of the International WAC/WID Mapping Project.

Kate Vieira is an assistant professor of English at the University of Wisconsin, Madison, in the program in composition and rhetoric. She is the author of *American by Paper: How Documents Matter in Immigrant Literacy* from the University of Minnesota Press.

Bo Wang is associate professor of English and Co-Director of the Writing Program at California State University, Fresno. Her research is focused on how transnational and feminist perspectives on rhetoric can be theorized to reconfigure research methods of rhetoric and composition. She has published in *Advances in the History of Rhetoric, CCC, College English, Rhetoric Review*, and *Rhetoric Society Quarterly*.

Xiqiao Wang is a fixed-term assistant professor in the Department of Writing, Rhetoric and American Culture at Michigan State University. Her research attends to multilingual students' literacy practices in transnational contexts and to writing pedagogical practices that can support literacy learning.

Kat Williams is an MFA candidate in creative writing (nonfiction) at the University of Wyoming, where she also teaches first-year composition. Her creative work deals with queer theory, gender identity, and disorders of all kinds.

Morris Young is director of English 100, professor of English, and faculty affiliate in Asian American Studies at the University of Wisconsin, Madison. Building on his previous work, *Minor Re/Visions* and *Representations: Doing Asian American Rhetoric* (with LuMing Mao), his current project conceptualizes Asian American rhetorical space.

Amy Zenger is an associate professor of English at the American University of Beirut, where she teaches rhetoric and composition. Her recent publications include *New Media Literacies and Participatory Popular Culture Across Borders*, coedited with Bronwyn Williams, and two chapters coauthored with Joan Mullin and Carol Haviland.

MLA's essential standard guide for graduate students, scholars, and professional writers

"The bastion of scholarly publishing etiquette."
—*Bookpage*

MLA Style Manual and Guide to Scholarly Publishing
3RD EDITION

The third edition of the *MLA Style Manual* offers complete, up-to-date guidance on writing scholarly texts, documenting research sources, submitting manuscripts to publishers, and dealing with legal issues surrounding publication. The third edition offers:

- simplified citation formats for electronic sources
- detailed advice on the review process used by scholarly journals
- a fully updated chapter on copyright, fair use, contracts, and other legal issues
- guidelines on preparing electronic files
- discussion of the electronic submission of a dissertation

"This third edition of the manual is . . . indispensable."
—*Choice*

AVAILABLE NOW.
xxiv & 336 pp.
Cloth $32.50
ISBN 978-0-87352-297-7

LARGE-PRINT EDITION
Paper $37.50
ISBN 978-0-87352-298-4

MLA guides present the most accurate and complete information on MLA style.

Modern Language Association **MLA**

bookorders@mla.org ▪ www.mla.org ▪ Phone orders 646 576-5161

More than just a new edition, this is a **NEW MLA STYLE.**

Forthcoming APRIL 2016

xiv & 146 pp.
Paper ISBN: 978-1-60329-262-7
List price: $12.00

Large-print edition
Paper ISBN: 978-1-60329-263-4
List price: $20.00

Also available in e-book formats.

Learn to Cite Any Source Easily.

Get the authoritative guide for research in the digital age.

Shorter and redesigned for easy use, this groundbreaking new edition of the *MLA Handbook* recommends one universal set of guidelines, which writers can apply to any type of source.

Buy the eighth edition of the *MLA Handbook* and learn how to master MLA style:

- Cite any source—no matter how unusual.
- Correctly organize and format a research project.
- Determine the reliability of research sources.

Discover Even More Online at *MLA Style Center.*

style.mla.org

The only authoritative Web site devoted to MLA style, *MLA Style Center* is the official, free online companion to the *MLA Handbook*.

- See how to format a research paper.
- Get answers to your questions.
- Read sample research papers.
- Find teaching resources.
- Search the book's index.
- Join the conversation about writing well.

style.mla.org • www.mla.org

Call for Proposals – 2016 Graduate Research Network

The **Graduate Research Network (GRN)** invites proposals for its 2016 workshop, May 19, 2016, at the Computers and Writing Conference hosted by St. John Fisher College, Rochester, NY. The C&W Graduate Research Network is an all-day pre-conference event, open to all registered conference participants at no charge. Roundtable discussions group those with similar interests and discussion leaders who facilitate discussion and offer suggestions for developing research projects and for finding suitable venues for publication. We encourage anyone interested or involved in graduate education and scholarship--students, professors, mentors, and interested others--to participate in this important event. The GRN welcomes those pursuing work at any stage, from those just beginning to consider ideas to those whose projects are ready to pursue publication. Participants are also invited to apply for travel funding through the CW/GRN Travel Grant Fund. Deadline for submissions is April 19, 2016. For more information or to submit a proposal, visit our Web site at http://www.gradresearchnetwork.org or email Janice Walker at jwalker@georgiasouthern.edu.

PARLOR PRESS
EQUIPMENT FOR LIVING

Congratulations to These Award Winners & WPA Scholars!

The WPA Outcomes Statement—A Decade Later
  Edited by Nicholas N. Behm, Gregory R. Glau, Deborah H. Holdstein, Duane Roen, and Edward M. White
  Winner of the Best Book Award, Council of Writing Program Adminstrators (July, 2015)

GenAdmin: Theorizing WPA Identities in the Twenty-First Century
  Colin Charlton, Jonikka Charlton, Tarez Samra Graban, Kathleen J. Ryan, & Amy Ferdinandt Stolley
  Winner of the Best Book Award, Council of Writing Program Adminstrators (July, 2014)

Mics, Cameras, Symbolic Action: Audio-Visual Rhetoric for Writing Teachers
  Bump Halbritter
  Winner of the Distinguished Book Award from *Computers and Composition* (May, 2014)

New Releases

Antiracist Writing Assessment Ecologies: Teaching and Assessing Writing for a Socially Just Future
  Asao B. Inoue. 345 pages.

  Inoue helps teachers understand the unintended racism that often occurs when teachers do not have explicit antiracist agendas in their assessments.

First-Year Composition: From Theory to Practice
  Edited by Deborah Coxwell-Teague & Ronald F. Lunsford. 420 pages.

  Twelve of the leading theorists in composition studies answer, in their own voices, the key question about what they hope to accomplish in a first-year composition course. Each chapter includes sample syllabi.

www.parlorpress.com

www.ingramcontent.com/pod-product-compliance
Lightning Source LLC
Chambersburg PA
CBHW031319160426
43196CB00007B/586